DESIGN BASICS 3D

DESIGN BASICS 3D

RICHARD ROTH
Virginia Commonwealth University

STEPHEN PENTAK
The Ohio State University

Australia • Brazil • Japan • Korea • Mexico • Singapore • Spain • United Kingdom • United States

Design Basics: 3D, International Edition
Richard Roth, Stephen Pentak

Publisher: Clark Baxter

Senior Development Editor: Sharon Adams Poore

Assistant Editor: Ashley Bargende

Editorial Assistant: Elizabeth Newell

Associate Media Editor: Kimberly Apfelbaum

Marketing Program Manager: Gurpreet S. Saran

Senior Content Project Manager: Lianne Ames

Senior Art Director: Cate Barr

Senior Print Buyer: Mary Beth Hennebury

Rights Acquisition Specialist, Image: Amanda Groszko

Production Service: Lachina Publishing Services

Text Designer: Anne Carter

Cover Designer: Anne Carter

Cover Image: Abstract view of the Pompidou Center, France, © VIEW GLOBAL/Alamy

Compositor: Lachina Publishing Services

International Edition:
ISBN-13: 978-1-133-31048-8
ISBN-10: 1-133-31048-6

Cengage Learning International Offices

Asia
www.cengageasia.com
tel: (65) 6410 1200

Australia/New Zealand
www.cengage.com.au
tel: (61) 3 9685 4111

Brazil
www.cengage.com.br
tel: (55) 11 3665 9900

India
www.cengage.co.in
tel: (91) 11 4364 1111

Latin America
www.cengage.com.mx
tel: (52) 55 1500 6000

UK/Europe/Middle East/Africa
www.cengage.co.uk
tel: (44) 0 1264 332 424

Represented in Canada by Nelson Education, Ltd.
www.nelson.com
tel: (416) 752 9100 / (800) 668 0671

Cengage Learning is a leading provider of customized learning solutions with office locations around the globe, including Singapore, the United Kingdom, Australia, Mexico, Brazil, and Japan. Locate your local office at: **www.cengage.com/global**

For product information and free companion resources: **www.cengage.com/international**

Visit your local office: **www.cengage.com/global**

Printed in the United States
1 2 3 4 5 6 7 15 14 13 12 11

To Susan and Justin
R.R.

To Debbie, Jamie, Kate, and Craig
S.P.

CONTENTS

CHAPTER 1

3D DESIGN INTRODUCTION 1

CHAPTER 2

IDEAS AND APPROACHES 20

CHAPTER 3

3D DESIGN ELEMENTS 64

CHAPTER 4

3D DESIGN PRINCIPLES 86

CHAPTER 5

CHAPTER

6

CHAPTER 7

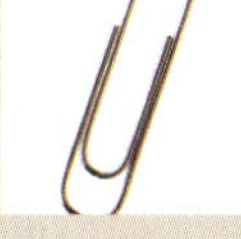

CHAPTER 8

FIGURATION 160

CHAPTER 9

FORMING AND FABRICATION 168

PREFACE

Design Basic: 3D aims to illuminate the elements, principles, and conceptual foundation of three-dimensional design and to render them accessible tools. We have utilized the same highly effective format of *Design Basics* to explain fundamental 3D principles. *Design Basics: 3D* covers a wide spectrum of historical and contemporary art and design ideas in words and images culled from all points on the globe, and from a diverse array of cultures and disciplines. In addition, *Design Basics: 3D* deals with the pressing issues of concept, fabrication, meaning, new technology, and sustainability. We hope you will come to appreciate this book as a collection of images and ideas that transcends the textbook function, becoming a book worth keeping as a catalogue of both classic examples and contemporary objects and explorations.

When we were young artists and new faculty members at The Ohio State University Department of Art (along with Georgia Strange, now Director of the Lamar Dodd School of Art at the University of Georgia), our assignment was to energize and restructure the OSU foundation program. Though we were three very different personalities with unique aesthetic viewpoints, we shared a genuine belief in the value of the foundation experience. We felt then that some of the most mind-expanding and intense explorations of form, material, and process occurred during that critical first year, and that these explorations were easily capable of emitting a light as bright and long-lasting as subsequent studies within specific art and design disciplines.

Now as before, we are committed to the notion that basic design is much more than the simplification or dumbing down of complex principles; quite the contrary—basic design, when done right, is the investigation of deep, core principles. This has been the work of design students and emerging artists since the era of apprentices and guilds, and the experiments of the twentieth century, as it is today in our current digital environment. Basic design study involves first principles and seminal art and design ideas. It has the potential to forever alter perception, opening eyes as well as hearts and minds.

Richard Roth
Professor, Virginia Commonwealth University

Stephen Pentak
Professor Emeritus, The Ohio State University

FLEXIBILITY

Get the resources you need the way you want …

Pentak/Roth/Lauer, *Design Basics: 2D and 3D*, 8e 978-0-495-90997-2	Lauer/Pentak, *Design Basics*, 8e 978-0-495-91577-5	Pentak/Roth, *Color Basics* 978-0-534-61389-1

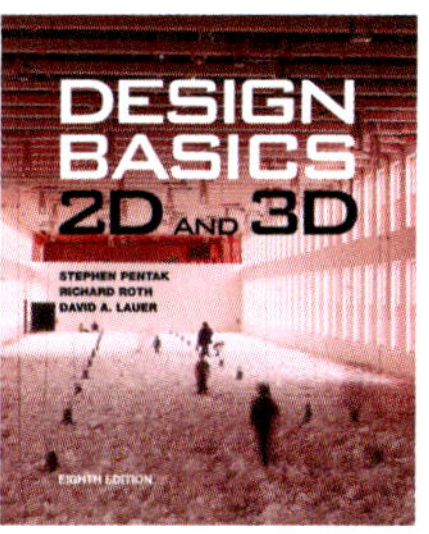

RESOURCES

Art CourseMate supports the printed book with resources including an ebook, interactive foundations tutorials, and design projects.

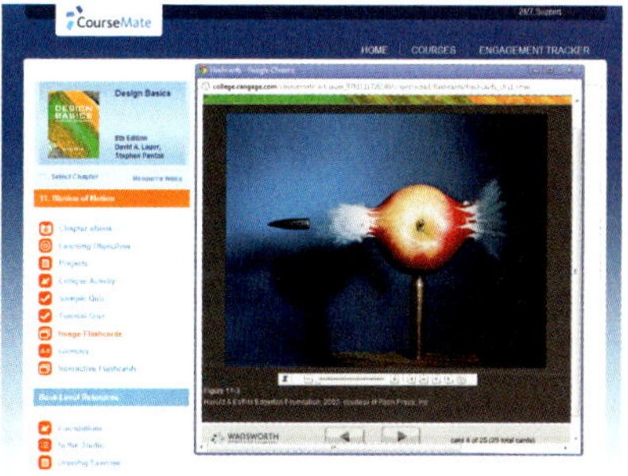

ArtStudio provides a secure, password-protected online image and video upload and grading program that enables you to critique students' assignments as well as facilitating student peer-review, allowing students to see and respond to the work of others in an interactive, non-judgmental environment. ArtStudio includes pre-built assignments and grading rubrics in core topic areas, which you can choose to use or modify—or, you can build entirely new assignments.

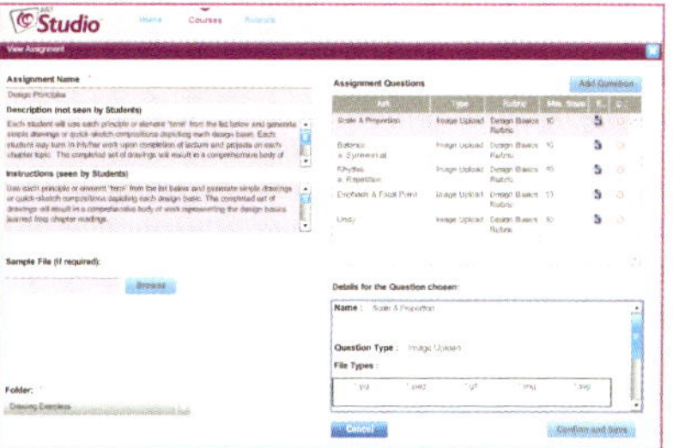

F/A-18 Hornet aircraft breaking the sound barrier.

CHAPTER 1

3D DESIGN INTRODUCTION

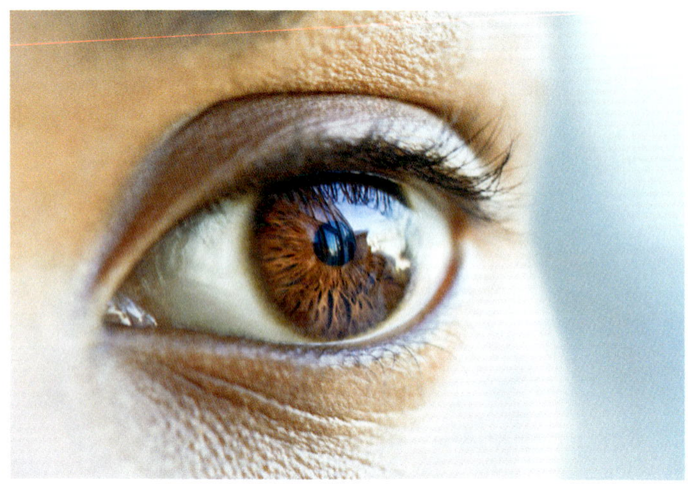

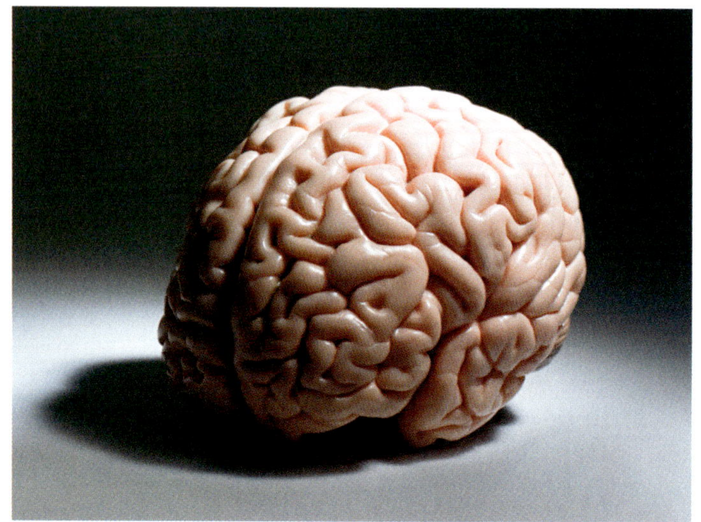

ORGANIZING FORM

Artists, designers, and architects organize form, placing elements in relationship to each other in order to make useful products, meaningful objects, and ordered experiences.

To some extent, everyone is a designer, and if we think of **design** as an organizing activity, everything in the built world has been designed. Daily life requires that each individual shape his or her environment, order priorities, and organize time. If you arrange the furniture in your living room or adjust the handlebars on your bicycle to get a better position—you are organizing form. Through education and experience, artists and designers become sensitive to nuance and engage more serious and complex issues, expanding on everyday aspects of design, like a master chef who creates sophisticated dishes that celebrate and elaborate on basic home cooking.

All the Senses

While vision is the primary sense involved in art and design, three-dimensional design concerns all the senses—visual, **haptic**, acoustic, and olfactory. Your computer might imitate the sound of crinkling paper when you toss a document into the trash icon, giving you important acoustic feedback confirming that the task has been completed. Your appreciation of a good hammer **(A)** is likely to be more tactile than visual. Does it fit your hand? Is it the right weight for you? Does its balance permit a comfortable and accurate swing?

Attention

There is perhaps no frame of mind more important to design thinking than attention! Without interest and care, nothing will happen. The writer Guy Davenport said, "Art is always the replacement of indifference by attention." Excitement with things in the world enables us to see and understand more. Attention propels invention.

Good Design

While we all aspire to create good design, we must recognize that there are no simple recipes to follow—and if there were, design wouldn't be the challenging and exhilarating activity it is. Good design and quality in the arts are notions that are forever in flux. Those who simply learn rules and recipes will inevitably be left behind, producing objects that might have been considered good in an earlier time or another place. Good design, provocative sculpture, and magnificent architecture are achieved by those who are passionate, visually sensitive, informed, open-minded, and inventive. It is toward the development of these qualities that this book is directed. As artists and designers of the future, it is up to you to determine the values of your time and to create its significant objects.

> *(Art) is the impress of those who live in full play of their faculties. The individual passes, living his life, and the things he touches receive his kind of impress, and they afterwards bear the trace of his passing. They give evidence of the quality of his growth.*
>
> *Art appears in many forms. To some degree every human being is an artist, dependent on the quality of his growth. Art need not be intended. It comes inevitably as the tree from the root, the branch from the trunk, the blossom from the twig. None of these forget the present in looking backward or forward. They are occupied wholly with the fulfillment of their own existence. The branch does not boast of the relation it bears to its great ancestor the trunk, and does not claim attention to itself for this honor, nor does it call your attention to the magnificent red apple it is about to bear. Because it is engaged in the full play of its own existence, because it is full in its own growth, its fruit is inevitable.*
>
> —Robert Henri

→ **A**

S2 Framing Hammer. 18 oz., length 1' 6". Vaughan, manufacturer.

DESIGN DEFINED

The word design has many meanings. Design is often used as a noun: *the design* (referring to the result of the process of design) or *design*—the professional discipline of design, as in product design, graphic design, information design, interior design, and so forth. It is also used as a verb: *to design*—referring to the activity of designing, planning, or organizing. Design, as primarily used in this book, refers to design's more general definition—design as an organizing activity.

Basic Design

To complicate matters, there is also *basic design*—the course of study that most art and design students take in their foundation year before majoring in a specific discipline. The basic design course is, traditionally, a series of visual exercises that teaches the fundamental concepts of visual form and organization, and develops sensitivity to visual phenomena. Basic design is usually subdivided into three parts: two-dimensional design, three-dimensional design, and time design, sometimes called 4D. Two-dimensional design deals with all that is flat—such as composition, pattern, illusion, and color. Time design involves phenomena that exist in time; it deals with movement and the sequential. Three-dimensional design covers all concepts relating to 3D form and structure, as well as related spatial issues.

Origins

Many of the seminal ideas taught today in art, design, and architecture foundation programs around the world were developed in the revolutionary, experimental German design school, the **Bauhaus (A)**, during the years 1919–1933.

The Bauhaus brought architecture, art, craft, design, and technology together under one roof. Artists and designers were encouraged to utilize machines, mass production, new materials, and technology in order to create design for their own time. The Bauhaus existed during a crippling economic depression; it made utility and economy of means paramount, and promoted the belief that design should arise from first principles and experiment, not from precedent. Though the school was eventually disbanded by the Nazis, the Bauhaus spirit and philosophy are very much alive in contemporary art, architecture, and design as well as in their pedagogical underpinnings. Prior to the Bauhaus, the training of artists and designers was an apprenticeship system: students learned their masters' techniques. The "new" approach emphasized student discovery, which remains relevant in this era of digital design, rapid prototyping, and new materials.

The paper-folding project at the Bauhaus aimed to teach students to understand the structural possibilities of paper and to utilize its unique properties—its paperness! In **B**, artist and instructor Josef Albers conducts a critique of student work.

One of the most important and decisive experiences for me was the Vorkurs (foundation course) conducted by Josef Albers. Every student had to go through this preliminary course to prove his abilities, before he was accepted.

I remember vividly the first day of Vorkurs, Josef Albers entered the room, carrying with him a bunch of newspapers, which were distributed among the students. He then addressed us, saying something like this: "Ladies and gentlemen, we are poor, not rich. We can't afford to waste materials or time. We have to make the most out of the least. All art starts with material, and therefore we have first to investigate what our material can do. So, at the beginning we will experiment without aiming at making a product. At the moment we prefer cleverness to beauty. Economy of form depends on the material we are working with. Notice that often you will have more by doing less.

Walter Gropius. 1925–1926. Bauhaus Building, Dessau, Germany. © 2011 Artists Rights Society (ARS), New York/VG Bild-Kunst, Bonn.

Our studies should lead to constructive thinking. All right? I want you to take the newspapers you got and try to make something out of them that is more than you have now. I want you to respect the material and use it in a way that makes sense—preserve its inherent characteristics. If you can do without tools like knives and scissors, and without glue, the better. Good luck." And with these words he left the room, leaving us quite flabbergasted. He returned hours later and asked us to put the results of our efforts on the floor.

There were masks, boats, castles, airplanes, and all kinds of cute little figurines. He referred to all this as kindergarten products which could often have been made better in other materials. He pointed then at a study of extreme simplicity, made by a young Hungarian architect. He simply had taken the newspaper and folded it lengthwise so it was standing up like a folding screen. Josef Albers explained to us how well the material was understood and utilized—how the folding process was natural to paper, because it resulted in making a pliable material stiff, so stiff that it could stand up on its smallest part: the border of the paper. He further pointed out to us that a newspaper lying on the table would only have one page visually active, where as the rest would be hidden. Now that the paper was standing up, both sides had become visually active.

. . . Through the Vorkurs a whole new world of seeing and thinking opened up to us. Most students had come to the Bauhaus with set ideas about art and design. They were usually romantic cliché ideas. But we soon learned that habitual thinking was in the way of creative thinking. The Vorkurs was a kind of group therapy. Seeing the solutions made by other students, we learned quickly to recognize the most elegant solution to a given problem. We also learned to exercise self-criticism, which was considered more important than criticism.

—Hannes Beckmann, on his experience in Josef Albers's Bauhaus, basic design course

Josef Albers assessing work from his Preliminary Course at the Bauhaus. 1928–1929.

William Wegman. *Contemplating the Bust of Man Ray.* **1978. Photograph. JPMorgan Art Collection.**

ATTENTIVE OBSERVATION

We are moved by the beauty of the natural world, devoted to the face of a loved one, and inspired by art, design, and architecture. In all these instances, observation is essential. It is at the very heart of art and design. Attentive observation is also a survival skill. Artists and designers are voyeurs—the entire world elicits fascination.

Sensitivity

We often look without really seeing. Try drawing the front of a one-dollar bill from memory. You will find that although you have looked at the dollar bill countless times, you have not really seen it. Most people can recall only a few rudimentary aspects—George Washington in the center, numeral ones on some corners, and a border of sorts. The proportions, the text, the ornate scrollwork, and the colors are usually missing or incorrect. Don't even try to recall the back of the dollar bill! Rigorous observation demands effort. Art and design require seeing with sensitivity—they are disciplines that help develop analytical and insightful powers of observation. Drawing and sculpting from observation, for example, teach us to see more and to see with greater sensitivity.

Viewpoint

Looking implies a vantage point. To observe, you must situate yourself somewhere in space. The same object **(A** and **B)**, a section of vertebra, viewed from two different angles appears completely different. Does a viewpoint suggest that you must also have a point of view? Cezanne said, "Here on the edge of the river, the motifs are very plentiful, the same object seen from a different angle gives a subject for study of the highest interest and so varied that I think I could be occupied for months without changing my place, simply bending a little more to the right or left."

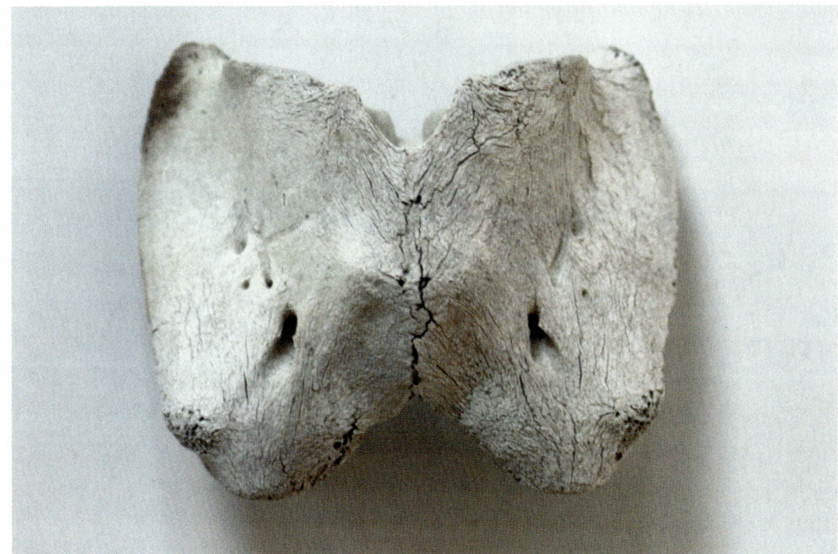

Vertebra section, view 1.

↑ B

Vertebra section, view 2.

SIMILARITIES AND DIFFERENCES

When observing two or more things, it is natural to perceive how similar or different they might be. This tendency, when thoughtfully utilized, is an extremely useful aid to sensitive seeing. Comparison helps us see in context and make insightful observations that inform our understanding of both objects.

Compare the sculpture *Bird in Space* **(A)** to the **functional** bird decoy, *Blue Heron* **(B)**. Most significantly, they share extremely **reductive** form—they depict only essential features, eliminate detail, and utilize a radical economy of means. Both express a very modern sense of lightness, appropriate to their subject matter. We may also observe that *Bird in Space* is polished bronze and represents a bird in flight, and therefore the movement and freedom of flight are also expressed. *Blue Heron* depicts a heron standing motionless and is made of

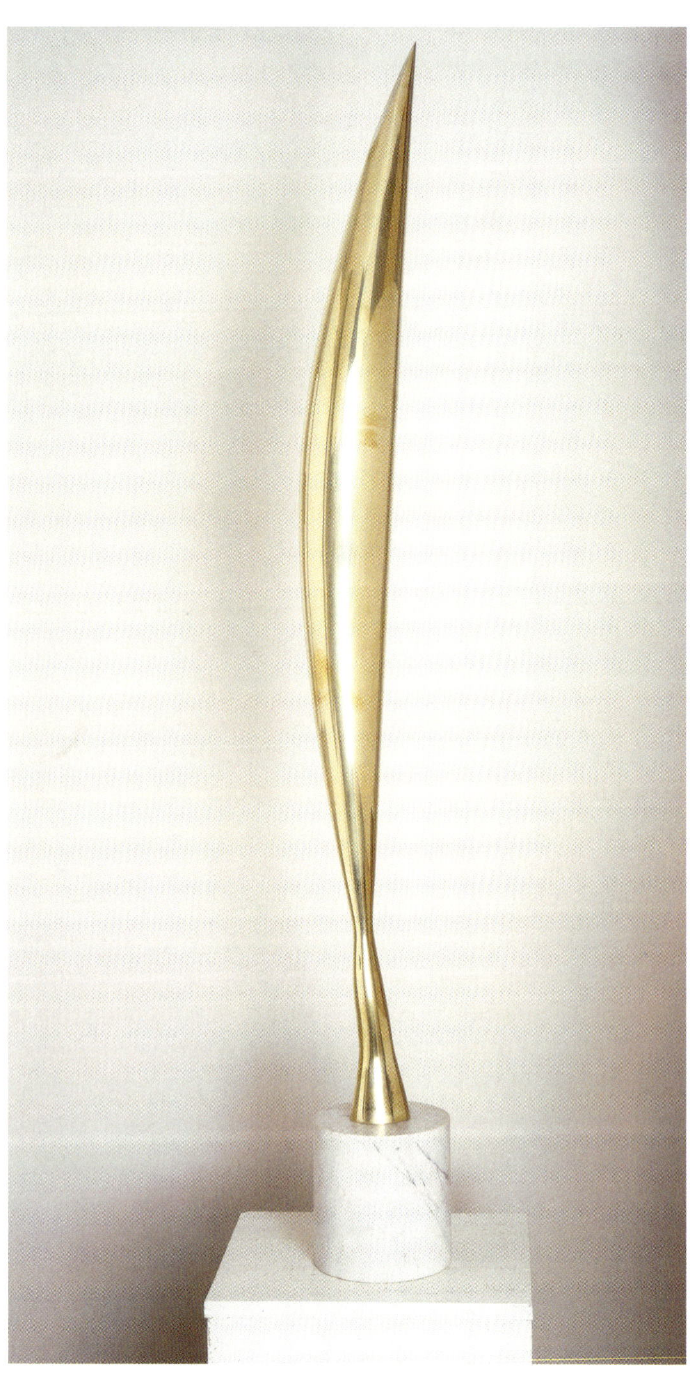

↑ A

Constantin Brancusi. *Bird in Space.* **1924. Bronze, 4' 2$\frac{5}{16}$" high.**

carved wood. *Bird in Space* is a single discrete form mounted on a pedestal (which may be considered part of the work). *Blue Heron* is composed of five parts and is intended to be placed directly in the ground.

We could continue in this manner for quite a while; comparing similarities and differences is a most useful technique for observation. It is interesting to note that Brancusi's sculpture was groundbreaking in its use of reductive form—*Bird in Space*, created in 1928, is an icon of modern art. *Blue Heron* was made by an anonymous craftsperson as a functional object, a humble decoy. Its primary purpose was simply to attract herons for hunting. It is, nonetheless, a completely delightful object that transcends its simple function. *Blue Heron* was created in New Jersey in 1907.

↑ **B**

Blue Heron **Decoy. 1907.**

CONNECTIONS

To appreciate and understand the world of 3D form and to make sense of experience in general, we make connections. We see or sense a commonality between one shape and another, or between one underlying concept or structure and another. Memory plays a role when we make connections between shapes or structures seen long ago. The mind is always seeking patterns and attempting to make sense of the world. Artists and designers work to nurture and heighten this natural inclination in order to invent new and useful configurations.

Underlying Patterns in Nature

The eminent Scottish biologist D'arcy Wentworth Thompson is revered for his observations that revealed the physical and mathematical laws that determine the forms of living things. The poet Edith Sitwell found numerous related structures in nature. She marveled at "the immense design of the world, one image of wonder mirrored by another image of wonder—the pattern of fern and of feather by the frost on the window-pane, the six-rays of the snowflake mirrored in the rock-crystal's six-rayed eternity—seeing the pattern on the scaly legs of birds mirrored in the pattern of knotgrass . . ."

↑ A

Afghanistan Markhor (*Capra falconeri megaceros*). Male.

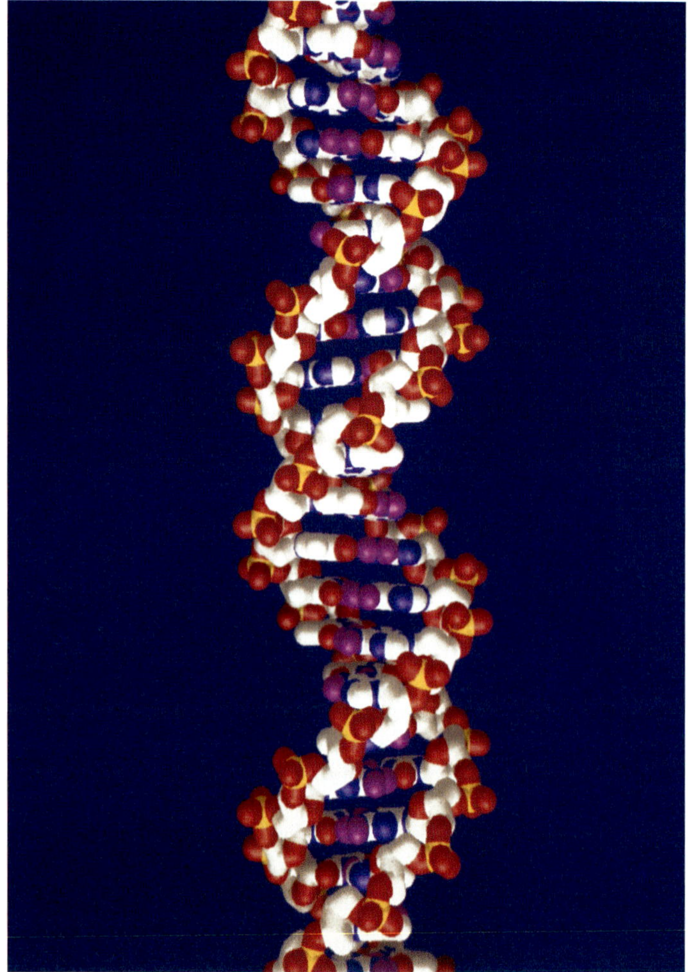

↑ B

Double Helix DNA model.

Such structural resemblances are seen everywhere in nature—from the ordinary to the majestic. The markhor's horn **(A)** and the double helix of DNA **(B)** share helical configurations. A spiral nebula that is more than 60,000 light years across **(C)** has the same fundamental form as the chambered nautilus **(D)**. Artists and designers, much like scientists, are always on the lookout for resemblances and hidden patterns connecting the world and their work, and within the work itself. How many spiral structures can you find in a day?

← **C**

Spiral Nebula (M51). NASA, Hubble Heritage Team. 2010. Photo.

→ **D**

Chambered nautilus, cross section.

TACTILE SENSATION

The sense of touch (tactile sensation) plays an important role in experiencing the 3D world. Though vision may be the primary mode of human perceptual experience, all the senses contribute to our ongoing need to decipher, navigate, and manipulate the three-dimensional realm.

Imagine that you are in a house, blindfolded, and need to find your way to another room. You would undoubtedly do so with your arms extended in front of you. Your two hands, probing for obstacles, serve as antennae and function as a primitive form of sight.

Vision and Touch

Vision and the sense of touch, working in tandem, constitute a partnership that is an extremely successful perceptual agent. The woodcarver in **A** must observe visually and sense with his hands, simultaneously. The craftsperson sanding a piece of wood will visually examine the completed work to make sure the surface is adequately smooth. Next, he or she will inevitably feel the wood, lightly sliding a hand across the surface in order to ascertain the accuracy of the initial visual observation. The use of touch in this manner is an example of feedback. The sensitive hand communicates specific information concerning surface imperfections, enabling one to sand efficiently and complete the task. When it comes to judging texture or the gracefulness of a curving surface, whether in the making or the appreciation, the hand is an extraordinary sensory tool.

↑ **A**

Hands carving wood.

The Hand

Though touching art in museums is widely forbidden, it is not unusual to see a particular spot, a beautiful curved form on an accessible bronze sculpture, that has had its **patina** rubbed off and its surface polished by museum visitors who could not resist reaching out to touch it as they walked by. While museums, of necessity, must forbid touching, most sculptors are extremely engaged with the tactile qualities of their work.

The industrial designer Raymond Loewy believed that judging an automobile's design required running one's hands over it. The automobile is but one of the numerous objects and structures that engage the tactile. The clay car model **(B)** involves shaping complex curves and necessitates using the hand to test for gracefully flowing form. Many functional objects engage the viewer's touch. How does the cup feel in your hand? How does it engage your lips when drinking? Does the cup when filled with tea get too hot to hold?

↑ **B**

Clay model, 2010 BMW 550I Gran Turismo. © BMW PressClub.

A SHAPING FORCE

Objects communicate their characteristics and take on meaning not in isolation but in context. All objects exist in relationship to other objects and to their environments. The perceived qualities of objects change when other objects are placed in proximity or when placed in a new environment. Such changes affect both form and meaning. We cannot help comparing the formal characteristics of objects, as we always see each in comparison to the other. A small book may seem large when it sits next to an even smaller book. Every object-group and site also involves complex social and psychological effects that are, like form, relative and contextual. Artists and designers must be sensitive to the formal, social, and psychological implications of context. Spaces and situations are never neutral.

Artist Haim Steinbach is a master of context. His practice has for many years consisted of placing groups of found objects on shelves. The Ajax can in the sculpture in **A** is a component of a work of art. Transporting objects from one social context to another is now a commonly understood art strategy. Under your kitchen sink, the Ajax can means something quite different than it would in an art gallery. This work, though, deals with context in another way as well; it pits one found object against another. It also raises the important issue of the pedestal in sculpture. The Ajax can is elevated in status due to its place of honor on the subservient shelf; but the shelf, a rustic handmade object, possesses more qualities associated with traditional art than does the Ajax can. Steinbach's sculpture gives us a glimpse of shifting contextual relationships between two mute objects.

↑ A

Haim Steinbach. ***Shelf with Ajax.*** **1980. Mixed mediums. Fisher Fine Arts Library Image Collection.**

Recontextualizing

The artist Fred Wilson was invited to the Maryland Historical Society in 1992 to rearrange the collection. The resulting exhibition, "Mining the Museum," **recontextualized** the art and artifacts in the museum collection by creating provocative new **juxtapositions**. One pairing—*Slave Shackles* (never previously exhibited) and *Silver Vessels in Baltimore Repoussé Style* **(B)**—critiques the ideological biases of institutions as well as history.

See also *Scale: Comparative Size*, page 118.

Fred Wilson. *Mining the Museum: An Installation.* **1992. Detail: Silver Vessels in Baltimore Repoussé Style, 1830–1880, and Slave Shackles, maker unknown. c. 1793–1872. Baltimore.**

SITE SPECIFIC

All objects exist in context, but artworks, architecture, and design installations that make context essential are called **site specific**. Such works are made for particular places. If moved from their intended sites, they become unintelligible or acquire new meaning.

Architecture is especially involved with issues of site. A new building must contend with the landscape it resides in, as well as neighboring structures. Site issues can become contentious when high-rise buildings are planned for low-rise residential neighborhoods or pristine natural sites, or when an extension is planned for a building that happens to be an architectural landmark.

Frank Lloyd Wright's *Fallingwater* **(A)**, a house in rural Pennsylvania, makes a waterfall its central feature. *Fallingwater* appears to become an extension of the overhanging rock formations of the landscape. Using natural materials and sandstone from a local quarry further reinforced its site-specific spirit.

Surrounded Islands **(B)** is a sculpture installation that used 6.5 million square feet of woven polypropylene fabric to surround eleven islands in Biscayne Bay. The intense pink fabric floated on the surface of the water for the two-week duration of this temporary work. The flamboyant gesture that is *Surrounded Islands*, removed from its site, would be nothing, just a pile of fabric. In fact, what is *Surrounded Islands* really? Is it simply the fabric, which the artists had fabricated, or does it encompass all of Biscayne Bay, including its islands, boats, people, and weather?

In a digital print **(C)**, Wim Delvoye simulates an amusing site-specific installation. The message, "Out walking the dog, back soon. Tina," would, of course, not be funny if it were on an ephemeral Post-it attached to a door; it would just be another daily bit of information. By recontextualizing the note, putting this mundane sentence into a wildly inappropriate context, one more suitable for a monument or a presidential memorial, Delvoye disrupts our expectations.

↑ **A**

Frank Lloyd Wright. Kaufmann House (*Fallingwater*). 1937. Bear Run, Pennsylvania. © 2011 Frank Lloyd Wright Foundation, Scottsdale, AZ/Artists Rights Society (ARS), New York.

Wolfgang Volz©1983 Christo

↑ B

Christo and Jeanne-Claude. *Surrounded Islands, Biscayne Bay, Greater Miami, Florida, 1980–83.* **Copyright Christo & Jeanne-Claude.**

→ C

Wim Delvoye. *Out Walking the Dog.* **2000. C-print on aluminum, 3' 3" × 4'.**

BECOMING INFORMED AND AWARE

In art and design, as well as life in general, few activities are more important than learning. Many of the things we do in the arts are intended to enrich and inform the maker, not simply to arrive at a product . . . or perhaps, the maker can also be considered a product to be shaped. Artists and designers are fortunate to have practices that require perpetual learning.

Art and design foundation programs (first-year programs) are created to teach students the basics of visual form, introduce materials and structural principles, develop technical skills and the ability to research and articulate ideas, foster visual sensitivity, communicate effectively, and above all, become informed, inventive, thinking makers who are beginning to develop an awareness of the history and the nature of the disciplines of art and design, against a global backdrop.

Problem-Solving in the Art Foundation

Problem-solving assignments have been created to accomplish these formidable educational tasks. We have inherited many assignment ideas from the Bauhaus. Successful projects have been passed along from teacher to teacher, often adjusted to create variations on the original, and some are completely new. In 3D classes projects range from the highly structured to the expressive, and from the observational—depicting various displayed objects in clay, cardboard, or wire, perhaps—to studies in structure (towers or bridges constructed of wood dowels that must support a brick or other weight, for example).

Box Beam Workshop

Every assignment is designed to teach a lesson or a bundle of lessons. Let's examine one project in order to gain some insight into the workings of the 3D foundation experience.

In the art foundation program of the School of the Arts at Virginia Commonwealth University (a foundation program that includes both art and design students), Professor Matt King has assigned the "One-Week Box Beam Workshop" **(A** and **B)**. He states the problem: "Using box beam construction, create a cardboard structure that suggests an extraordinary or unexpected relationship to gravity." With only corrugated cardboard, hot glue, and brown paper tape, the students work in groups of three to four. Professor King sets some of the following parameters: "The piece must be taller than the tallest person in the group; the cardboard may only have three points of contact (two on the floor and one on a stool or chair); the stool must remain unattached to the cardboard structure." Student solutions are accomplished in accordance with a specific procedure, requiring the creation of 1:8 scale preliminary models, investigation of the stresses involved, and finally translating the scale model into a full-size structure.

→ **A**

Student project. Professor Matt King, instructor. Virginia Commonwealth University, Art Foundation Program.

However delightful the students' solutions may be, they are, more importantly, the vehicle for significant lessons. Students learn to work collaboratively, requiring them to put their ideas into words. They learn to be inventive, generate ideas through the use of models, think in scale, measure, and develop fabrication skills. Their structures must be carefully balanced; thus they learn to deal with issues of gravity and **cantilever**, as well as structure. By means of the instructor's criticism and the final group **crit**, students learn to be articulate about things visual and structural, and they learn the importance of self-criticism.

↑ **B**

Student project. Professor Matt King, instructor. Virginia Commonwealth University, Art Foundation Program.

Jessica Hiltout, photographer. Nine homemade soccer balls, Africa.
From the book *Amen: Grassroots Football*, 2010.

CHAPTER 2

IDEAS AND APPROACHES

RESEARCH

Artists, designers, and architects utilize research in numerous ways. On one level, research in design is similar to research in the humanities. An artist/designer might go to the library or the web, or travel to find out more about the history of the Civil War, if intending to design a commemorative monument in Richmond, Virginia. Research in the arts sometimes resembles play, but, just as often, it can be similar to scientific investigation.

Biomimicry

Biomimicry is a discipline in which engineers, scientists, and product designers research and emulate nature's designs and processes to create products, solutions, and strategies to solve human problems. The sandcastle worm builds its dwelling **(A)** by gluing sand and bits of shell together underwater. Scientists are studying this phenomenon in order to develop adhesives that will be able to bond broken bones and seal incisions in the moist environment of the human body. Self-cleaning surfaces, such as glass and paint used in architecture, are examples of bioinspired products developed by studying the self-cleaning properties of plant leaves. The design process and research are inseparable.

Experiments and Questions

Another type of research in art and design takes the informal path. In this research mode, the artist/designer asks a series of questions: What will happen if I put the structural elements of my building on the outside instead of hidden internally? What will happen if I design a product that spoofs "good" design? What will happen if I construct a chair with the least amount of material possible? What will happen if I place a round, wood form above a faceted steel polyhedron? Then, after enacting a response (altering material) and answering the question, more questions follow: That doesn't work, but what if I split it in half? Then the designer attempts that, and so forth. Whether this process is highly structured or simply involves exploring material properties, this kind of research can lead the designer on a journey of connected discoveries leading to a new, original and unexplored terrain.

Testing

A racing bicycle **(B)** is tested in a wind tunnel to arrive at the most **aerodynamic** and efficient form. The Cervélo Baracchi **(C)** was designed from scratch and subjected to an intense testing regimen that involved real-life road racing, as well as wind tunnel analysis, to create the ultimate aerodynamic racing bike.

A

Tube-shaped dwelling of sandcastle worm (top); two beads of a worm's home microscopically enlarged (bottom). © Russell Stewart.

B

Cervélo bicycle in wind-tunnel test.

Design Research

Subjecting **prototypes** of aircraft, automobiles, sports equipment, and most other products to testing provides valuable information for improving performance. Wind tunnel testing, structural stress testing, real-world use, and interviewing and videotaping users of new products are just some of the many modes of contemporary product testing. It is useful to all makers, on every level, to subject the objects they create to testing.

Research Methodology in Art

The working method of some contemporary artists resembles that of the scientist. Natalie Jeremijenko created a sculpture installation, *Tree Logic* **(D)**, in which she suspended six live trees upside down from an armature. This was an experiment to examine the effects of gravity and phototropism on the growth and shape of trees.

C

Cervélo Baracchi bicycle.

D

Natalie Jeremijenko. *Tree Logic.* **1999. MASS MoCA, North Adams, Massachusetts.**

PROCESS

To one who has watched the potter at his wheel, it is plain that the potter's thumb, like the glass-blower's blast of air, depends for its efficacy upon the physical properties of the clay or 'slip' it works on, which for the time being is essentially a fluid. The cup and the saucer, like the tube and the bulb, display (in their simple and primitive forms) beautiful surfaces of equilibrium as manifested under certain limiting conditions. They are neither more nor less than glorified 'splashes,' formed slowly, under conditions of restraint which enhance or reveal their mathematical symmetry.

—D'Arcy Wentworth Thompson, On Growth and Form, *1917*

The Relationship of Process, Material, and Form

While the form of many objects, products, and structures today is to a great extent determined by function, form is also significantly the result of its fabrication process and material. A chair constructed of wood and steel **(A)** and one of resin and fiberglass **(B)** might share the same function—to seat diners around a table. The formal difference between two such chairs can be attributed to factors that include the dissimilar processes and materials involved in their fabrication and the designer's values and sensibility.

Form Is a Diagram of Forces

The industrial process of extrusion is an example of a fabrication procedure that determines very specific kinds of forms. As heated aluminum, rubber, or other malleable material is forced

Jean Prouvé. Standard chair. 1950. The Museum of Modern Art, New York.

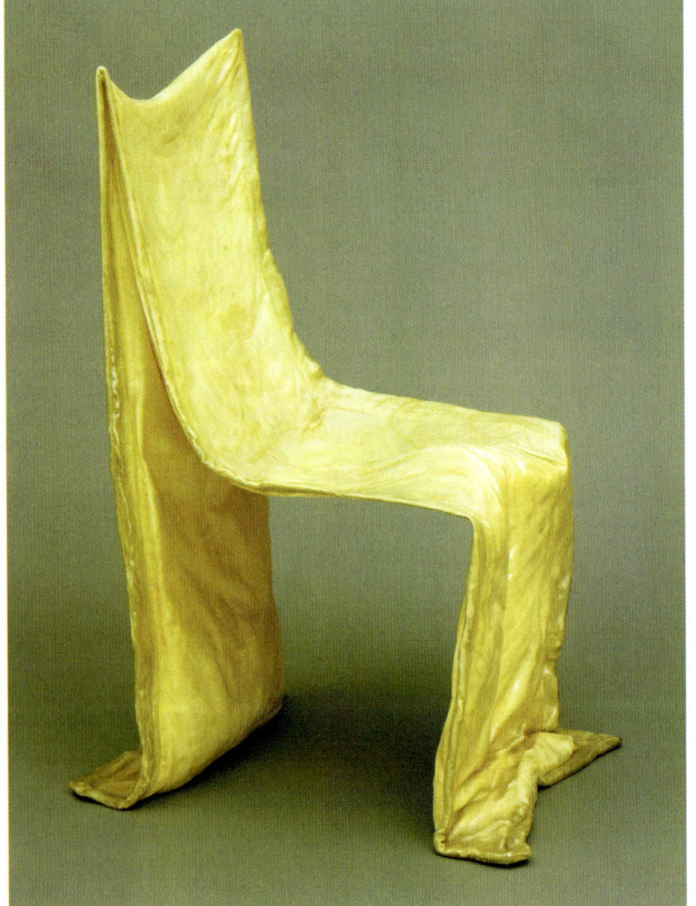

Gaetano Pesce. *Golgotha Chair.* 1972. Dacron filled and resin soaked fiberglass cloth, 3' 3" × 1' 6½" × 2' 3¾". The Museum of Modern Art, New York.

through an aperture of specific shape, it achieves the form of a long rod or tube with a configuration derived from the shape of the aperture. In **C**, a pliable, flour paste is extruded to form rigatoni, one of the many pasta shapes that may be determined by the simple change of aperture.

Biologist D'Arcy Wentworth Thompson said, "In short, the form of an object is a diagram of forces; in this sense, at least, that from it we can judge of or deduce the forces that are acting or have acted upon it; in this strict and particular sense, it is a diagram." The extrusion process is a good example of Thompson's proposition: it produces forms that are easily identifiable as extrusions and illustrates developmental forces.

Process and Feedback

Feedback is an important component of many fabrication processes. Consider the work of a potter **(D)**. The potter's wheel predetermines fundamental formal qualities—it naturally and efficiently produces round and cylindrical shapes. As the potter squeezes the pliable wall of a spinning clay vessel, he or she is constantly sensing the thickness of the wall. This ongoing feedback is essential to the achievement of the desired outcome. Feedback and process are interactive partners.

Process and Invention

Artists and designers often utilize process as a research tool. The exploration of materials and their properties can result in useful and surprising discoveries. Gaetano Pesce is an Italian designer known for his freewheeling experimentation with new materials. Looking again at **B**, note how Pesce combines unlikely materials—Dacron-filled, resin-soaked fiberglass cloth—to invent a playful, **anthropomorphic** chair.

C

Rigatoni extrusion in pasta machine.

D

Ceramic artist at potter's wheel.

THE VESSEL

> *It is significant that in speaking of craft objects, people use terms such as savor and style. The beauty of such objects is not so much of the noble, the huge, or the lofty as a beauty of the warm and familiar. Here one may detect a striking difference between the crafts and the arts. People hang their pictures high up on walls, but they place their objects for everyday use close to them and take them in their hands.*
>
> —*Sōetsu Yanagi*

The tradition of the vessel (a receptacle or container) extends back to prehistory; it is an **archetypal** form, worthy of our special attention. From the cups, glasses, pots, and bowls we use every day, to highly technical scientific and industrial vats, the vessel is born of utility. Vessels are everywhere around us: paper cups, glass and plastic bottles, and cookware; even cardboard boxes, cabinets, and dressers may be considered vessels, and so too, rooms and buildings. While we are thinking broadly, let's not forget the bathtub, the toilet bowl, and the swimming pool. Boats and ships are also referred to as vessels; they contain cargo and people and volumes of air that displace water.

Glass and Ceramics

The disciplines of glass and ceramics hold an esteemed place for the vessel, ranging from the purely functional to vessels that primarily explore form and disregard utility. The potter may take flat slabs of clay, pinching them together at the seams, to create a vessel, or roll out long lines of clay and coil them in circles, one above the other, to construct a bowl **(A)**. Of course, pots are most commonly thrown on the potter's wheel, harnessing the spinning forces and the potter's hand, used as an instrument of extrusion, to naturally produce spherical and cylindrical forms. Similarly, the glassblower's breath and the spinning of the molten glass at the end of the blowpipe produce round and cylindrical vessels—byproducts of the process **(B)**.

Another way of producing ceramic vessels **(C)** is by pouring slip (liquid clay) into molds. As with all ceramic objects, after drying, the vessels are fired in kilns. In a related manner, glass may be blown into forms to produce precise shapes.

New Processes

Designer Stefan Lindfors re-imagines and elevates the humble motor oil can **(D)**. The blow-molded polyethylene container is produced by an industrial process in which air is blown into polyethylene plastic. The air pressure forces the plastic against the walls of a mold where the container's shape is determined.

See also *Replication Technologies: New Approaches*, page 192.

Aztec hand-coiled domestic pottery. 16th century. Mexico.

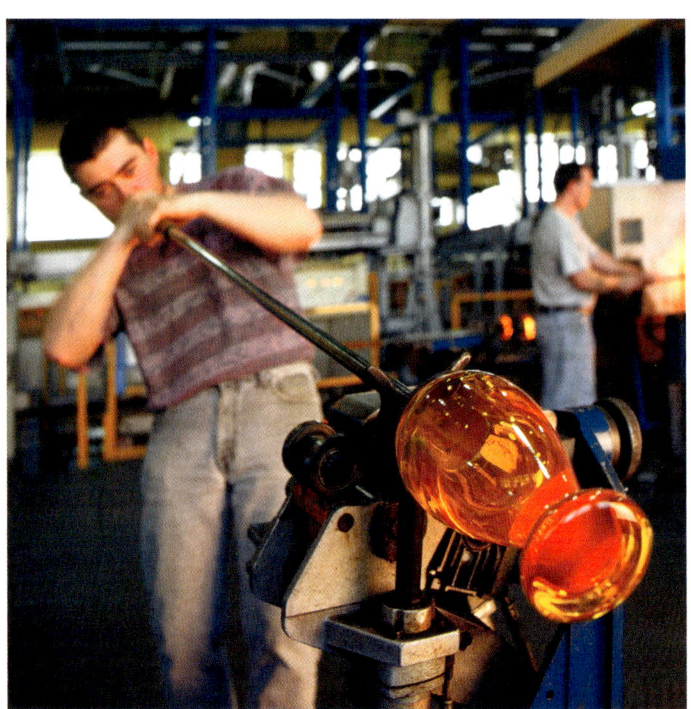

Glassblower at Waterford Crystal, Ireland.

↑ C

Russel Wright. American modern dinnerware. 1937. Manufacturer: Steubenville Pottery, East Liverpool, Ohio. The Museum of Modern Art, New York.

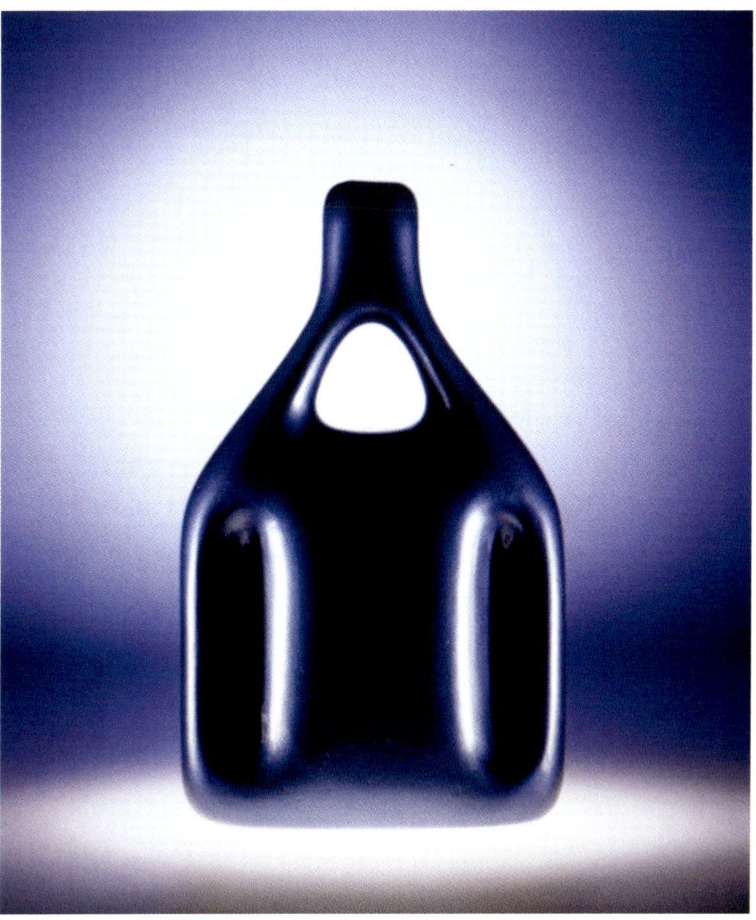

→ D

Stefan Lindfors. *Oil.* Four-liter motor oil container prototype for Neste Oil. 1994. Blow-molded polyethylene.

NATURE

We might not think of nature as designed, but the fact is, all form and matter, whether organic or inorganic, must of necessity be generated and shaped by forces, conditions, and processes. In this sense, nature might be seen as the ultimate designer as well as the first and foremost source of design inspiration—the design school without equal.

The Grand Canyon **(A)** is one of the most awe-inspiring natural monuments. The rock of the Colorado Plateau was carved away bit by bit for a duration spanning millions of years by the eroding force of the Colorado River. Its form was and continues to be determined by natural processes—the creation of the plateau by forces of plate tectonics followed by the perpetual interaction of limestone and sandstone with ice, wind, gravity, and a turbulent river.

Sand and wind combine to generate spectacular dunes **(B)** in Peach Canyon, Arizona. Here, sand acts as a perfect recording device for atmospheric conditions. Wind blows, sand piles up, collapses and slides down, seeking equilibrium, then begins all over again. Every breeze is transcribed.

The Hooded Oriole nest **(C)**, made of artfully woven plant fibers, hangs attached to the underside of leaves and is perfectly suited to its purpose. The Oriole utilized not just the usual natural fibers, but much like any savvy contemporary designer, it incorporated whatever worked and was available in the vicinity—in this case, green holiday tinsel!

Grand Canyon.

↑ B

Bruce Barnbaum. *Hollows and Points, Peach Canyon.* 1984. Photograph.

→ C

Richard Barnes. Hooded Oriole nest. Photograph.

EXTENDING CAPABILITY

It was once thought that humans distinguished themselves from other animals by their use of tools. It is now common knowledge that animals also utilize tools. Some chimpanzees and bonobos use sticks as probes to extract ants and termites from their hives. To crack open mussels, flying birds drop them on rocks below. Some crows have been observed placing walnuts on roads so passing cars can break them open!

The first human tools were most likely repurposed found objects—such as shells used for digging, cutting, and drinking, and stones used as hammers and weapons. The earliest human-made prehistoric stone tools **(A)** were simple hand axes. Today, tools are everywhere and are increasingly complex. It is almost impossible to imagine life without tools.

Tools enable us to perform special and complex tasks that would otherwise be impossible. Levers and pulley systems allow us to lift heavy weights; lenses bring distant objects near and make small objects appear large; computers perform many tasks by making huge calculations instantly. Art and designed objects look as they do, in part, because tools generate particular forms. It is safe to say that many contemporary buildings would simply not exist without computer-aided design.

The traditional jack plane **(B)** is perfectly suited to its task. It is a hand tool for smoothing flat, wood surfaces, one thin shaving per stroke. It is efficient, adjustable, and exquisitely simple. From the hand ax to the ever-present and increasingly complex computer, tools continue to extend human capability. Industrial welding robots **(C)** produce perfect welds at great speed.

Today artists and designers utilize a wide array of tools. For example, sculptors use hammers and chisels to carve wood and stone, molds to replicate forms, welders and laser cutters to shape steel, and **CNC** routers (computer controlled carving machines) to shape many materials. Designers utilize **CAD** (computer aided design programs) and **rapid prototyping** (3D printers), as well as traditional hand tools. An important part of a basic 3D design course consists of mastering tools and technology.

↑ A

Paleolithic stone hand ax.

Now the camera, camcorder, and computer have been added to the list of essential tools.

A famous moment in the movie *2001: A Space Odyssey* neatly summed up the evolution of tools on earth when it portrayed an early, ape-like human ancestor throwing a bone high in the air after discovering that it could be used as a weapon. At the top of the bone's trajectory, bridging millions of years in an instant, the film cuts to an image of a rotating space station.

> *I love the tools made for mechanics. I stop at the windows of hardware stores. If I could only find an excuse to buy many more of them than I have already bought on the mere pretense that I might have a use for them! They are so beautiful, so simple and plain and straight to their meaning. There is no "Art" about them, they have not been made beautiful, they are beautiful.*
>
> —*Robert Henri*

B

Traditional jack plane. Peck Tool.

C

Welding robots at an auto plant in Fukuoka prefecture on Japan's southern island of Kyushu.

TRANSCENDING PHYSICALITY

The requirement that raw material be transformed, changed from mere matter to something greater, something transcendent, is a commonly accepted notion in the arts. Clay is nothing but mud. In the hands of a great sculptor, clay can be transformed into human flesh. The **aesthetic** expectation that matter be altered evokes historic myths of transformation—alchemy's transmutation of base metals into gold, as well as creation stories.

By depicting nuanced human form garnered from careful observation, Gian Lorenzo Bernini coaxed life out of cold, hard marble **(A)**. Prior to Bernini, it was rare to see indentations (due to the pressure of a grasp, for example) depicted in sculpture. This telling detail completed the illusion of the transformation of stone to flesh.

Tara Donovan stacked thousands of ordinary clear plastic drinking straws against a gallery wall to create *Haze* **(B)**. When first viewing *Haze*, one does not perceive the completely ordinary material of its construction. The initial experience is spatially disorienting and perceptually ambiguous. *Haze* appears to be a cloud-like formation, more like a mirage than an object. Upon close inspection **(C)**, seeing that it is made of drinking straws startles and amazes.

> *A musical instrument is a mysterious thing, inhabiting a complex sort of space: it is both an ordinary three-dimensional object and a portal to another world; it exists as a physical entity solely so that it—and, indeed, physicality—can be transcended.*
>
> —*Joyce Carol Oates*

Transformation as a Conceptual Act

In 1975, sculptor Scott Burton took an old and quite ordinary wooden chair left behind by the previous tenant of his apartment and had it cast in bronze **(D)**. He did not alter the chair in any other way. He performed one simple modification: he converted a wooden chair to a bronze chair. This simple conceptual act had profound ramifications. Identical to the original chair in every way, except material, the chair was no longer a chair; it was sculpture. As sculpture that was *about* a chair, it became philosophical. The Burton chair was profoundly transformed by a simple act. It is cold to the touch, rock hard, and extremely heavy, but it looks exactly like a chair and . . . you can sit in it!

→ **A**

Gian Lorenzo Bernini. ***The Rape of Proserpina*****, detail of Pluto's hands. 1621–22. Marble, height 9' 8". Galleria Borghese, Rome.**

Tara Donovan. *Haze.* 2003. Installation with translucent drinking straws, dimensions variable.

Tara Donovan. *Haze*, detail. 2003. Installation with translucent drinking straws, dimensions variable.

Scott Burton. *Bronze Chair.* 1979. Solid cast bronze, 3' 8⅛" × 1' 9½" × 1' 10½". © 2011 Estate of Scott Burton/Artists Rights Society (ARS), New York.

ALTERING FORM

Variation

Why do designers and artists create variations on a theme? Isn't one version enough? There are compelling reasons for this design tactic; one is—to get it right. The first, second, and third versions (also referred to as **iterations**) might not express exactly what needs to be stated, so perhaps a fourth version is required. The end result is four interesting and related objects, but with varying attributes. Another reason for working with variations is simply the fact that certain issues and themes suggest numerous responses. When a single conclusion will not suffice, different points of view are required to fully understand the subject.

Henri Matisse created four versions, in bronze relief, of the female back **(A, B, C, D)**. Matisse did not create these pieces as a series; they were generated by a theme of great interest that he returned to repeatedly during a period of more than twenty years. These monolithic reliefs allowed Matisse to use sculpture to inform his painting—relief is the flattest form of sculpture and can be rectangular—in this way, relief is painting's kindred spirit. In these four works, Matisse explored ideas of realism and pursued a development toward greater abstraction. The back in **D**, the final piece, evolved into a figure that is primarily about form—the vertical masses of the bifurcated back and their relationship to the rectangular frame.

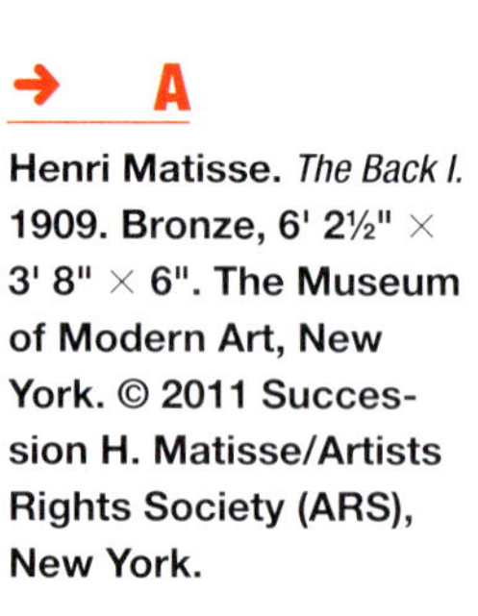

→ **A**

Henri Matisse. ***The Back I.*** **1909. Bronze, 6' 2½" × 3' 8" × 6". The Museum of Modern Art, New York. © 2011 Succession H. Matisse/Artists Rights Society (ARS), New York.**

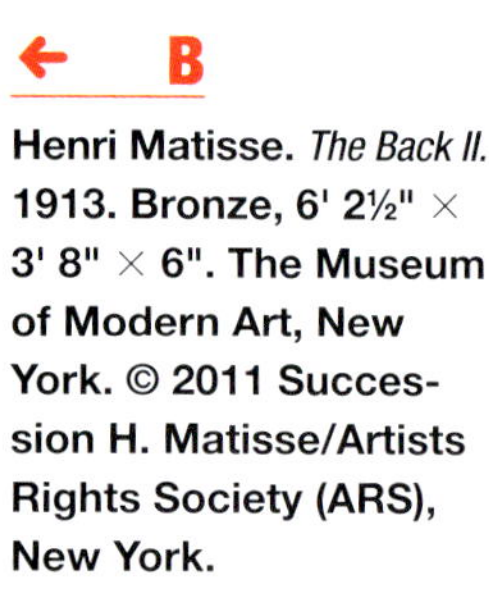

← **B**

Henri Matisse. ***The Back II.*** **1913. Bronze, 6' 2½" × 3' 8" × 6". The Museum of Modern Art, New York. © 2011 Succession H. Matisse/Artists Rights Society (ARS), New York.**

→ **C**

Henri Matisse. ***The Back III.*** **1916–1917. Bronze, 6' 2½" × 3' 8" × 6". The Museum of Modern Art, New York. © 2011 Succession H. Matisse/Artists Rights Society (ARS), New York.**

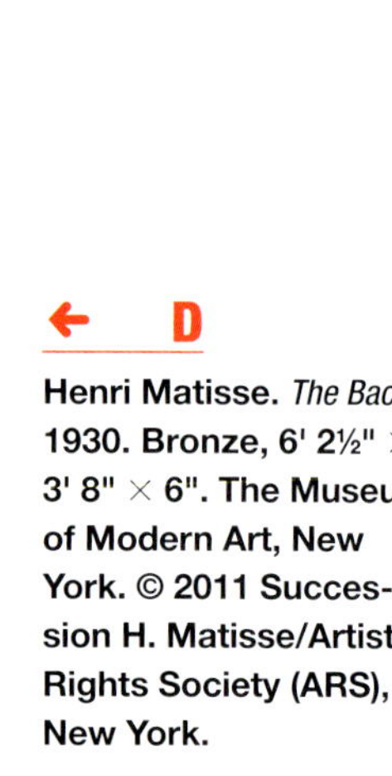

← **D**

Henri Matisse. ***The Back IV.*** **1930. Bronze, 6' 2½" × 3' 8" × 6". The Museum of Modern Art, New York. © 2011 Succession H. Matisse/Artists Rights Society (ARS), New York.**

Images **E** and **F** are two variations of many that the architecture firm SITE designed for a company that owned numerous big-box stores in the 1970s. SITE preserved the basic, efficient box structure of the buildings but decorated the façades in inventive and destabilizing ways, riffing on antiquity and suburbia, and creating variations that once seen are never forgotten.

Deformation

Deformation plays an important role in art, design, and architecture. It involves rethinking and reinventing established forms or pre-existing elements. It can entail anything from a complete restructuring to a subtle tweak. In some way, all creation involves a deformative act, as there is always a prior format or genre.

George Ohr took a common form of **ceramic** vase and had a great deal of fun with it **(G)**. He dented the side of a freshly thrown clay vessel until its side collapsed, creating a new vase in which the original form as well as the process of its deformation remain clearly visible.

The painter Jasper Johns suggests, "Take an object. Do something to it. Do something else to it. Do something else to it."

Peeling Project. 1971. Richmond, Virginia. SITE architecture, art and design.

Indeterminate Façade Building. 1974. Houston, Texas. SITE architecture, art and design.

↑ G

George Ohr. *Lighthouse pot.* c. 1895.

FOCUSED INVESTIGATION

Throughout history, artists and designers have worked in series. Monet painted numerous versions of water lilies, haystacks, and Rouen Cathedral. Degas returned repeatedly to ballet dancers and their classic positions. The rise of scientific method as well as modern mass production enhanced interest in the series—consider the automobile production line or the similar yet different houses in a suburban development. Nature as well loves the series—scientists estimate over 9,000 species of birds in the world. Matisse observed that every fig leaf is different, but all are always unmistakably fig leaves.

In the arts and design, a series can be based on a theme, a form, a process, or an idea. Each element in a series varies from the others while maintaining a distinct similarity. Series allow creators to investigate issues more deeply than a single work would permit.

Conceptual Series

Sol LeWitt created a **conceptual** sculpture series titled *Incomplete Open Cubes* **(A)** that included all 122 variations of an open-sided cube missing between one and nine of its edges. To create this work, LeWitt followed his initial concept rigorously—122 permutations based on a generating principle. It is exciting to see the range of formal variation and expressive form resulting from such a methodical approach.

Sol LeWitt. ***Incomplete Open Cubes.*** **1974. Installation: painted wood structures, gelatin silver prints, and drawings on paper, sculptures: 8" × 8" × 8", framed works: 2' 2" × 1' 2", base: 1' × 10' × 18'. Collection SFMOMA. © 2011 The LeWitt Estate/Artists Rights Society (ARS), New York.**

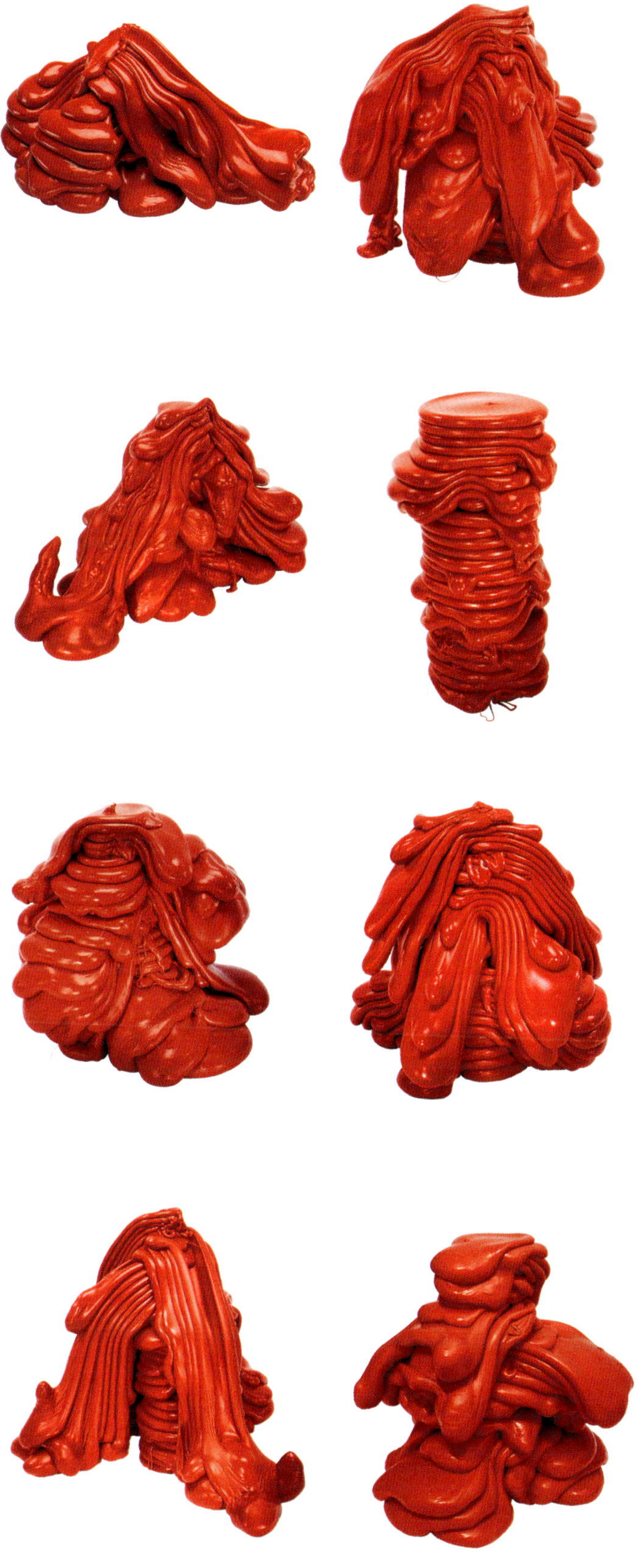

↑ B

Roxy Paine. Eight sculptures. All 2003 except lower left 2007. Low density polyethylene, dimensions vary from 1' 6" to 2' 6" h. Courtesy the artist and James Cohan Gallery, New York/Shanghai.

Seriality and Process

Roxy Paine used a modified industrial extruding process and a set of computer instructions to create a sculpture series **(B)**. "Engaged ambivalence" is how he refers to his involvement in this automated fabrication process. His sculpture machine discharges piles of layered polyethylene to create a series that is at once thoroughly consistent and exuberantly diverse.

Thematic Series

Some series are based on observed reality. The goose decoys on a frozen lake **(C)** depict geese in varying positions. Only the series would allow the maker to articulate an array of archetypal positions.

↑ C

Goose decoys on a frozen lake.

THE IDEA BECOMES A MACHINE THAT MAKES THE ART

"If the idea is there, the brush can spare itself the work." This Chinese painter's proverb makes it very clear that concepts have always been important to the arts. Art and design involve ideas; consequently, it might be safe to say that all art and design are conceptual. Some traditional genres, such as Realism, that have very long histories might seem devoid of concept, but this is only because we have so completely assimilated their histories and methodologies that they appear "natural," obvious, inevitable. In fact, Realism is quite a rich conceptual domain.

Let's look again at Sol LeWitt's *Incomplete Open Cubes* **(A)**. They were generated entirely by a single operational idea—construct all 122 permutations of an open-sided cube missing between one and nine of its edges. LeWitt has written, "In conceptual art the idea or concept is the most important aspect of the work. When an artist uses a conceptual form of art, it means that all of the planning and decisions are made beforehand and the execution is a perfunctory affair. The idea becomes a machine that makes the art."

Cloaca **(B)** is an installation that explores the operation of the digestive system of the human body. Though it *looks* nothing like its subject (constructed of glass vats, tubes, pumps, and digestive enzymes), it does *function* like a digestive system. Cloaca is "fed" real food; fecal matter is the end product. This sculpture, with its straightforward conceptual approach, would be equally at home in a science laboratory. It is a good example

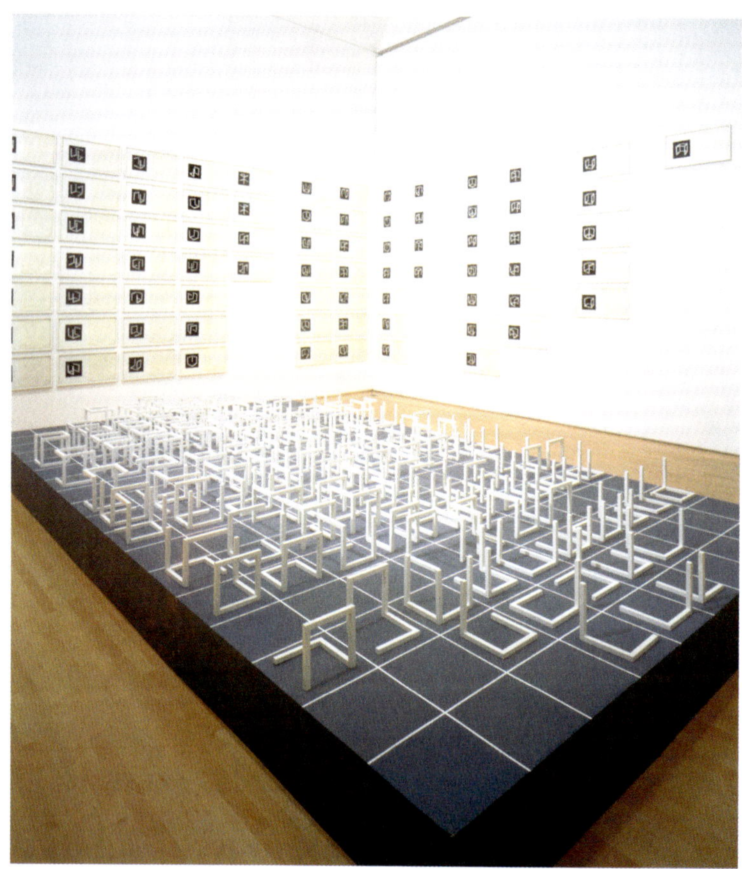

Sol LeWitt. *Incomplete Open Cubes.* **1974. Installation: painted wood structures, gelatin silver prints, and drawings on paper, sculptures: 8" × 8" × 8", framed works: 2' 2" × 1' 2", base: 1' × 10' × 18'. Collection SFMOMA.**

of a work of art that completely avoids traditional aesthetic values, while perhaps suggesting a new aesthetic model.

Extreme Concept

AN OBJECT TOSSED FROM ONE COUNTRY TO ANOTHER.

Some conceptual work is all concept, no object. In the above statement (in blue text) created in 1969, artist Lawrence Weiner made language the vehicle of his art. Whether painted on a wall or printed here, the words, "an object tossed from one country to another," *are* the art. Whether this work is read or performed, and whether you consider it sculpture, theater, or literature, you must admit that, with the lightest of touches, it delivers so much. In 1968 Weiner wrote this statement of intent:

1. THE ARTIST MAY CONSTRUCT THE WORK
2. THE WORK MAY BE FABRICATED
3. THE WORK NEED NOT BE BUILT

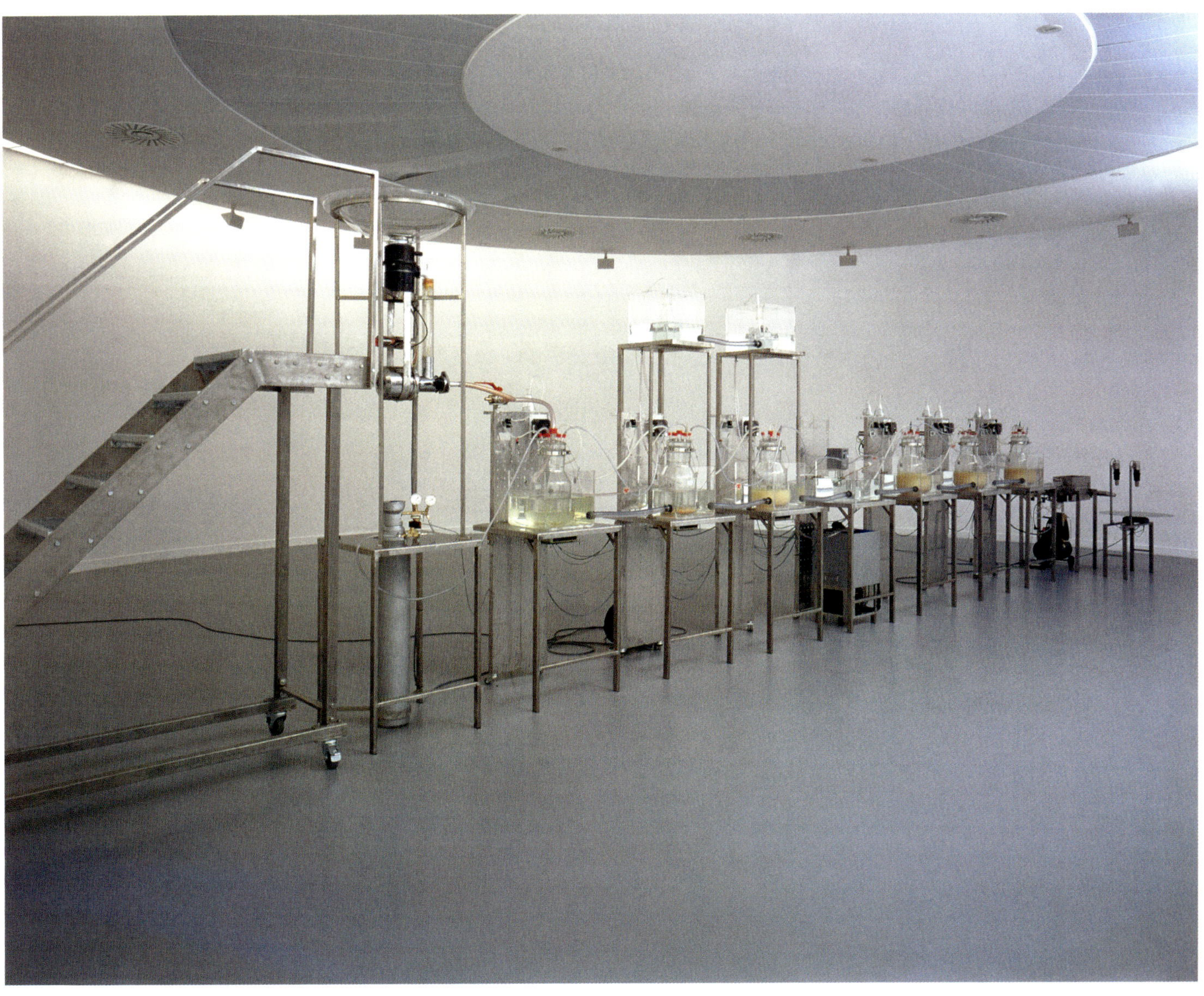

↑ **B**

Wim Delvoye. ***Cloaca.*** **2000.**

DISCOVERY

Let my playing be my learning, and my learning be my playing.

—Johan Huizinga

Play

In 1938 the Dutch scholar Johan Huizinga wrote the book *Homo Ludens* (Man the Player). Huizinga made a powerful case for the importance of the play element in culture. To Huizinga, play is not a cultural amusement; it is a necessity! Artists and designers perform acts of serious play in order to arrive at new discoveries.

Casually constructed of such materials as wire, wood, cork, and cloth, *Cirque Calder* **(A)** is a miniature version of a circus. *Cirque Calder* is not only a sculpture but a set of props that Alexander Calder used to enact live performances. This childlike involvement with the circus and the rudimentary nature of the craft utilized by one of the major sculptors of the twentieth century affirm the importance of play to creativity.

Both hearts and teapots are liquid-bearing vessels, but to actually construct a teapot in the form of a realistic human heart and its arteries, as Richard Notkin does in **B**, is a bold leap that renders a functional object whimsical and surreal.

Invention

Seeing similarities and differences, and playfully combining and manipulating forms, can enable us to discover objects in our environment and utilize them in new ways. In 1942 Picasso took a bicycle seat and handlebars, and through an act of great imagination created a quite realistic bull's head with horns **(C)**.

Those who simply love the language and materials of art and design, and spend countless hours playfully exploring, create a surprising amount of great work. Play need not lead only to playful creations. Play, as a methodology or a sensibility, can lead to serious discoveries.

Problem Solving

Innovation and invention are achieved via numerous paths. While the element of play is a major factor for many, more systematic problem-solving methods are also extremely valuable, especially in the design disciplines. There are many problem-solving methodologies, and the various disciplines favor specific approaches. Some principles common to a number of such systems include brainstorming (especially with an interdisciplinary team), breaking down large problems into small discrete units, lateral thinking (avoiding the obvious direct approach), and research (investigating existing solutions to related problems).

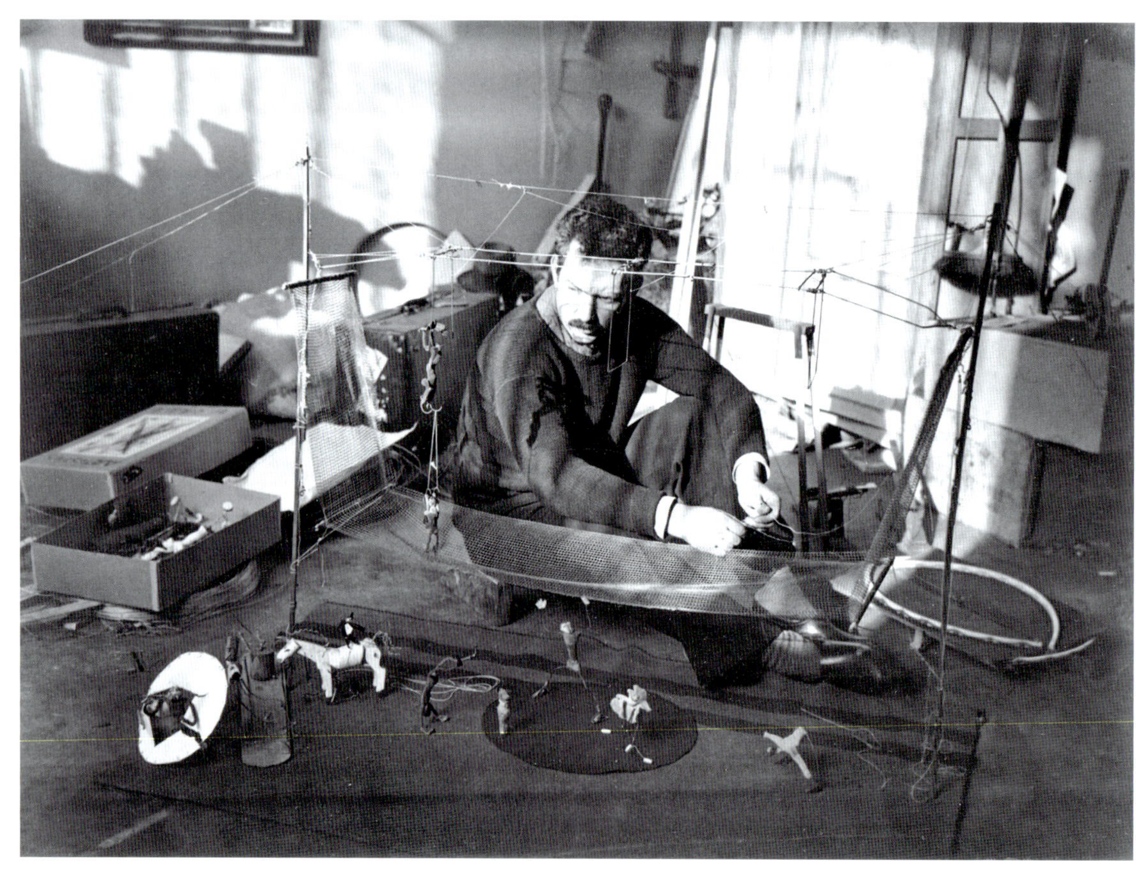

 **A**

Alexander Calder with his *Cirque Calder* (1926–1930).

 B

Richard Notkin. *Heart Teapot: The Pump II,* Yixing Series. 1990. Stoneware, 6⅛" × 10½" × 4⅞".

Pablo Picasso. *Bull's Head.* Assemblage, bicycle seat and handle bars, 1' ½" × 1' × 7½". © 2011 Estate of Pablo Picasso/Artists Rights Society (ARS), New York.

REDUCTIVE SENSIBILITY

Simplicity is not an objective in art, but one achieves simplicity despite oneself by entering into the real sense of things.

—*Constantin Brancusi*

It would be difficult to overstate the importance of reductive strategies in art and in life. When we think of reductive form, **Minimalism** and International Style architecture, with their tenet "less is more," might first come to mind. Minimalist sculptors like Donald Judd clearly made pure form—devoid of figuration and decoration—the central focus of their attention. The unadorned plywood and geometric structure of the sculpture in **A** celebrates essential, formal relationships in a severe and straightforward manner.

We may also think of reductive form as a strategy for bracketing out the world. Jettisoning the noise and cacophony of daily life, simplicity allows the viewer to experience a perceptual slowing down and heightened awareness.

Many artists, designers, and artisans throughout history have demanded that simplicity come first, but even fields removed from what we think of as conventional design disciplines can embody the general sensibility of a culture. The sushi in **B** exemplifies the reductive spirit of traditional Japanese design. Sushi is not only visually reductive, one or two elements juxtaposed, but one or two tastes are carefully balanced. And sushi is not cooked—simplicity extends even to its preparation.

One common mistake of the beginning student involves the tendency to put everything he or she *likes* into a single work. Yes, it is good to be motivated by that which excites you, but, if you made a stew, would you put in everything you like? Steak, apples, mustard, and ice cream? In art and design, as in the creation of a meal, carefully considered proportions of very specific elements are the key to success.

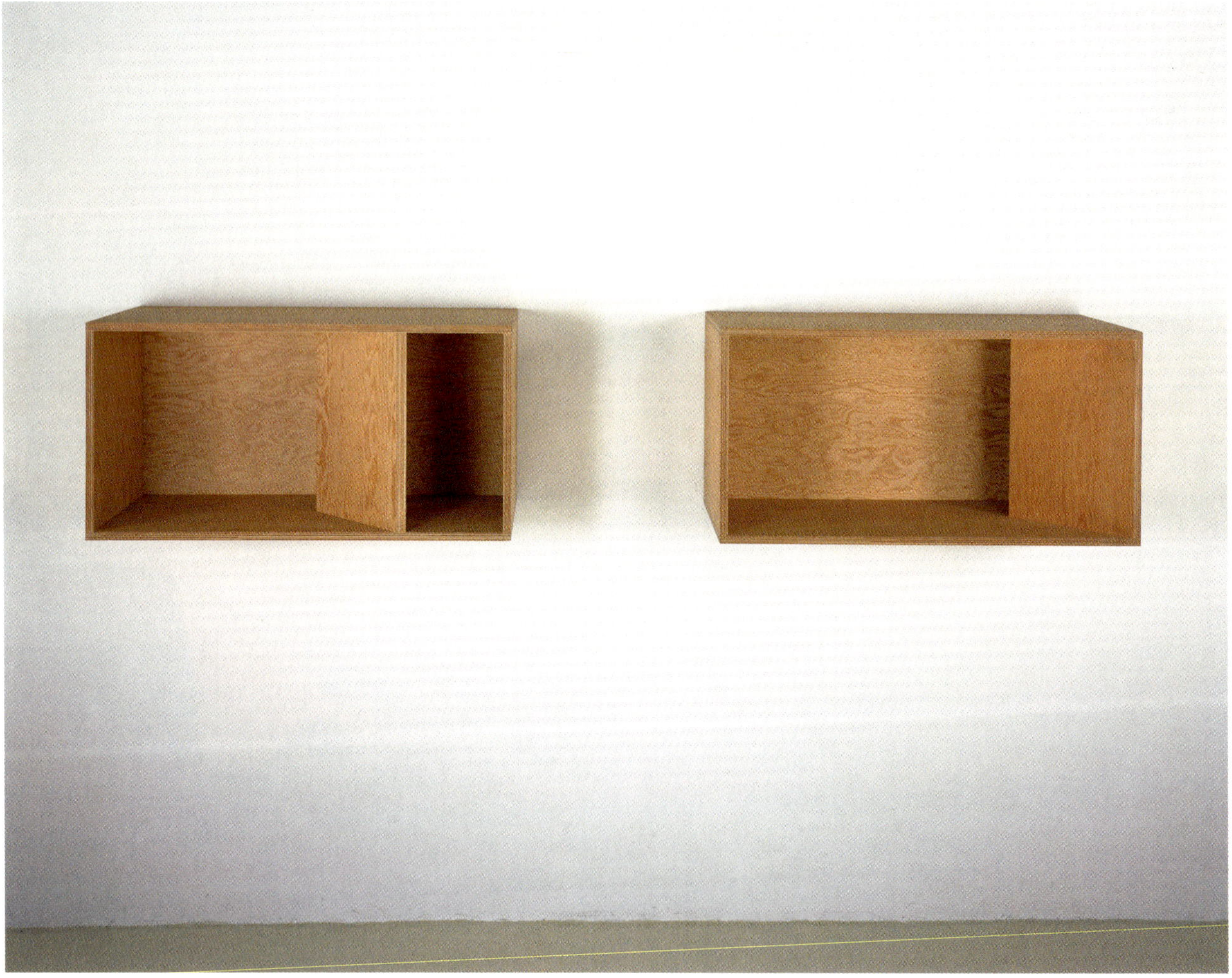

 **A**

Donald Judd. ***Untitled.*** **1989. Two plywood units, 1' 7$\frac{11}{16}$" × 3' 3$\frac{3}{8}$" × 1' 7$\frac{11}{16}$" × each. Donald Judd Photography by Ellen Page Wilson, courtesy The Pace Gallery. © Judd Foundation. Licensed by VAGA, New York.**

Economy of Means

Perhaps even more important than the appreciation of minimal form is the interconnected idea—economy of means. This idea manifests itself in both simple and complex forms; it is not a concern limited to abstract artists or designers with a geometric style. Paring down form and communication to *only that which is essential* has always been important.

Robert Maillart's barrel-vaulted shell **(C)** was a bold, early experiment in reinforced concrete construction. It spanned 53 feet with a shell thickness of a mere 2⅜", testing the structural limits of a new material (sprayed concrete and steel mesh). Maillart's shell, along with objects such as racing bicycles and jet airplanes, are pared down forms utilizing as little material as possible. You can sense the designers thinking, "How light can we go?"

Economy of means raises the question "what is essential?" It also suggests the good old-fashioned values of frugality. These ideas reverberate with new meaning as we confront the prospect of diminishing natural resources and endangered ecosystems worldwide.

On your next project, try asking yourself, "What is unnecessary? What can be eliminated?"

See also *Sustainability: Reuse and Green Design*, page 134, and *Structural Economy: Efficient Form*, page 140.

> *Vigorous writing is concise. A sentence should contain no unnecessary words, a paragraph no unnecessary sentences, for the same reason that a drawing should have no unnecessary lines and a machine no unnecessary parts. This requires not that the writer make all his sentences short, or that he avoid all detail and treat his subjects only in outline, but that every word tell.*
>
> —*William Strunk, in* The Elements of Style

> *Perfection is reached not when there is nothing more to be added but when there is nothing to be taken away.*
>
> —*Antoine de Saint Exupery*

 B

Tako Octopus Sushi (foreground).

Robert Maillart. Cement Industries Hall, Swiss National Exhibition. 1939. Zurich, Switzerland. The Museum of Modern Art, New York.

IDEATION

It is hard to imagine anything more important to the design process than sketching, model making, and prototyping. Sitting still and attempting to simply *think up* ideas just isn't effective. Developing solutions to design problems and creating art require both thought and action.

Sketching and making models and prototypes are activities that facilitate successful **ideation** and invention. Making a sketch or model allows you to see and test your idea, and that prompts modifications as well as the opportunity to detect something unexpected, something that can lead to new and better ideas. Sketches and models need not be beautiful or highly crafted; in fact, many sketches seem dashed off, and models may be rough and crude—mock-ups that contain the bare bones of only that which needs to be present.

Sketching

The sketches for the Guggenheim Museum in Bilbao, Spain **(A)**, are more like energy diagrams than accurate depictions; nevertheless, they perfectly express the dynamic fluidity of the finished building (see Guggenheim, Bilbao, page 188).

> *As soon as I understand the scale of the building and the relationship to the site and the relationship to the client, as it becomes more and more clear to me, I start doing sketches.*
>
> —*Frank Gehry*

Model Making

The sculptor David Smith used cardboard boxes taped to his studio window **(B)** to develop ideas for his large-scale, welded steel sculpture **(C)**. In the model, he has total freedom to move his forms around, searching for the most powerful relationships, and he can do it with a speed that is simply impossible when hoisting and welding heavy stainless steel boxes. A model that is reduced in scale, like the one in **B**, is also called a **maquette**.

↑ **A**

Frank Gehry. Sketch of Guggenheim Museum Bilbao. Bilbao, Spain.

David Smith assembling liquor boxes as models for his sculptures.

Prototypes

In **D**, the designer utilizes simple paper silhouettes to test her idea for the shape and placement of the handle on her prototype pitcher. A prototype is a unique object that is a full-scale working model of the product being designed. It can be used and tested for effectiveness. Often, a number of prototypes are produced in succession, each attempting to improve an aspect of the previous one. In the case of the pitcher **(D)**, the prototype can be used to evaluate its form (from every angle), judge the comfort of the handle in use, or ascertain the spout's pouring characteristics. After a successful pitcher prototype is arrived at, molds are made and the pitcher goes into production.

C

David Smith with completed sculptures *Cubi IV* and *Cubi V*. Art © Estate of David Smith/Licensed by VAGA, New York.

D

Eva Zeisel working on a model.

CLOSE ATTENTION

God is in the details.

—Ludwig Mies van der Rohe

Observing and interacting with designed objects and buildings in which primary form is in synch with minor characteristics can be exhilarating. It is not enough to have a good idea if it is executed without care.

Consider traditional handcrafted wood joinery. If the facets are not cut perfectly flat, if the corners are not clean and sharp, and if the angles are not exact, the joinery will not be structurally sound. Here, attention to detail is required for functionality.

Looking again at the chair in **A** reveals a very special attention to detail. The designer made numerous drawings, studies, and prototypes to get the details right, carefully considering the size and placement of the welds, the size and number of crimps to bend a tube, and the proportions of every element.

Totalizing Detail

The dining room interior **(B)** is defined by the primary elements of space, structure, and proportion, but the architect Frank Lloyd Wright went well beyond these elements. He designed every aspect of this room—table, chairs, lamps, and built-in seating, shelving, and decorative elements. From macro to micro, this extreme attention to detail allowed the architect to extend and amplify his design sensibility.

Jean Prouvé. Standard chair. 1950.

Frank Lloyd Wright. Robie House, dining room. 1910. Chicago.

Precision

Precision in the past was less available and more difficult to achieve. To a large extent, only nobility and the wealthy could afford the expert craftwork that resulted in precision products such as fine handmade watches, perfectly balanced swords, precise measuring devices, and intricate textiles. Today, technology and industrial production have made precision available to multitudes. In this regard, precision might be considered a modern phenomenon. Consider laser cutting technology, the computer, computer memory chips **(C)**, integrated circuit boards, satellites, surgical technology, digital imaging, cell phones, and the automobile engine.

Appropriate Craft

Attention to detail requires neither high craft and finish **fetishism**, nor that all aspects of a sculpture, product, or building be pristine or geometric, only that everything be considered and *appropriately* crafted.

↑ C

Computer memory chip, Intel Core 2010 (microscopic view).

AN INTERPRETIVE ACT

Meaning

In 1994 a four-foot-tall, bullet-shaped chunk of granite **(A)** was discovered by Hindus and New Agers in a remote section of Golden Gate Park and fast became a sacred shrine. Believed to be a symbol of the divine Siva, throngs of devotees left offerings of flower garlands, milk, and sandalwood paste. The rock, probably, originally a parking barrier, was deposited at the site by a worker practicing with heavy equipment, said a city official. It was eventually removed. A park representative said, "It is basically a piece of rubble. It's not part of the park."

The problem of meaning has long fascinated philosophers and cultural critics. In the deepest sense, meaning is now understood to be a notion assigned to objects by viewers, not simply something that is built into objects and hardwired. It is a dialogue between viewers and the properties of objects and events. Meaning is also relative—it varies from culture to culture and changes over time. It is an interpretive act, requiring effort on the part of the viewer.

Improvised shrine in Golden Gate Park. c. 1994. San Francisco. Photographer: Susan Spann. Image scanned from January 16, 1994 *New York Times.*

Value

Value (here referring to significance) is one of the most slippery and important concepts in the arts. We all need to assign value to things and ideas in the world. Failing in this would render us unable to decide how to order our lives, how to proceed, and what to make. Works of art in the museum have achieved significance over time, either by consensus or by expert opinion. One would be imprudent to ignore the wisdom that has accrued over the ages, and the values of one's time; nevertheless, it is up to every individual to formulate a personal value system, without which we would be deprived of the thrill of new ideas and condemned to remake the art and architecture of the past.

The photograph in **B** shows Nelito, a boy from an impoverished region of Mozambique, and his homemade soccer ball. He had to be resourceful, gathering and assembling scarce materials to make his own, simulated soccer ball. Compared to a new, regulation, Adidas ball, what value would you assign to Nelito's? Compared to a diamond ring?

 **B**

Jessica Hiltout, photographer. *Nelito's Ball.* **Nhambonda, Mozambique. From the book *Amen: Grassroots Football*, 2010.**

GENERATING CREATIVE ENERGY

Artists and designers are always on the prowl for information and inspiration. Bountiful wellsprings, repeatedly turned to, are called sources. **Source** material can come from anywhere; it only needs to inspire and generate creative energy. Artists and designers are nourished by their sources and often come to cherish them.

The source for many artists and designers is, not surprisingly, other art and design, both contemporary and historical; but nature, geometry, and culture at large are especially valuable influences as well. An artist's or designer's source may often be barely observable in the work or completely invisible—it may be a spiritual or conceptual inspiration. Sometimes the source is overt and extremely evident.

The work of Marcel Duchamp has long cast a powerful spell on countless artists. Dropping a meter-long thread from the height of one meter, three times, Duchamp created three new, meter-long templates that were all different lengths—*Three Standard Stoppages* **(A)**. Using chance operations to determine form, Duchamp commented on the arbitrary and relative nature of standards and hierarchies.

Forty-eight years later, Robert Morris created a sly, pop culture homage to Duchamp's *Three Standard Stoppages*, titled *Three Rulers*. Three found, wood, hardware store yardsticks were hung together, side by side on a wall. Such yardsticks were once given free to store patrons. Due to their cheap and sloppy fabrication, Morris's rulers are all slightly different lengths.

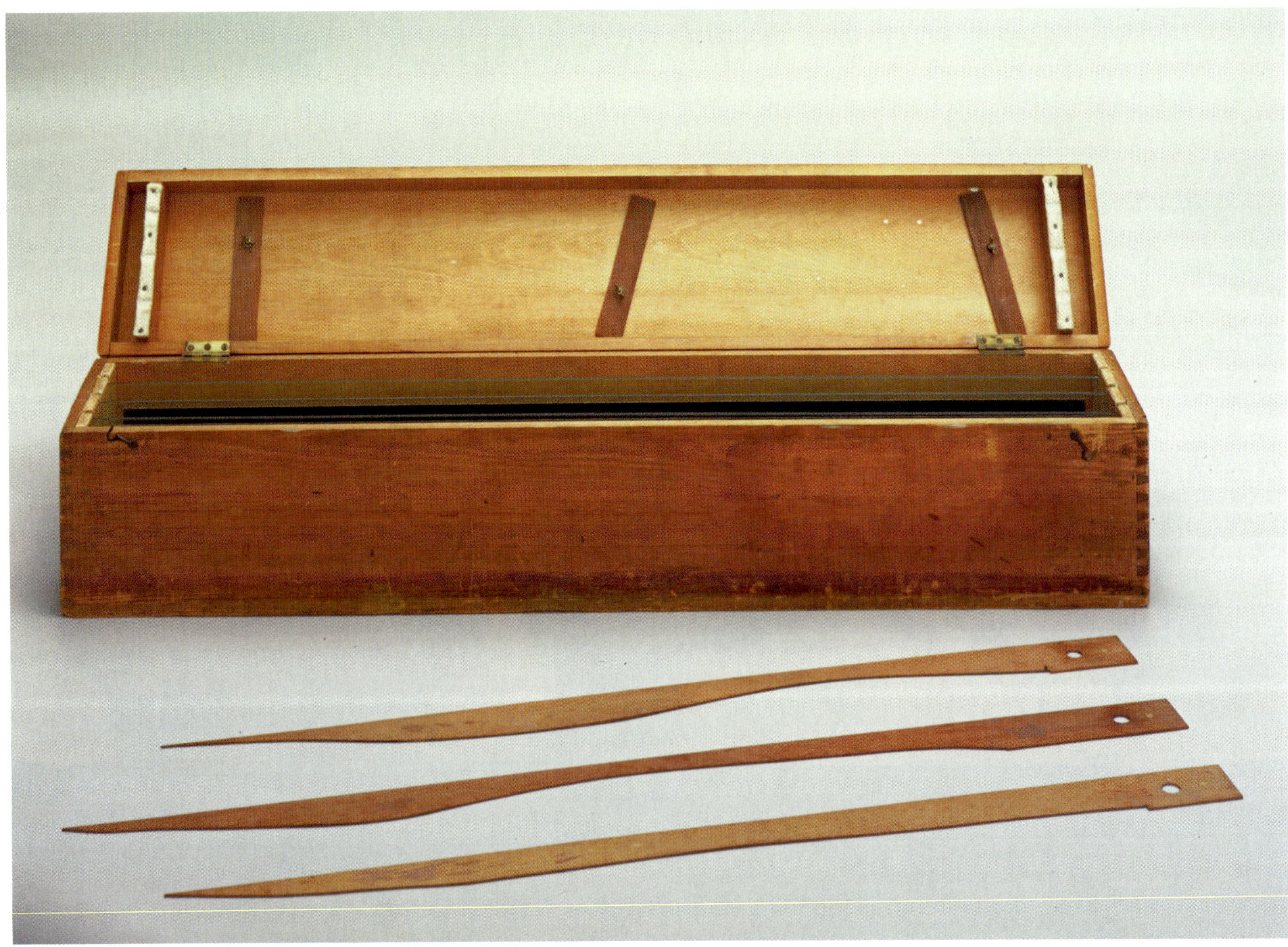

↑ A

Marcel Duchamp. *3 Standard Stoppages.* 1913–1914. © 2011 Artists Rights Society (ARS), New York/ADAGP, Paris/Succession Marcel Duchamp.

Influence

For a recent line of clothing, the designer, Raf Simons, was inspired by the French mid-century ceramist Pol Chambost (who was himself inspired by natural forms). The formal similarities between Chambost's ceramic vessel **(B)** and the soft fabric coat **(C)** are quite evident—biomorphic structure and interior/exterior color.

Obsession

Sometimes an inspiring source becomes an obsession. For example, many painters found inspiration in the work of Picasso, but Arshile Gorky was more intensely preoccupied than most. When Gorky said, referring to Picasso, "If he drips, I drip," the line between source and obsession was blurred.

References

When a visual similarity to another artwork or any built or natural form is observable in a work of art, design, or architecture, we call it a reference. When you sense natural forms, rock and bone, in the abstract sculpture of Henry Moore, you can say that the sculpture refers to nature or that nature is a reference.

B

Pol Chambost. ***Vase.*** **c. 1954. © 2011 Artists Rights Society (ARS), New York/ADAGP, Paris.**

C

Raf Simons, designer. For Jil Sander. Fall 2009 Ready to Wear.

NATURE

Nature is the ultimate source. It envelops all. Artists, designers, and architects have always looked to nature for ideas and inspiration. The scale and spectacle of its realm and its overwhelming diversity—plants, insects, fish, mammals, rock formations, oceans, weather, and the cosmos at large—render nature the source of all sources, and humbles us as we stand before its magnitude and deep mysteries. We are inspired even while knowing, as fellow creators, we will always be decisively outperformed.

Biomorphism

Nature, especially in the form of rock, shell, and bone, was a vital source and inspiration for the sculptor Henry Moore. Most of us who are inspired by nature find ourselves collecting bits and pieces of it wherever possible. Moore was no exception. A selection from his collection of bones **(A)** clearly demonstrates the reciprocal nature of collecting source material. Moore's sculpture **(B)** looks a lot like the bones he collected, and the bones he collected were those that resembled his sculpture.

Henry Moore was enamored of twisting forms, gracefully flowing forms, holes that penetrate form, and textural variation. Nature provided him with an extensive range of models. The term **biomorphic** is used to categorize design and art that, like Moore's, utilize flowing organic form reminiscent of nature.

Art Nouveau also found inspiration in organic form. The design of the Art Nouveau ornamental ironwork in **C** is derived from plant forms and the exuberant, twisting patterns of growing tendrils.

 **A**

Henry Moore's collection of bones. Reproduced by permission of The Henry Moore Foundation.

There is recorded in a Zen book an episode which took place a long time ago in China, when a novice came to see Shô Zenji, a Zen master who lives at Sekken, and, wishing to study under him, asked the master, "I have come to be in my novitiate for the first time. From where shall I enter into the study of Zen?" The master, thereupon, asked him in return, "Canst thou hear the sound of that mountain stream?" The novice answered, "Yes, I hear it." The master told him, "Then enter from there."

—Zenkei Shibayama

For the artist communication with nature remains the most essential condition. The artist is human, himself nature, part of nature within natural space.

—Charles Biederman

He who is in harmony with Nature hits the mark without effort and apprehends the truth without thinking.

—Confucius

 **C**

Hector Guimard. Entrance gate of Castel Berenger, Paris. 1898.

 **B**

Henry Moore. ***Standing Figure.*** **1962. Bronze height 9'4". Reproduced with permission of the Henry Moore Foundation.**

GEOMETRY AND MATHEMATICS

God always geometrizes.

—*Plato*

Mathematics and geometry are omnipresent in the built world. Look around and you will see straight lines, squares, cubes, triangles, and circles everywhere, as well as number and proportion. The vast majority of contemporary structures, from individual rooms to houses and buildings, are based on the rectangle. In bridges, towers, and other structures with strict functional requirements, the triangle reigns supreme. Triangulation results in extremely stable structures.

Geometry and Philosophy

Some 3D forms are of special historical importance, such as the five Platonic solids of geometry **(A)**. They possess special properties, unique configurations, and flawless symmetry.

In Plato's *Dialogues*, Socrates proclaims,

> *. . . what the argument points to, is something straight or round, and the surfaces and solids which a lathe or carpenter's rule and square produces from the straight and round. I wonder if you understand. Things of that sort, I maintain, are beautiful, not, like most things, in a relative sense; they are always beautiful in their very nature, and they offer pleasures peculiar to themselves, and quite unlike others. They have that purity which makes for truth. They are philosophical.*

Geometry and Mathematics in Nature

Forms that reveal a marked mathematical and geometrical structure are also widely evident in nature. There are countless examples: crystals, sunflowers, bubbles, rainbows, growth patterns, spiral nebula, and DNA's double helix. The bee's honeycomb **(B)** is a network of hexagons, and hexagonal rods are among the twenty-two polyhedrons or combinations of polyhedrons that allow for the most efficient packing of space.

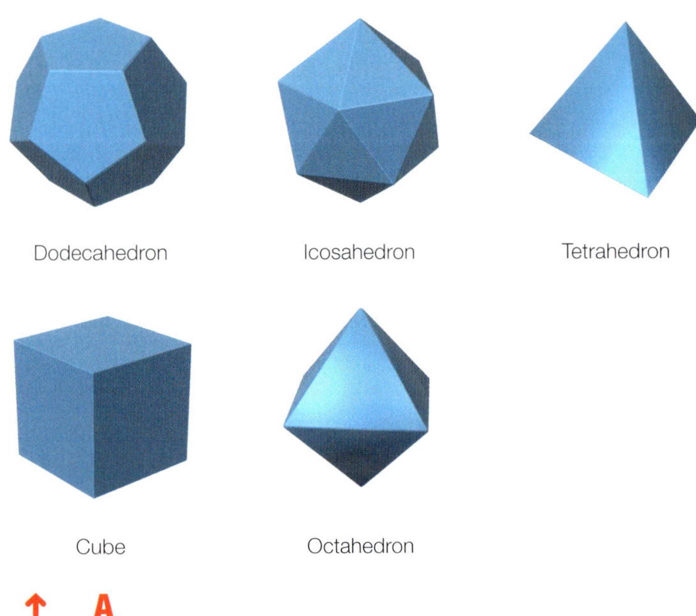

↑ A

Five Platonic solids.

→ B

Honeycomb and honeybee.

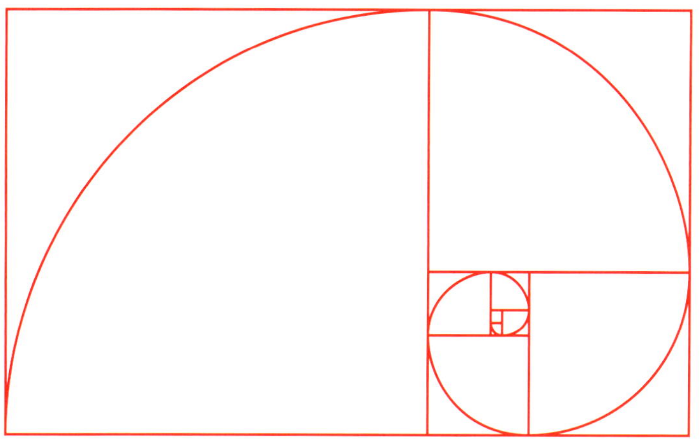

C

Golden Spiral in golden rectangle.

No discussion of mathematics in nature could be complete without mentioning the Fibonacci series and its relationship to the golden rectangle and the spiral. The numbers of the Fibonacci series are 1, 1, 2, 3, 5, 8, 13, 21, 34, and so forth. Add two consecutive numbers together to create the next. Rectangles with a 3 to 5 ratio are known as golden rectangles, and the 3:5 ratio is the **golden mean** (symbolized by the Greek letter ø). A series of consecutively smaller golden rectangles can be placed to describe the path of a golden spiral **(C)**, and the golden spiral is the spiral of the chambered nautilus **(D)** and many other spirals found in nature. Many artists and designers have used 3:5 proportions in their work, believing that the golden rectangle has unique harmonic properties.

D'Arcy Wentworth Thompson studied the physical and mathematical laws that determine biological form. In **E** he shows how the porcupine fish on the left may appear transformed into a sunfish (right) due to a different growth pattern, a pattern that is represented by a simple deformed grid.

D

Chambered nautilus, cross section.

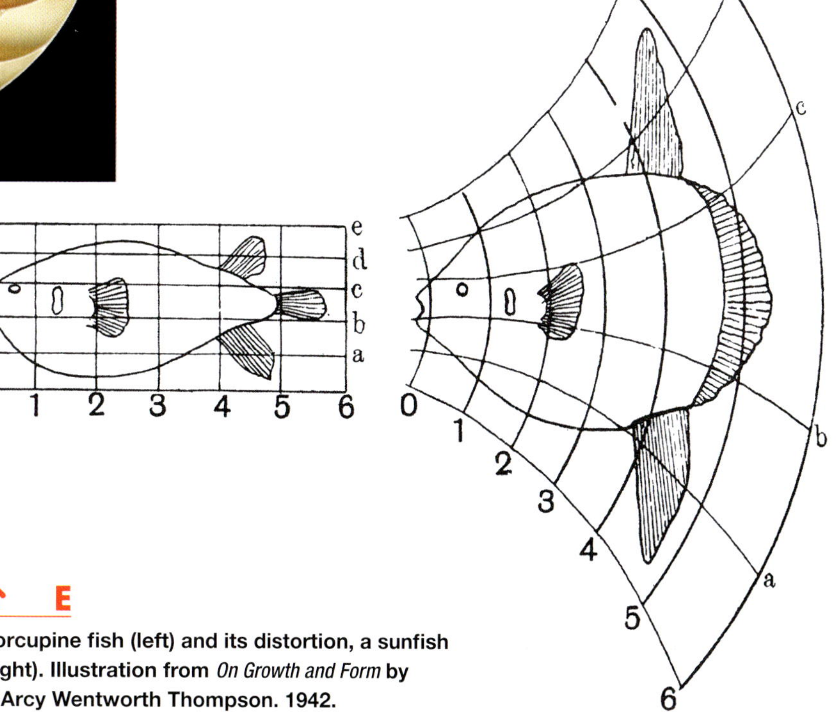

E

Porcupine fish (left) and its distortion, a sunfish (right). Illustration from *On Growth and Form* by D'Arcy Wentworth Thompson. 1942.

CULTURE

The wide realm of culture is a source of increasing importance. Film director Werner Herzog said, "My friends are wondering why did I watch Anna Nicole Smith's show. Why do I watch Wrestlemania? My answer is . . . the poet must not avert his eyes. . . ."

Cultural anthropologists originated one of the most significant changes in our perception of art and design! In the past, the word *culture* most often implied the fine arts, classical music, the great books—the most refined esthetic forms. Today, thanks to anthropologists and the philosophers and theorists who also contributed to this paradigm shift, culture is increasingly understood to be *all* the customs and products of human beings—from everyday cooking to dating rituals. To the anthropological eye, the low is as important as the high, and maybe more important. If you were visiting Earth from another planet and you wanted to find out what human beings were all about, where do you think you would learn more—at the symphony or . . . a flea market?

Andy Warhol. ***Brillo Boxes.*** **1964. 2011. Synthetic polymer paint and silkscreen on wood, each 1' 5⅛" × 1' 5" × 1' 2". © 2011 The Andy Warhol Foundation for the Visual Arts, Inc./Artists Rights Society (ARS), New York. The Museum of Modern Art, New York.**

The Vernacular

This change of attitude was not lost on artists, architects, and designers. Since the early twentieth century, artists and designers increasingly turned to the **vernacular**, a hallmark of both **modernism** and **postmodernism**, and in so doing, they democratized subject matter. The **ash-can school** artists went up on tenement rooftops and down to the subways to find beauty and meaning in the ordinary, the everyday, and the humble. Edward Hopper painted the gas station, and Stuart Davis the Champion spark plug logo. John Cage said, "Everything you listen to is music, everything you don't listen to is noise." Duchamp invented the "**ready-made**," and Warhol discovered the Brillo box **(A)**.

Guild House **(B)**, a housing project for the elderly, was inspired by vernacular, commercial architecture. In other words, the architects, Robert Venturi and Denise Scott Brown, looked to the "lowest," most ordinary kinds of architectural sources instead of the most sophisticated buildings. They favored "ugly and ordinary" architecture over "heroic and original." In 1977 they took a class of Yale graduate architecture students on a trip to seriously study something so vulgar most architects at the time could only sneer—Las Vegas, the ultimate commercial strip.

Guild House opened in 1964 with an oversized, gold anodized TV antenna **(C)** mounted conspicuously above the building's entrance. Not a functioning antenna, it served as sculpture, a symbol intended as a nod to its elderly occupants' involvement with television. Perceived as disparaging, eventually the antenna was removed.

B

Robert Venturi and Denise Scott Brown. Guild House. 1964.

C

Robert Venturi and Denise Scott Brown. Guild House, detail of antenna/sculpture. 1964.

BELIEF SYSTEMS

The practices of art and design do not take place in a vacuum. Artists and designers are immersed, as all people are, in a particular culture and in a particular historical moment. Every culture is imprinted with numerous beliefs, philosophical inclinations, biases, infatuations. In addition, particular individuals, groups, and professional disciplines within a culture develop their own philosophical views—attitudes that shape everything they create. For example, during a period of scarcity and spiraling economic inflation in Germany, the artist/designers of the Bauhaus elevated the ideas of *doing as much as possible with the least amount of material* and *favoring efficient new industrial fabrication technologies* to fundamental design tenets. The Bauhaus chair **(A)** not only utilizes less material than the traditional stuffed chair, but its innovative use of bent steel tubing allowed hand fabrication to be replaced by mass production. Such a radical idea for a chair would have been unthinkable without the socioeconomic conditions that preceded it.

↑ A

Marcel Breuer. ***Club chair.*** **1927. The Museum of Modern Art, New York.**

Taking a Stand

It is important that contemporary artists and designers be educated in the broadest possible way. Simply being sensitive to the visual is not sufficient. An educated, critical, and impassioned worldview is a vital component of the visual disciplines. G.K. Chesterton said, "Art consists of drawing a line somewhere." This aphorism has a double meaning: yes, art must begin with an initial act, in this case drawing, but more importantly, art means taking a stand!

New Conditions = New Ideas

The abstract expressionists believed that the most important human emotions and expressions were those that were subconscious. Consequently, they avoided straightforward representation and analytical inquiry and favored the spontaneous and the accidental, which they believed were expressions of greater emotional depth. It is not surprising that the abstract expressionists were influenced by **surrealism**, **automatic writing**, Jung's ideas on myth, and Freudian psychology—the power of the unconscious, dream interpretation, and slips of the tongue. While most **abstract expressionists** were painters, there were forays into sculpture. Willem de Kooning's sculpture **(B)** displays the quick fluid gestures of its making. This process was intended to encourage aspects of the deep subconscious to bubble up and become visible. At a later stage, skilled craftspeople were required to make molds and cast them in pewter.

What ideas and events contribute to the formation of your worldview? How do your beliefs influence your approach to art and design?

↑ **B**

Willem de Kooning. ***Untitled.*** **1972. Pewter, 6½" × 11" × 2⅝". © 2011 The Willem de Kooning Foundation/Artists Rights Society (ARS), New York.**

MODERNISM

Modernism may sound like a synonym for "contemporary" in art or design. In fact, it is a historic period traced to the nineteenth century. It is still present as a cultural force, but most historians now agree that we are in a "postmodern" era (we will discuss the implications of this concept in the next section).

Modernism is an idea that embraced originality and progress (a love of the new), and aspired to be an international style, creating useful and beautiful products for the working masses. "Less is more" and "truth to materials" replaced decoration in architecture and design. Representation made room for abstraction in art. Built on the foundation of the Enlightenment (the global project of reason, and the rejection of superstition) and spurred by developments in science, industrialization, and photography, modernism would, it was believed, lead us to a utopian world.

During the Bauhaus years, which were critical to modernism's development, factories were producing machine-made furniture that looked like the ornate, hand-made furniture of the past. This was unacceptable to Bauhaus designers. They believed that industrially produced furniture and products should not disguise the new materials and processes of industrialization; new products should reflect their industrial fabrication and express the new era.

Rationality, the Grid, and Industrial Fabrication

The sculpture in **A** is a minimal work with high modernist inclinations. Its fabrication utilized industrial methods, its repetition of identical parts pays homage to mass production, and its composition owes a debt to rational systems. The Eames House **(B)** is based on the grid and is built primarily of off-the-shelf, prefabricated parts ordered from building catalogues. The grid ultimately became known as the signature structure of modernist design.

Utopian Modernism

> *A designer is an emerging synthesis of artist, inventor, mechanic, objective economist and evolutionary strategist.*
>
> *—R. Buckminster Fuller*

The visionary inventor and futurist R. Buckminster Fuller designed the model of the house in **C** (actually named the *Dymaxion Dwelling Machine*). The Dymaxion house was made of aluminum and was intended to be mass-produced. The bathroom was a sealed copper pod that included a "fog gun" for instant hygienic cleaning. In the 1940s, the Dymaxion house was far ahead of its time. Bucky Fuller went on to imagine floating cities and methods for the global distribution of food. He is the author of numerous books, including *Operating Manual for Spaceship Earth*. His utopian approach to rethinking design on a global scale, for human needs, has, over the years, become increasingly relevant.

↑ **A**

Donald Judd. ***Untitled.*** **1980. Steel, aluminum and perspex, 9" × 3' 4" × 2' 7". Tate, London/Art Resource, NY © Judd Foundation. Licensed by VAGA, New York.**

B

Charles and Ray Eames. The Eames House. 1949.

C

R. Buckminster Fuller. *Dymaxion Dwelling Machine,* model. 1944–1946. Aluminum and plastic, h. 1' 8", diam. 3'. The Museum of Modern Art, New York.

POSTMODERNISM

You do not have to read and concur with contemporary theory to be postmodern; you need only to be living in the present moment. Many cultural critics believe we are all postmodern now. Although the exact nature of postmodernism remains vague, it is considered the **Zeitgeist** (defining spirit) of the contemporary world. Postmodern ideas have decisively influenced the disciplines of art, architecture, and design.

Postmodernism arose from the perceived exhaustion of modernism that for many had lost its original idealism, becoming another form of imposition by a dominant culture. This led to art and design that countered modernist principles: sincerity was replaced by **irony**, *more* became more (in answer to modernism's dictum that less is more). Multiplicity replaced an aspiration for an international style. A new generation of critics, curators, and historians gave credence to overlooked cultures and voices.

Artists and designers characterized as postmodern feel free to work in different styles simultaneously, scavenge the media, **appropriate**, quote, and playfully mix styles from past to present. The idea of **collage** has come to be known as the signature structure of postmodern design.

After Modernism

The word *post* means after—postmodernism comes after modernism. Daniel Clowes, in the comic book story *The Future* **(A)**, puts his finger on the very postmodern notion that recombining existing ideas is all that is left for us. Looking to past models, whether playfully or in earnest, is a liberating freedom for this era in contrast to modernism's striving for the new.

A

Daniel Clowes. Frame from *The Future,* Eight Ball Comics, number four.

Michael Graves. The Portland Building. Portland, Oregon.

Multiplicity and History

The building in **B** is a postmodern classic by architect Michael Graves. It incorporates stylized design elements from the past as well as pattern and ornament. Its multiplicity of references is a far cry from modernist purity. The decorative elements are like a coat of paint, rather than being integral to the building's structure. For example, the pink keystone shape is a purely visual element here: it does not serve to anchor an arch as it once did in Roman architecture.

Jenny Holzer utilized a Spectacolor electronic sign in Times Square **(C)** to illuminate various messages, called Truisms by Holzer. Her Truisms are shape-shifters; they appear in numerous forms including T-shirts, projected light, stone benches, and websites. Often displayed in public spaces, and using commercial modes of communication, she critiques power and exposes oppression. In contrast to modernist zeal for form and function, Holzer emphasizes content and language.

Irony

The *Duct Tape Chair* in **D** is a good example of irony in design. The "duct tape" is actually fine leather, and the chair is not an old, used flea market find; it is a high-end designer chair that appropriates the look of a shabby easy chair, repaired in the most expedient manner. The humor in this is obvious to anyone who has had either fussy, design-conscious relatives or a cranky old uncle who won't give up his favorite recliner.

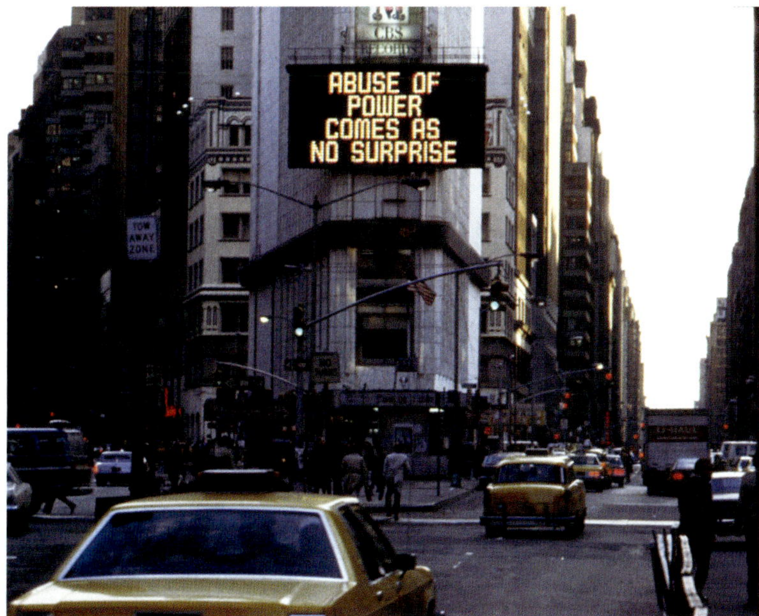

Jenny Holzer. *Truisms.* 1982. Spectacolor electronic sign, 20' × 40'. Times Square, New York. © 2011 Jenny Holzer, member Artists Rights Society (ARS), New York.

Jason Miller. *Duct Tape Chair.* 2006. Cotton/wool upholstery and leather over a wood frame, 2' 5" h.

Subatomic neutrino tracks showing electrons and muons caught in a nano second. Fermi National Accelerator Laboratory in Batavia, Illinois.

CHAPTER 3

3D DESIGN ELEMENTS

FORM

Form is the overall 3D shape of an object, the complete configuration of its mass. (Shape usually refers to flat silhouette.) The word form is also is used to describe *all* visual/structural aspects (as opposed to subject matter and content) of 2D, 3D, and time-based events. When form is used in this way, it is in reference to the **formal** aspects of art and design (color, shape, composition, and so forth).

The Three in 3D

What makes 3D form different from 2D shape? It is the all-important, extra dimension that lifts three-dimensional form up and off the plane; it is the flat page of this book, compared to the page of a pop-up book. To explain three-dimensional objects, three views are required **(A)**, and these views participate in a virtual matrix with three axes, most often referred to as x, y, and z. To fully understand a 3D object, six views are best—front and back, left and right side, top and bottom.

Form and Content

The sculpture in **B** is **figurative**, and it obviously has much to say about the seated, draped human figure (its subject matter). It is also a three-dimensional form, and it has formal qualities. This sculpture, as a form, is a static, rounded **monolith**. In addition, its hooded top creates a shadowed void. This sculpture is a grave marker. What contributes more to its content (death)—its subject matter or its form?

The Visceral Experience of Form

Form is powerful. We react to form **viscerally**, experiencing it in our bodies and our minds as we empathize with such characteristics as curvilinear flow or severe right angles.

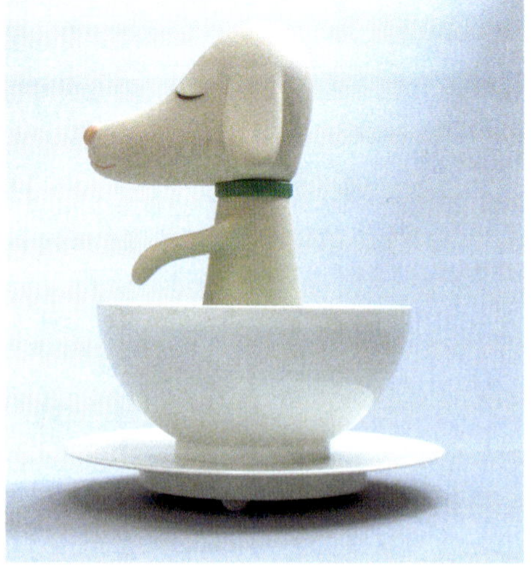

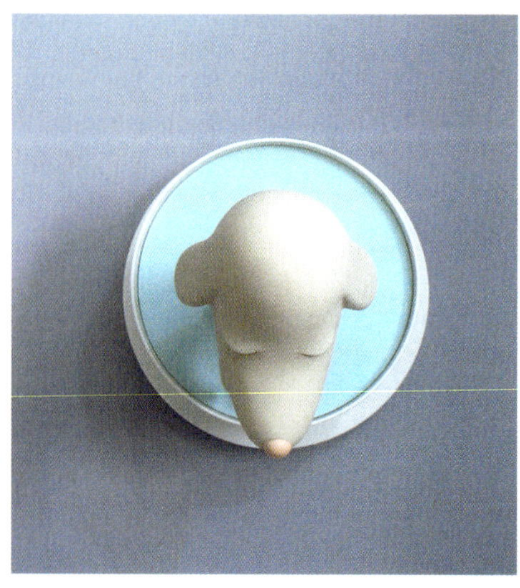

↑ A

Three views of Yoshitomo Nara's Pupcup. Bozart Toys Inc. 8½" high.

B

Augustus Saint-Gaudens. ***Adams Memorial.*** **Bronze, modeled 1886–1891, cast 1969. Bronze, 5' 9⅞" × 3' 3⅞" × 3' 8½".**

In Wolfgang Köhler's classic 1927 Gestalt psychology experiment **(C)**, subjects were asked to match two images with two made-up words. Most viewers immediately paired *takete* with the jagged geometric image and *maluma* with the curvilinear shape (*takete* sounds jagged, with sharp staccato syllables; *maluma* sounds soft and gently undulates), illustrating the human propensity to intuitively experience form as well as the ability to recognize related structural qualities in visual and auditory experience.

Aspects of 3D Form

A form is a positive element, and the space around it is **negative space**. A form can be geometric or **curvilinear**, concave or convex, **static** or **dynamic**. It can have an interior and an exterior, or pockets of negative space. It can be something that must be experienced in the round—as an object in space that one must walk around—or it might be planar, like relief sculpture, with a single frontal viewpoint. Form can embody any combination of these qualities and have numerous other properties as well.

When one walks around and in between the curved planes of oxidized steel, the full experience of Richard Serra's sculpture **(D)** unfolds. The viewer, dwarfed by steel "walls" over twelve feet high, "feels" the pressure of those tilting planes and curved paths. This is not an intellectual experience; it is a felt experience, emotional and visceral, and it is the overall form that is doing all the communicating.

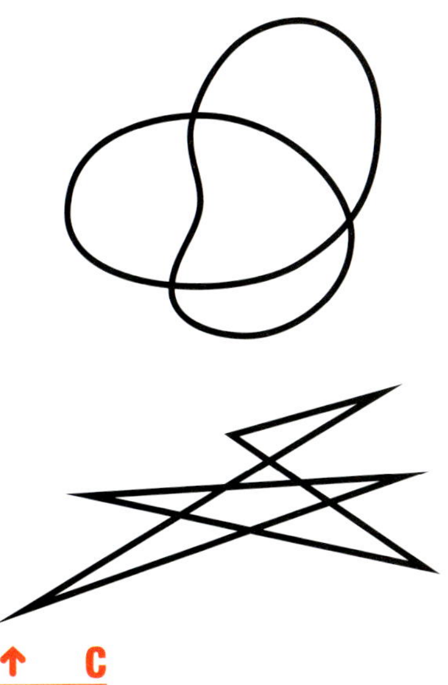

C

Takete and Maluma. Rendering based on an illustration in Wolfgang Köhler's ***Gestalt Psychology.***

D

Richard Serra. Installation view of the exhibition "Richard Serra Sculpture: Forty Years." 2007. Oxidized Steel. The Museum of Modern Art, New York. © 2011 Richard Serra/Artists Rights Society (ARS), New York.

THE CUBE

The cube, as a form, is so ubiquitous and so perfect that it merits special mention. One of the five Platonic solids, the cube is a form with a long history in art, design, and architecture. Like its sister, the sphere, the cube is iconic and ideal.

According to Islamic history, the Kaaba **(A)** was the first sacred structure on earth—built by Adam, rebuilt by Abraham and Ishmael and reconstructed many times in the course of its history. The present-day Kaaba is a cube approximately forty

A

Pilgrims circle the Kaaba inside the Grand Mosque during the Haj. Mecca, Saudi Arabia.

B

Donald Judd. ***Untitled.*** **1971. Anodized aluminum. Collection Walker Art Center, Minneapolis Gift of the T.B Walker Foundation, 1971 © Judd Foundation. Licensed by VAGA, New York.**

feet high. It is located in the courtyard of the Great Mosque in Mecca, Saudi Arabia. The Hajj, the annual Muslim pilgrimage, culminates at the Kaaba, the most sacred site in Islam. From the origins of Islam to the philosophy and mathematics of ancient Greece, the cube quickly achieved special status as a form among forms.

Minimal sculptors were drawn to the purity of the cube. In **B**, six cubes sit together informally on the floor. These pristinely fabricated forms resist being understood to represent anything other than their physical presence.

Minimal form, the grid and the cube are archetypes of high modernist art. Observing the staying power of these forms is interesting, even as we enter the realm of a more freewheeling postmodernism. From Andy Warhol's famous *Brillo Box*, a near cube, to Charles Ray's *Ink Box*, which is actually an open steel box filled to the brim with printer's ink, the cube sheds its "neutral" status. *Ink Box* and the sculpture in **C** have been infused with new meaning through their use of content-laden materials. The cubes of chocolate and lard in **C** were literally gnawed on by the artist as part of a complicated process in which chewing resulted in the production of candies and lipstick. Whether you might understand this work to be a primal form of carving, a statement about overabundance in the industrial world, or a feminist take on eating and cosmetics, the cube remains (however altered)—occupying space with severe dignity.

From the sublime cube of the Kaaba and Plato's philosophy, to the absurdities of popular culture, the cube has retained its value and fascination for thousands of years. The "square" watermelons of Japan **(D)** are grown in adjustable cube-shaped molds. They ship more efficiently than round watermelons, but, ultimately, they have become cult commodities because, like bonsai, they perfectly express the traditional Japanese interest in altering and idealizing living natural form.

↑ **D**

Square watermelon. Japan.

→ **C**

Janine Antoni. *Gnaw.* 1992. Chocolate, lard, and 150 lipsticks, overall dimensions variable. © 1992, Janine Antoni. Courtesy of Janine Antoni and Luhring Augustine, New York.

THE ART OF THE HOLE AND THE LUMP

The significance of mass and space (also referred to as positive and negative space) to three-dimensional design is perhaps best summarized in Auguste Rodin's famous dictum, "Sculpture is the art of the hole and the lump." Mass and space always exist in tandem, whether an object is pierced by voids, like a block of Swiss cheese, or is simply a solitary lump, for even the lump is surrounded by space that is altered by its intrusive form.

Mass

The sculpture in **A** is all about mass. Its intentionally funky, faux rock-like forms celebrate sheer bulk in sculpture.

Space

Louise Bourgeois's sculpture **(B)** is in many ways the opposite of **A**. Instead of using mass to occupy space, she uses mass to delineate space. Matter here embraces and defines a space. With a light touch, Bourgeois's sculpture envelops the viewer in its protective canopy. Similar to the towering interior arches of the gothic cathedral **(C)**, matter is used primarily to shape meaningful spaces.

A

Franz West. Sculpture at 52nd Venice Biennale, Arsenale. 2007.

B

Louise Bourgeois. *Maman.* 2005. Bronze, stainless steel, and marble, 32' 10" high. © Louise Bourgeois Trust/Licensed by VAGA, New York.

C

Interior of Laon Cathedral (looking northeast), Laon, France. Begun c. 1190.

D

Henry Moore. ***Large Two Forms.*** **1969. Bronze, length 20'. © 2011 The Henry Moore Foundation. All Rights Reserved/ARS, New York/DACS, London.**

Mass/Space Interaction

Paying attention to the interaction of negative and positive space results in dynamic form. In Henry Moore's sculpture **(D)**, the two main forms are separated by a space that both divides and unites the forms. This carefully considered **interstitial** space becomes a phantom third "form" and an important player in the work. The hole in this sculpture is not an empty space created by the simple act of cutting a hole in a form; it is a hole that is the by-product of a form that appears to have organically grown around it.

The sculpture in **E** is a homage to negative space. The artist performed a simple transformative operation—she exchanged the places of mass and space. Where there was matter, there is now void; where there was space, there is now substance. The sculptor took the underside of a table and chair, and with the aid of molds, filled all the voids (the negative space) with rubber and polystyrene, then removed the table and the chair. Solid versions of the spaces beneath are all that remain.

E

Rachel Whiteread. ***Table and Chair (Green).*** **1994. Rubber and polystyrene, 2' 3" × 4' × 2' 8". © 1994, Rachel Whiteread. Courtesy of Rachel Whiteread and Luhring Augustine, New York.**

A POINT SET IN MOTION

One of the simplest elements in design, line is nonetheless quite important and infinitely versatile. We look to the endpoints of a line segment and imagine them extending—in this way, lines are directional forces. Lines can be as true and straight as a laser beam or as graceful as the arc of a perfect circle; they can also form gentle irregular curves as in cursive **calligraphy**.

Charles Ray made powerful use of line in his deceptively simple sculpture **(A)**. On one hand it is a sculpture that refers to Minimalist Art and appears to be nothing more than a black line extending vertically from floor to ceiling. Understood formally in this way the sculpture encourages the viewer to perceive the entire space in a new way, as a field that revolves around a line that connects the floor to the ceiling. This simple linear element is in fact neither a wire nor a rod, but a stream of black printer's ink that literally flows downward from an aperture in the ceiling to a hole in the floor. The hapless viewer who attempts to touch this seemingly static line might be splattered with ink. Like a shooting star, this work refers to the geometric definition of line—a point set in motion.

Alexander Calder. ***Sow.*** **1928. Wire construction, 7½" × 1' 5" × 3". The Museum of Modern Art, New York. © 2011 Calder Foundation, New York/Artists Rights Society (ARS), New York.**

Claes Oldenburg and Coosje van Bruggen. ***Ago, Filo e Nodo*** **(Needle, Thread and Knot), installation detail. 2000. Brushed stainless steel and fiber-reinforced plastic, height 59'. Piazzale Cadorna, Milan, Italy.**

Charles Ray. ***Ink Line.*** **1987. Ink and pump, dimensions variable.**

Gesture

Line can also become an expressive **gesture**, as in the delightful, bent wire pig **(B)** or playful monumental sculpture by Claes Oldenburg and Coosje van Bruggen **(C)**.

The colossal, site-specific *Running Fence* **(D)** was a 24.5-mile-long, white nylon fence (18 feet high). It was designed to be understood in relationship to the Northern California landscape that gave it its gently rolling form. Though *Running Fence* was actually a thin plane in space, due to its extreme length it read as a line in the landscape. *Running Fence* was viewed primarily from that other monumental linear earthwork, the public highway system **(E)**.

Whether actual or implied, line is a dynamic element—expressing direction and activating the space that surrounds it.

D

Christo and Jeanne-Claude. *Running Fence, Sonoma and Marin Counties, California, 1972–76.* **Copyright Christo & Jeanne-Claude.**

E

Freeway interchange, aerial view.

THE TWO-DIMENSIONAL ELEMENT

Points, lines, planes, and rectangular solids are related visually and structurally in numerous ways. In geometry, a moving point generates a line, a moving line generates a plane, and a moving plane—a rectangular solid.

Planes are ubiquitous design elements: the walls of your apartment, the painting on the wall, the windowpane, and the paper you write on. The built world is planar and geometric.

Planar Representation

Picasso's *Guitar* **(A)** uses planes of metal, almost exclusively, to depict an existing object, a guitar, which is in itself built of planes. Beyond simple depiction, Picasso celebrates its essential features, its "guitarness," while also creating a more dynamic form than the original could ever hope to be. The viewer connects to the fabrication process and the material of *Guitar*, as the quite ordinary sheet metal as well as its hand-cut shapes are extremely evident.

Interpenetrating Planes

The Barcelona Pavilion **(B)** is fundamentally planar. This icon of modernism, using a strict vocabulary of horizontal and vertical elements, displays its form and structure with extreme clarity. It takes advantage of the simplicity of the plane, while exploiting its essential dynamism, interpenetrating planes slicing through space. Vertical planes are used as long, low space activators. As they enter the area defined by the horizontal roof plane, they become enclosing walls.

Curved Planes

The curved plane and the folded plane have great structural integrity. The building in **C** uses complex curves in planar form to span vast spaces, exploiting the amazing strength of the curved plane while creating a soaring, graceful visual spectacle. Richard Serra's sculpture (see page 67) shows that curved form need not be simple—curved form can be nuanced. The Serra is a ribbon of gradually changing complex curves that alter space and experience.

↑ **A**

Pablo Picasso. ***Guitar.*** **1912. Sheet metal and wire, 2' 6½" × 1' 1⅞" × 7⅝".**

B

Ludwig Mies van der Rohe. Barcelona Pavilion. Barcelona, Spain. 1929.

Santiago Calatrava. Tenerife Opera House. 2003. Santa Cruz de Tenerife, Canary Islands, Spain.

THE RELATIONSHIP OF THE PLANAR TO THE DIMENSIONAL

The ordinary cardboard box begins life as a flat piece of corrugated fiberboard. It is then die-cut, scored, and folded to become a fully three-dimensional container. In this way, 3D form may be generated from 2D, planar material. Flat shapes cut from steel or aluminum sheets, for example, may be folded to form many objects, from electrical utility boxes to sculpture.

Origami, the traditional Japanese craft of paper folding, similarly begins with a flat rectangle or square and proceeds, fold upon fold, until the desired configuration is obtained. In **A** instructions to make an origami praying mantis are presented in the form of a diagram. Origami is much like folding cardboard to form a box, but the forms are often extremely complicated and may even result in movable parts.

The chair in **B** folds completely flat when not in use, resembling the two-dimensional condition of its origin—a sheet of three-quarter inch plywood.

Flatland

Two-dimensional shape has long contributed to the development of three-dimensional form, and the relationship between these dimensional realms is rich and diverse. In the1880s Edwin A. Abbott wrote *Flatland*, a mind-bending book about a fictional society that existed in two dimensions; geometric shapes such as squares and triangles lived in a completely flat, planar world. The narrator, a square, attempts to understand the third dimension—Spaceland. The drawing **(C)** illustrates how a sphere would be understood by the occupants of Flatland. The sphere would be incomprehensible, appearing simply as a circle, increasing or decreasing in size as the sphere penetrates the plane of Flatland. Abbott's book raises the interesting issue concerning our ability to understand dimensions beyond our own three-dimensional realm.

Google SketchUp is a free computer program that allows the user to easily construct 2D representations of 3D form around x, y, and z axes. Like many CAD programs, it is a useful aid to planning, understanding, and diagramming 3D structure. One SketchUp tool—*Push/Pull* **(D)**—allows the user to generate virtual three-dimensional solids, such as cubes, from squares drawn on the ground plane, with the simple move of the cursor.

Robert J. Lang. Origami praying mantis, length 4", and fabrication instructions in the form of a diagram. The mantis is made from a single square sheet of uncut paper.

↑ B

Ufuk Keskin and Efecem Kutuk. *SheetSeat* folding chair. Wood laminate, ¾" thick. Ufuk Keskin and Efecem Kutuk (efecemkutuk.com and ufukkeskin.com).

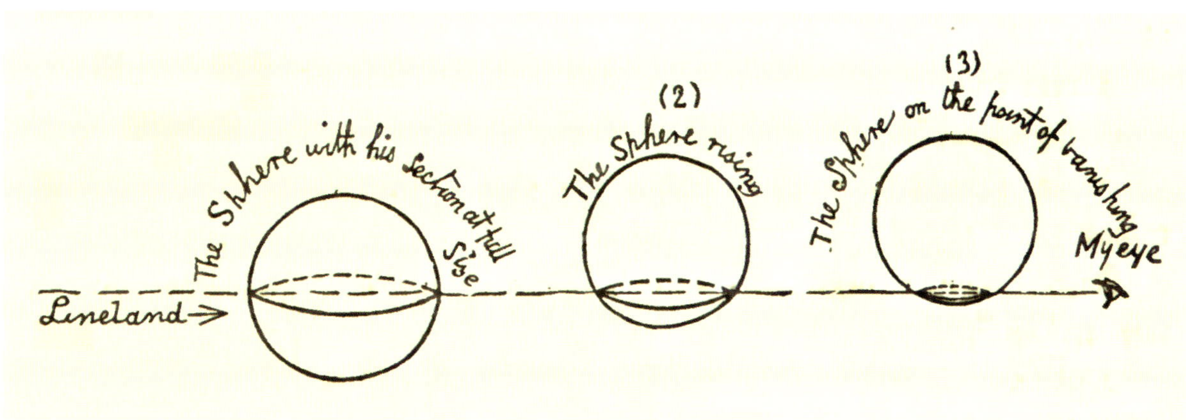

↑ C

Edwin A. Abbott. Illustration from *Flatland: A Romance of Many Dimensions*. 1884.

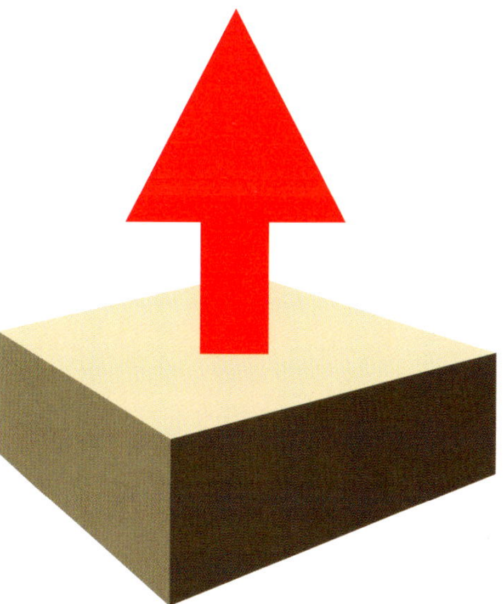

→ D

Rendering based on the push/pull icon from Google SketchUp.

TEXTURE

Surface is one of the first characteristics of form perceived by a viewer. Surface is skin on the human body, the shell of the egg, the rind of an orange, the fur of a bear, the wrinkled, gray hide of an elephant. The specific characteristics of skin, hide, and shell make a huge difference in our perception of an object. Surfaces can be soft, hard, moist, dry, smooth, rough, and any color. Determining a surface for a sculpture, product, or building has significant implications.

Texture is that aspect of a surface that we can experience tactilely. Texture is also, of course, an important visual characteristic of objects, but visual observation is not required. Rub your hand over any surface and you will experience its textural qualities—rough like gravel, sandpaper, or mown grass perhaps; soft like a kitten; or smooth like paper or glass. Seed Cathedral **(A** and **B)** is a pavilion with an extreme textural presence. Its surface is studded with 60,000 fiber-optic rods, each 24 feet, 7 inches long. The rich textural experience of Seed Cathedral is rare, even radical on this scale. It would be more familiar as a seedpod or flower blossom you could hold in your hand.

The essential form of *Cloud Gate* **(C)** is not that different from *Seed Cathedral*, but *Cloud Gate's* highly polished surface results in a completely different textural experience. The stainless steel exterior not only conveys the impression of a slippery "bean," as it is commonly referred to, but it reflects light and creates and distorts reflected images of viewers, the city, clouds, and sky.

Texture Relativity

Texture, like many design elements, is contextual. Smooth is smoother when contrasted with rough, and rough becomes rougher when in proximity to smooth. Play one off the other to heighten textural characteristics. The stone path in **D** achieves full perfection in its juxtaposition of stone and gravel.

Structural Surface Qualities

In addition to the visual and tactile, surface qualities involve other important issues. Corten steel, for example, is a steel alloy that develops a unique protective coating of rust that eliminates the need for painting. This weatherproof steel is easily identified in contemporary sculpture and architecture by its rich, velvety orange surface. Other treatments, such as anodizing, galvanizing, and etching, serve to alter surface properties. When metal is tempered by additional periods of cooling and heating during the fabrication process, the surface is hardened.

A

Seed Cathedral. **2010 Shanghai World Expo. Thomas Heatherwick Studio.**

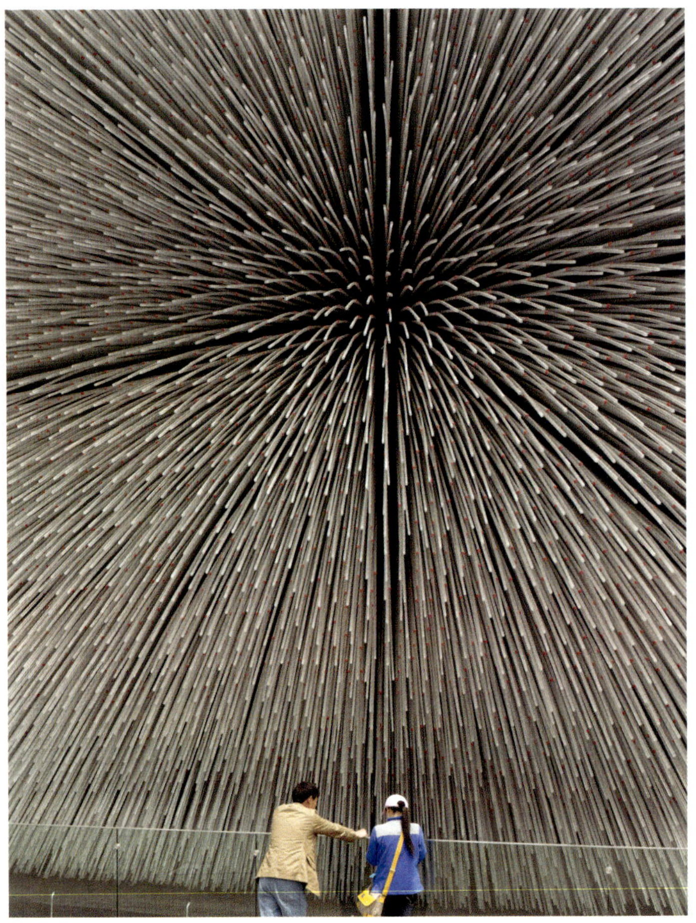

B

Seed Cathedral, **detail. 2010 Shanghai World Expo. Thomas Heatherwick Studio.**

C

Anish Kapoor. *Cloud Gate.* 2004. Polished stainless steel, height 33'. Millennium Park, Chicago.

D

Stone path in Japanese garden.

COLOR

Intrinsic Color

Unpainted plaster, a raw concrete wall, a mahogany door—white, gray, and dark brown—are examples of intrinsic colors. Intrinsic color refers to objects that retain the natural color of the material that forms them. A surprisingly rich palette is available in this realm of found color. Intrinsic color was favored by modernist architects and artists interested in the notion of truth to materials.

Applied Color

Color can also be applied. Surfaces can be painted, coated, glazed, enameled, oxidized, anodized, galvanized, patinated, and so forth. Applying paint to a surface is the most common way to alter the color of an object. It is easy, inexpensive, and, in most cases, serves to protect surfaces from weather or wear. Used to decorate ancient Egyptian artifacts and Greek temples, paint is one of the oldest methods for altering objects. Historians now believe that the iconic, pure white temples of Greece that we have come to love were actually ornately painted.

Patina involves natural changes to metallic surfaces, such as when copper oxidizes over time and takes on a powdery green cast. Patination is a traditional method of altering surface color in sculpture. The ancient Greek *Charioteer* **(A)** is an example of an almost iridescent, green patina on bronze. When the natural characteristics of patination are harnessed, it becomes an art and a science, and its practitioners must know their chemistry. There are numerous methods and formulas for creating a wide array of color possibilities. A patina sample displays a mottled green surface in **B**.

Polychrome Form

Form and color are always present. Monochrome refers to objects of a single color, such as a carved marble figure, or a very close color range, like the bark of a tree. When an object displays more than one color, we call it **polychrome**. The world we live in is largely polychrome. Differentiating the parts of an object or a building, using color, is a powerful and widely utilized design tool.

In **C** (a detail of a larger installation), the artist spray-painted various objects as well as the floor. This simple application of paint resulted in profound changes to the objects and the environment. Paint becomes light and shadow, illuminating and differentiating the spheres.

Luis Barragan's architecture is enlivened by color. In **D**, color serves to make each segment of wall a unique entity with its own personality. If left unpainted, the segments would appear blandly homogeneous. Barragan united modernist architecture (that previously favored a stark intrinsic color) with the applied colors of Mexican folk traditions.

↑ **A**

Charioteer of Delphi. **478–474 BCE. Bronze, 5' × 11". Greece.**

↑ **B**

Patina on copper.

C

Katharina Grosse. *Atomimage*, detail. 2007. Acrylic on wall, PVC carpeting, canvas, and latex balloons, height 13'.

D

Luis Barragan. The architect's house. © 2011 Barragan Foundation, Switzerland/Artists Rights Society (ARS), New York.

Transparency and Translucency

Color can also be transparent and translucent. The glass vessels in **E** celebrate surface color as it approaches becoming pure light. Unlike applied and intrinsic color, which are examples of reflected light, colored glass filters light directly.

E

Glasswork by Venini of Murano, Italy.

CHROMATIC LUMINOSITY

Just two hundred years ago, the sun and the stars and fire and lightning were the only sources of light on Earth. Now there are numerous industrially manufactured, light-producing devices—such as incandescent bulbs, fluorescent tubes, sodium vapor lamps, lasers, neon, and LEDs.

Reflected Light

Light illuminates form and casts shadow, enabling us to perceive form. In this capacity, light is essential. The structure of the monastery in **A** is made visible by light, not just in the simple sense that we require light to see, but in the sense that these forms were intended to be defined and caressed by light. In **A**, the light source is on the right, casting shadows to the left, revealing planes and voids. Color temperature is in play as well—the shadows are cool; the illuminating light is warm.

In general, white best reveals form, as it is the most reflective color; black objects absorb most of the light that falls on them, causing them to appear less nuanced. Architecture and sculpture in the landscape share the additional challenges and opportunities of existing in a light that is continually changing—from morning till night, season to season, and in all kinds of weather.

Luminosity

Some objects emit light; they contain their own source of illumination. Such luminous objects have dual natures—they are objects with structure and they are light-emitting vehicles. The sculpture in **B** consists of standard fluorescent fixtures (its structure), and as such it might be understood to be a kind of Pop or Found/Dada sculpture, appropriating an ordinary, quotidian product. As a light-emitting object, however, this work takes on a more theatrical and ethereal presence—it transcends its humble origin, completely transforming the corner of the room with its luminosity.

Light as Pure Medium

While great use is made of light in the theater, the use of light as a sole medium devoid of objects remains a kind of utopian dream in the arts. Something approximating this ideal was created in a piece titled *Your atmospheric colour atlas* **(C)**. In a room filled with fog, housing red, green, and blue lights programmed to mix in response to viewer movement, the empty space was made visible and substantive; the dense fog became a luminous chromatic environment.

Tribute in Light **(D)** was a temporary event that took place annually for a number of years to commemorate the tragic events of September 11th. Twin beacons, representing the two towers, illuminated the night sky from a location adjacent to the World Trade Center site.

The other subject of **D** should be acknowledged—it is the City of New York. This sprawling, night photograph reminds us that light in contemporary culture often takes the form of spectacle. From the kinetic displays of Times Square to the illuminated Statue of Liberty, and the millions of illuminated windows, New York is, itself, a sublime light-work on a massive scale, and no less symbolic than the twin commemorative beacons.

A

Monastery of Panagia Hozoviotissa. 11th century. Amorgos, Greece.

B

Dan Flavin. ***Untitled (to Donna) 6.*** **1971. Fluorescent lights, overall: 8' × 8'. © 2011 Stephen Flavin/Artists Rights Society (ARS), New York.**

C

Olafur Elliason. *Your atmospheric colour atlas.* 2009. Four installation views. Fluorescent lights, aluminum, steel, ballasts, and haze machine. 21st Century Museum of Contemporary Art, Kanazawa, Japan. 2009–2010.

D

Proun Space studio. *Tribute in Light,* 9/11 Memorial, New York. Photograph by Charlie Samuels.

KINETIC STRUCTURE

The traditional marble sculpture on a pedestal in a museum is still and fixed in place. It is static; nevertheless, like all experiences, it involves time and motion. To perceive it in its entirety you must walk around it—in doing so, new aspects of the sculpture reveal themselves in time. Viewing the work in a different order will result in a unique unfolding of experience. In addition, this frozen, still, mute object becomes a foil against which the movement of your own body, other museum visitors, and the hum of the ventilation system, for example, become more perceptible.

The **futurist** artist Umberto Boccioni created a static sculpture, *Development of a Bottle in Space* **(A)**, in which he presented multiple views of a bottle simultaneously, simulating a walk around it. Boccioni took on the challenging task of representing time and motion in a still object.

In **kinetic** structures, artists and designers utilize time and motion directly. László Moholy-Nagy projected light on a rotating, motorized structure **(B)** in order to modulate light and reflect it onto gallery walls, creating an enveloping symphonic experience.

The contemporary artist Tony Oursler uses motion, time, and sound, combined with objects to create psychologically charged scenarios. In **C**, video images of a face are projected on two hemispheric objects, accompanied by a soundtrack of a screaming man. In spite of the complete and intentional artifice, the result is disturbingly convincing.

Robotics

A visit to a contemporary automobile factory will reveal an amazing array of robotic production technology—huge machines for transporting, welding, and painting. Robotic technology is a rapidly developing realm that already has a far-reaching impact on our lives. One playful example that reached a wide audience as a commercial product is Sony's interactive robotic dog Aibo (**A**rtificial **I**ntelligence Ro**bo**t). Aibo **(D)** is a pet that recognizes spoken commands. It has facial expressions, welcomes its master, and is capable of learning. In spite of a cold plastic exterior, Aibos are much loved by their masters.

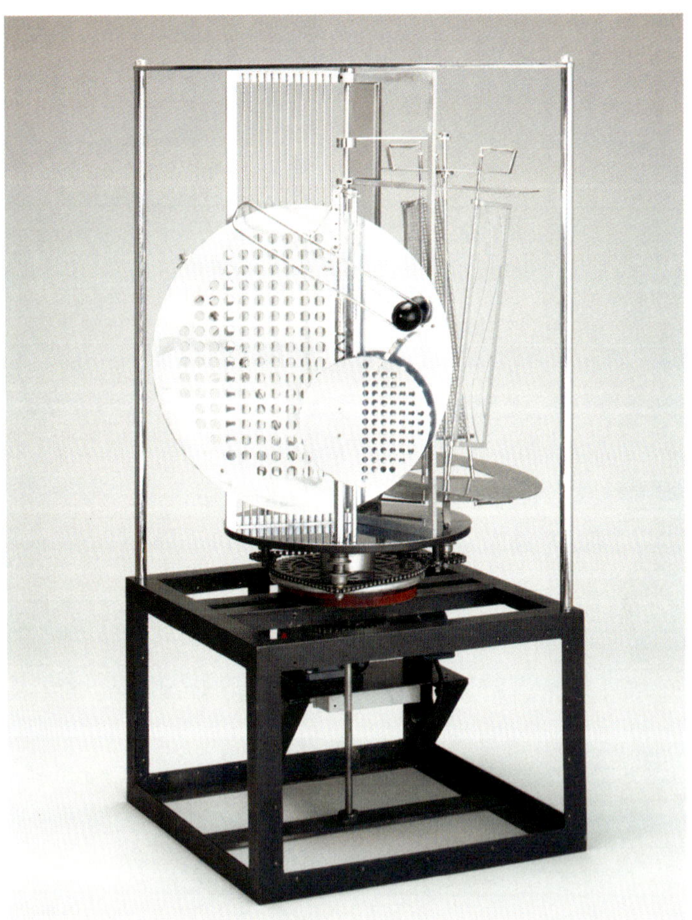

↑ **A**

Umberto Boccioni. *Development of a Bottle in Space.* **1912 (cast 1931). Silvered bronze, 1' 3" × 1' 11¾" × 1' ⅞". The Museum of Modern Art, New York.**

↑ **B**

László Moholy-Nagy. *Light Prop for an Electric Stage (Light-Space Modulator).* **1930. Aluminum, steel, nickel-plated brass, other metals, plastic, wood and electric motor, 4' 11½" × 2' 3½" × 2' 3½".**

Wonderful time/motion events also occur in everyday experience and in nature. These events await transformation by artists (they are raw material, sources of inspiration, and we can learn a great deal from them), but don't forget, they are also to be cherished just as they are.

Swarming behavior in insects and birds can create massive shifting forms that ebb and flow in a spectacular choreography. You can get a sense of the grandeur of such aerial action in the photograph of starlings over Rome **(E)**.

Tony Oursler. *Half (Brain).* 1998. 2 Sony CPJ 200 projectors, 2 videotapes, 2 Samsung VCRs, polystyrene foam, paint, performance by: Tony Oursler. Each 1' 2" × 1' 1" × 1' 1" (plus equipment).

↑ D

Aibo robotic dog. 1999. Sony Corporation.

Flock of Starlings. 2008. Rome, Italy. Photograph: Chris Helgren.

Antique bottle collection. Elliot Barnathan, photographer.

CHAPTER **4**

3D DESIGN PRINCIPLES

ORGANIZATION

Organization, the act of bringing separate elements together to form a unit or a structure, is a foundational component of the design process. The organization of form is facilitated by the knowledge and application of all the principles of design.

Preparing for an exhibition of Martin Puryear's sculpture, the curators and exhibition designers used small, scale models of each artwork, positioned on a diagram of the museum's floor plan **(A)**, to arrive at the best installation. Designing an exhibition is in an organizational activity.

Portia Munson created *Pink Project*, a collection of pink plastic products created for the "girl market." This collection is an artwork that has been exhibited in a number of different incarnations over the years. Let's consider three versions. The artist amassed hundreds of pink objects—the problem . . . how to present them? In **B** they are arranged neatly on a table top in groups of similar objects in a rough proximity (combs with combs, bottles with bottles). The objects in **C** are in two museum-style vitrines (with two very different approaches to display), and **D** takes the form of a chaotic pile on the floor.

Is one version of *Pink Project* better than the others? Is the pile in **D** disorganized, or is it just another kind of order? While there are no easy answers to such questions, it is worth noting that all three works have been thoughtfully organized by the artist, and in each, the objects take on an altered meaning. The subject matter of these works is as much about organization and the problem of presentation as it is about the material components. It should also be said that whatever kind of categorization or organization is used, the first principle is a visual one: all of the objects are pink, lending a commanding unity to whatever happens next.

A

Models for the Martin Puryear exhibition at the Modern Art Museum of Fort Worth.

B

Portia Munson. *Pink Project: Table.* **1995. 2' 6" × 8' × 14'.**

Portia Munson. *Pink Project: Vitrines.* **1995. 5' 8" × 2' 8" × 1' ½".**

Organization implies order, or at least *an ordering*, but this is not to say that design must be *orderly*. Yes, organization can be highly structured and logical, but it can also be generated by a complex blend of design principles, stylistic inclinations as well as random operations. The work in **D** is an interesting combination of opposing forces: a strong organizing principle—a unifying mound, plus the casual structure of random events.

The act of organization involves just about everything we do and create; it is not, of course, relevant only to the act of arranging separate objects, such as collections. Arranging and composing the materials and elements within a single work also involve organization. The house in **E** is an arrangement of planes in space (planes of varying proportion), rectangular perforations (windows), linear elements and colors—all organized to give physical form to the architect's ideals and values. The following sections in this chapter deal with a wide array of 3D principles and their use in organizing form.

← D

Portia Munson. ***Pink Project: Mound.*** **2006–ongoing. approx. 6' × 12'.**

→ E

Gerrit Rietveld. Schröder House. 1924–1925. Utrecht, The Netherlands. © 2011 Artists Rights Society (ARS), New York.

GESTALT

Unity is achieved when the whole is more important than the parts. A unified design may be, on the most basic level, a simple monolith or mass. More often, unity consists of many forms or objects brought together to construct a coherent whole.

The German word ***gestalt*** has proven to be quite useful for artists and designers. It is derived from the perceptual ideas of Gestalt psychology, and its full meaning has many facets. The way gestalt is most often used in art and design is a simplification, but it is a handy one. Gestalt (which means shape or form in German) suggests that experiences are greater than the sum of their parts. The individual notes of a musical tune—presented as completely separate entities—cannot provide the experience of the tune to the listener. A tune depends on the order of the notes and the intervals between them, and can only be recognized as an experienced totality. Most in the arts today use the word *gestalt* to suggest that one should experience the essence, the entire work, all at once!

Unity of the Figure

The human figure is a fundamental archetype of unity, like trees and boulders, cubes and spheres; consequently sculpture that depicts these subjects (and especially the human figure) achieves unity almost by default. So strong is the figurative image, that even the cartoon-like sculpture by Tom Friedman **(A)**, constructed of miscellaneous plastic parts, achieves unity with ease. Its monster eyeballs and loop of a mouth, however abstract and schematic, remain easily recognizable as a face.

Three-Dimensional Grid

The three-dimensional grid is a unifying force. The Seagram Building **(B)** is an example of extreme unity achieved by several contributing factors: its structure is a 3D matrix, it is a monolith, it stands isolated from other large buildings, and it has a unifying color.

Tom Friedman. *Green Demon.* 2008. Expanding insulation foam and mixed media, 7' 7" × 3' 7" × 3'. Courtesy of Tom Friedman and Luhring Augustine, New York and Stephen Friedman Gallery, London.

Ludwig Mies van der Rohe with Philip Johnson. Seagram Building. New York. 1956–1958.

Proximity

The marvelous window in **C** is the result of the architect taking two circles, decreasing the distance separating them (increasing their **proximity**) until they overlap, and forming one new and dynamic shape. This window could easily become a universal symbol of unity.

Unifying Pattern

The formal gardens of Versailles **(D)** consist of many elements: trees, bushes, paths, grass, and fountains, and all in numerous, unique shapes. One might expect such an array to be chaotic and break up into individual parts. The fact that this does not occur is the result of the garden's strong, symmetrical, unifying pattern. The whole is more important than the parts.

C

Carlo Scarpa, architect. Window at Brion-Vega Cemetary. 1970–1972. San Vito d'Altivole, Italy.

→ **D**

Gardens at the Chateau de Versailles. France.

DYNAMIC PARTNERSHIP

Unity and variety is a frequently utilized and universally applied design principle—it creates rich and powerful visual events almost effortlessly. Unification provides an overall and simplifying influence; the use of variation creates nuanced events and pockets of interest. Unity and variety are the dynamic duo of design.

Ryoanji **(A)**, a Japanese Zen rock garden, is unified by a rectangular framing format, a monochrome palette, and by its consistent elements—all natural rocks. Its sameness might be deadening, but Ryoanji is full of subtle variations that bring it to life. Each rock is a different size and a unique shape. There are many places from which the viewer can experience Ryoanji, and no matter where one sits, all fifteen rocks can never be seen at once—there is always at least one rock obscured. The secret of Ryoanji is in the spaces between the rocks and the variety of those spaces—it is an acknowledged masterpiece of Japanese culture because it makes silent voids tangible.

Since ***Zen*** is a word you will undoubtedly hear often in the arts, this might be a good opportunity to provide a brief

A

Rock Garden. Late 15th century. Ryoanji Temple, Kyoto, Japan.

B

Allan McCollum. ***Drawings.*** **1989–1991. Pencil on museum board, each unique. Installation: Centre d' Art Contemporain, Geneva, Switzerland.**

C

George Nelson. ***Marshmallow Sofa, extended version.*** **1956.**

explanation. Zen, a type of Buddhism, spread from China and India to Japan, from where it wielded most of its influence on the arts. Zen ideas are especially apparent in Abstract Expressionism, jazz, the writing of the Beat Generation, Dada, and conceptual art. Zen advocates not for things or even ideas but for the enlightened awareness of the practitioner. In this way, Zen—often called "the way of no way" and full of sassy, iconoclastic attitude—resembles the creative practices of art and design when performed at their highest levels.

The Grid

The installation in **B** is a highly ordered collection of small, framed drawings. This piece takes the form of a unifying **grid**. Its individual units are exactly the same size, and the drawings are similar—black silhouettes on white backgrounds. Its unity is clearly established. Its variety is based on the fact that every drawing is unique!

Color

The playful 1950s sofa in **C** displays an almost random variety of color disks, serving as an antidote to a unity of orderly repeated forms.

Continuation

While some work is equally balanced between unity and variety, others emphasize one quality or the other. *The Dance* in **D** leans more toward variety. It is a vigorous composition displaying a great range of forms, overlapping curves, and bodies in a wide array of configurations. Unity is evident in the symmetry of the arrangement, the monochromatic limestone, and most importantly, the use of **continuation**. The curve of an arm is visually continued by flowing drapery or by another arm, virtually making the two a single, extended curve. Continuation is used extensively in **D**, creating complex, interwoven forms that unify.

The sculpture *Study, 20 Elements* in **E** was created in response to *The Dance* in **D**, by invitation of the Musée d'Orsay for a project titled "Correspondences." Through abstract form alone, *20 Elements* perfectly captures the fusion of unity and variety in *The Dance*.

D

Jean-Baptiste Carpeaux. *The Dance.* **1863–1869. Limestone, 13' 9" × 9' 8 7/32" × 4' 9". Musee d'Orsay, Paris.**

E

Joel Shapiro. *Study, 20 Elements.* **2004.**

VISUAL AND STRUCTURAL

The ornament of Reims Cathedral **(A)** consists primarily of repeating elements that radiate like ripples in water: horizontally, vertically, and radially. This repetitive motif is, to some extent, functional, adding strength to walls, but it is also a device used to decorate surfaces and emphasize form.

Rodin's *Monument to the Burghers of Calais* **(B)** builds a powerful momentum through its use of repetition. In telling the story of the burghers, Rodin amplifies the perception of their tragic destiny by depicting all six figures, creating a series of dark crevices between the figures, repeating the heavy, hanging, vertical folds of their garments and the nooses around their necks.

Brancusi's *Endless Column* **(C)**, 1938, and the *Hole in the Ice* totem pole **(D)**, created over a century ago by First Nations craftspeople of British Columbia, have completely different reasons for being. They do, however, have a great deal in common formally. Both are thin, vertical columns, and both utilize vertical repetition to transform a mere column into a gravity-defying, extreme stack, suggesting unending extension.

The seemingly perfect form of many traditional, handcrafted objects is the product of countless anonymous artisans each adding a small improvement or minor variation over long periods of time. Though function may be the primary concern, delightful visual structure is often the result. The basket weaver in **E** uses the repetitive process of weaving to create a sturdy vessel that literally embodies the weaving process in its repetitive surface structure. Here, form, process, and pattern constitute an inseparable unity.

West Façade of Reims Cathedral. c. 1225–1290. Reims, France.

Auguste Rodin. *Monument to the Burghers of Calais.* **1884–1895.**

Constantin Brancusi. *The Endless Column.* 1938. Târgu Jiu, Romania.

Gitxsan totem pole, *Hole in the Ice*. c. 1900. Gitanyow (Kitwancool), British Columbia, Canada.

Artisan weaving a basket. Japan.

MODULARITY

A **module** is a standard unit. Modular forms such as bricks, concrete blocks, and sheets of plywood, like the tatami mats of Japan **(A)**, are not simply standardized building supplies; they have a profound influence on the design of the structures in which they are utilized. Rooms in Japanese architecture are traditionally described by the number of tatami mats required to cover the floor—a four-and-one-half-mat room is 9' × 9', for example. Due to mass production and industrial processes, the module has a large and increasing role in contemporary design.

If you played with blocks, Legos, or Tinker Toys **(B)** as a child, you already know a lot about modular systems. A diverse range of complex structures can be built from just a few basic elements—that is the value of the module! It is little wonder that the underlying structure of life and all matter is modular. With just over one hundred different kinds of atoms, an almost infinite range of molecules is possible, and that results in the incredible variety of forms in the universe. In **C**, James Watson and Francis Crick, utilizing molecular models constructed of modular elements not unlike the child's Tinker Toy, explain the structure of DNA.

Architect Moshe Safdie's Montreal building complex, Habitat '67 **(D)**, is one of the most well-known and earliest examples of modular architecture. Reminiscent of the efficient packing of the honeycomb, 354 prefabricated, individual, concrete modules are stacked and connected by steel cables—organized so that each apartment has a balcony on the roof of the apartment below. Modular architecture has clear advantages—notably the speed of on-site fabrication and the economy of prefabrication. Another kind of modular architecture is the modular house—it may be assembled from prefabricated parts at the site or shipped completely assembled as a single unit.

While architects today are increasingly involved in designing high-end, modular dwellings, it is good to remember that factory-built houses, as well as mobile homes, however maligned, are already in wide use.

A

Tatami room in a traditional Japanese house.

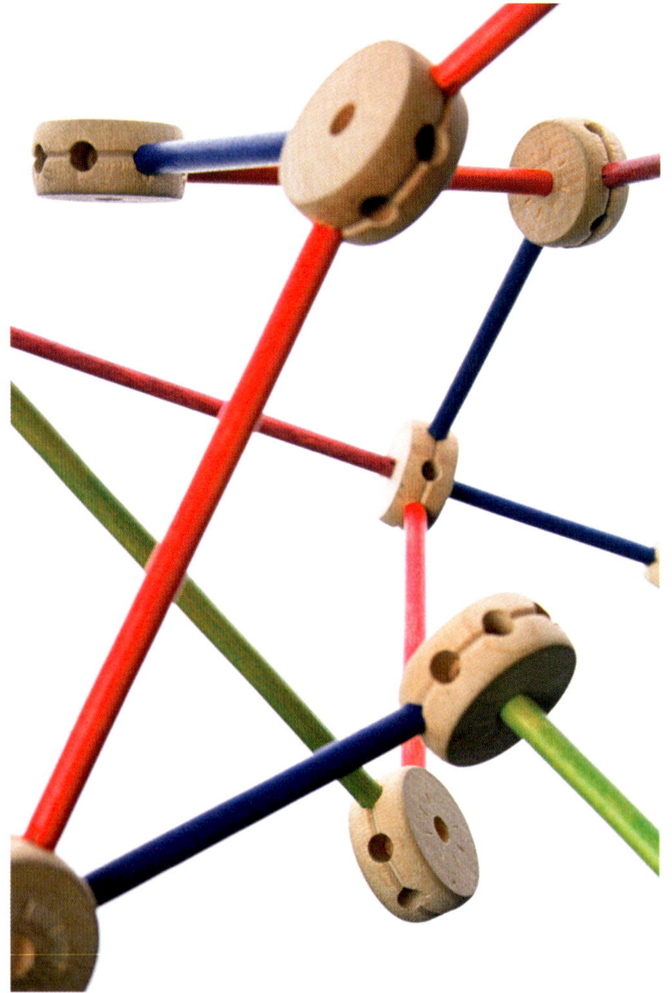

B

Tinker Toys.

 C

James Watson and Francis Crick with their DNA model at the Cavendish Laboratories in 1953.

 D

Moshe Safdie. Habitat '67. 1967. Montreal, Canada.

ORDERED REPETITION

Pattern, the ordered repetition of a visual element, is usually considered a two-dimensional issue. When pattern gets spatial, it becomes something other than what we usually consider pattern to be; it becomes more like 3D structure. Pattern is, however, an important aspect of the third dimension—especially in relief panels and when it exists on the surface of an object where it often serves to augment form.

 A

Erwin Hauer. ***Continua Series Design 1.*** **1950.**

3D Form as Pattern

Erwin Hauer is a master of the perforated surface. These panels **(A)** are all about pattern, and they create pattern uniquely, through three-dimensional form alone—no decorated surface here. These interwoven, organic forms result in perforations that are more like the flowing spaces under highway overpasses than simple holes. Repeated as modules, these biomorphic voids result in structures that are used architecturally in partitions, screens, and light-diffusing surfaces.

Repeat Pattern

Some patterns extend across a surface and never repeat; others utilize a modular unit, a section of pattern that may be endlessly replicated. These are called repeat patterns. The perforated surface in **A** is a repeat pattern.

Decoration

We often use the word *decoration* pejoratively, with the implication that decoration is simply a cosmetic substitute for interesting 3D form, but the exquisite detail, high craft, and range of juxtaposed patterns in the Mexican saddle **(B)** elevate the idea of decoration. Ornate embroidery, leatherwork, and embossed silver are characteristics of the artisans of Mexican cowboy culture. This saddle definitely makes one think: nothing in art and design is wrong if you do it right.

The glazed tile mihrab (niche) **(C)** in the Madrasa Imami, an Iranian mosque, is a mind-numbing display of pattern. This mihrab is considered a masterpiece of glazed ceramic tile—geometric and floral motifs are juxtaposed, calligraphic inscription and pattern are ingeniously integrated, and all edges receive special treatment—pattern delineates form.

Camouflage

Nature utilizes camouflage, dazzle patterns, and warning displays **(D and E)** to protect its creatures or to provide them with a predatory edge. Whatever the case, it must be acknowledged: nature loves pattern.

See also *Illusion: Camouflage*, page 164.

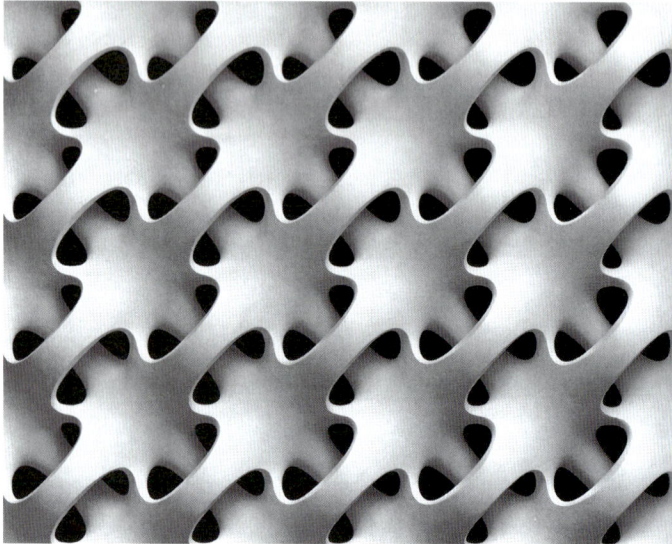

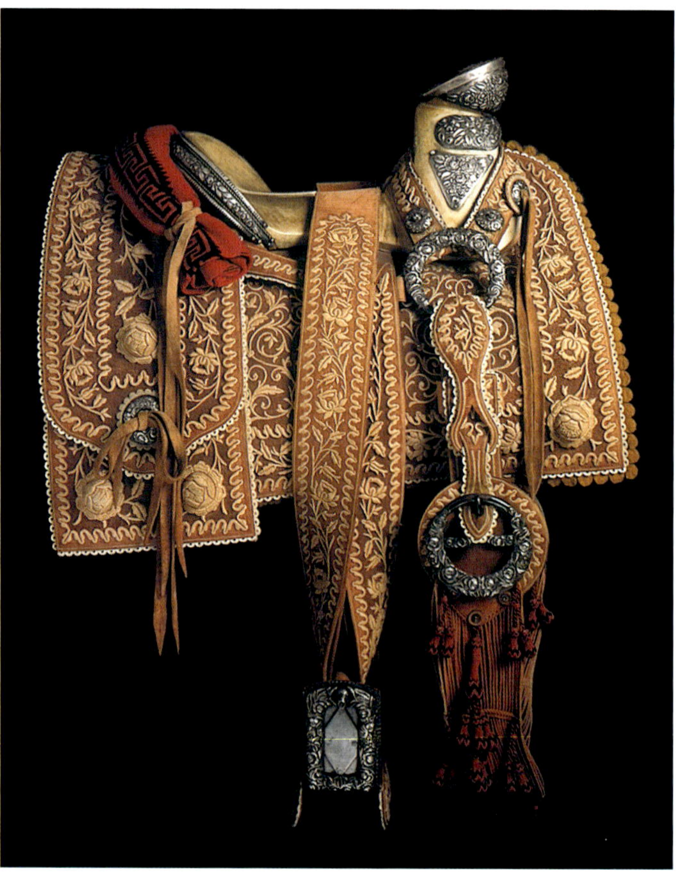

Gran Gala Charro Saddle. Early twentieth century. Leather, embroidery, sterling silver. El Potro Andaluz Saddlery. Puebla, Mexico.

↑ D

Coiled Dumeril's Boa.

↑ C

Mihrab. 1354. Mosaic of monochrome-glaze tiles on composite body set on plaster, 11' 3$\frac{1}{16}$" × 9' 5$\frac{11}{16}$". Isfahan, Iran.

↑ E

Grasshopper. India.

FLUID FORM

Visual **rhythm** and repetition are closely related. However, repetition is associated with a mechanical cadence of equal intervals while rhythm suggests a variation in tempo and more fluidity, not unlike rhythm in music or other time-based activities such as dance and sports.

Rhythm in Relief

The figures and drapery of the relief carving on the sarcophagus in **A** are arranged in a structure so rhythmic it appears that it might depict a dance. (The truth is far more grisly; Orestes plays out a violent Greek myth.) Different layers of rhythm are in operation, and they interact in a kind of syncopation—figures forming large wave-forms are below, and above, on the side of the lid, is a more delicate and shallow wave that is almost an echo.

Figuration and Form

A generally assumed or implicit issue in this book is worth reinforcing here. The principles of design do not just apply to abstract shapes or geometric form. Every building, sculpture, and object, even living things, have formal structures—they are forms! Within every realistic depiction, like the figures on the sarcophagus in **A**, a formal structure exists as well, and that structure affects us; it has its own independent life, regardless of the subject matter. Sometimes form and content work together, and sometimes they contradict each other. Whatever the case, there is no escaping form.

Sarcophagus with the Myth of Orestes. c. 140–150 CE. Roman. Marble, 2' 7½" h.

Eva Hild. ***Loop Through.*** **2007. Stoneware, 2' 11" × 2' 3½" × 1' ⅔". Eva Hild/© 2011 Artists Rights Society (ARS), New York/BUS, Stockholm.**

Rhythm in the Round

The rhythmic events on the sarcophagus in **A** take place on a two-dimensional surface in shallow relief. The sculpture in **B**, however, is an example of rhythm operating in full three-dimensional space. This is a fascinating and complex structure in which multiple rhythmic events occur from left to right, and top to bottom, and from inside to outside, and those rhythms continually rearrange themselves as the viewer circles the piece, assuming new vantage points.

> *Abstract sculpture now often looks like an exercise in topology, exactly because the sculptor shares the vision of the topologist.*
>
> —*Jacob Bronowski, 1970*

Staccato

In music another kind of rhythm, staccato, is about sound that changes abruptly—think drums instead of violins. The chair in **C** is a three-dimensional play on staccato rhythm. It has none of the curves we have been associating with visual rhythm; instead, there are short straight lines, planes, and points. The lines are all black, the points, yellow—this establishes a playful structure of syncopated staccato in painted wood.

→ **C**

Gerrit Rietveld. *Armchair Red and Blue.* **1918. Wood, paint. © 2011 Artists Rights Society (ARS), New York.**

ORIGIN AND IMPLEMENTATION

Aerodynamic Form

A three-dimensional design principle used to create the illusion of speed has its origin in a natural phenomenon: large things that move very fast are aerodynamic. We have come to associate movement and speed with such streamlined form. These forms are not simply capable of high speeds and great acceleration, they also look fast, even while standing still.

The illustration in **A** is a computer rendering of *The Bloodhound SSC*, a car being created to break the land speed record (it is expected to go 1,000 mph, faster than a bullet fired from a .44 Magnum). *The Bloodhound SSC* and the reef shark **(B)** share formal qualities associated with aerodynamic design—they are both long, pointy cylinders designed to minimize turbulence, allowing their sleek bodies to slip through the air or water. You will never see a shark, jet plane, or race car shaped like a brick.

Other ways to suggest motion are more commonly employed in two-dimensional design than in the 3D realm; they are, nonetheless, valuable principles.

Blur

The sculpture in **C** utilizes an illusion that is derived from photography. If your shutter speed is too slow when photographing a moving object, you get a blurred image. Subsequently, this fact has been used to great effect in photography and painting to express the illusion of motion. Blur is obviously more difficult to create in the realm of real objects. Sculptor Tony Cragg effectively blurs 3D form **(C)**—the bronze sculpture appears to be a figure in motion, twisting in space, and though the actual edges cannot blur, the features are vague and stretched, simulating blur and creating an illusion of motion.

Sculptors have also utilized what we now think of as the cinematic idea of representing motion—repetitive elements that appear as if they are a photographic multiple exposure. This can be effective at expressing a brief gesture, as in the Tantric figure **(D)**. Though its multiple arms are primarily symbolic, they nonetheless serve to animate this diminutive goddess.

The Bloodhound SSC (Super Sonic Car) is seen traveling at speed in this artist's impression.

B

Caribbean reef shark.

↑ C

Tony Cragg. *Bent of Mind.* 2005. Bronze. Frederik Meijer Gardens and Sculpture Park. Grand Rapids, Michigan.

D

Tantric Hindu Goddess. c. 17th century. Gilt copper. 6¾" × 5¾" × 3¾". Nepal.

ACTUAL AND IMPLIED

Balance, in the realm of three-dimensional structure, has two faces: (1) it is a phenomenon of nature ruled by gravity, operating in real space, and (2) it is a virtual or implied condition.

Real balance has to do with things like leaning backwards in your chair, just past your center of gravity, and crashing downward, or . . . walking a tightrope, as did Philippe Petit in 1974, from tower to tower of the World Trade Center **(A)**. Learning to be sensitive to the stresses placed on your body while balancing will inform your understanding of stress in the structures you construct.

Implied balance involves one's awareness of actual gravity and balance, but remains a strictly visual experience that has more to do with the organizational and aesthetic factors of visual weight.

Balance—Actual

Alexander Calder's mobiles (pronounced mö-bëls) are all about matter interacting with gravity. During the process of construction, Calder had to find balancing points in order to achieve the equilibrium that would permit resolution. In *Cascading Spines* **(B)**, Calder used many lighter rods to balance the heavier, black, sheet metal disks on the left. Furthermore, this mobile appears resolved and balanced in the implied, virtual sense as well; it illustrates the fact that the origin of implied balance is balance in the physical world.

The artist, Reinhard Mucha, rearranged ordinary furniture **(C)**, much as one would before mopping a floor, just to get everything up and out of the way. This informal and precarious sculpture refers to our everyday interaction with objects,

A

Philippe Petit walking a tightrope from tower to tower of the World Trade Center. 1974. Photograph by Jean-Louis Blondeau.

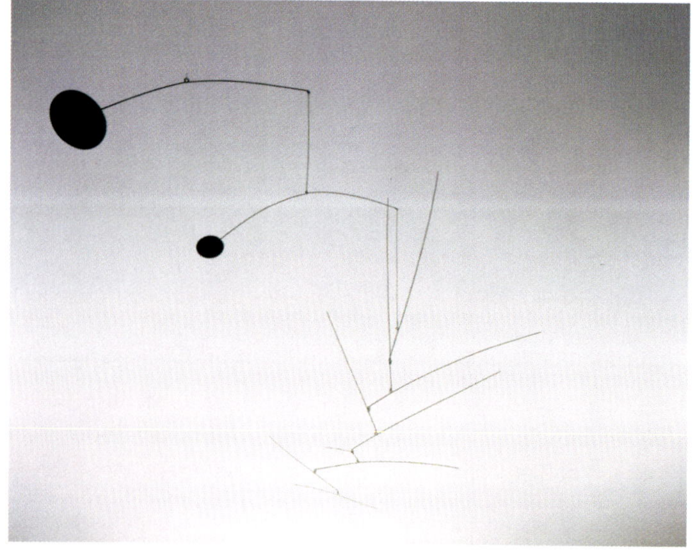

B

Alexander Calder. ***Cascading Spines.*** **1956. Sheet metal, wire, and paint, 4' 10" × 6' × 4'.**

 C

Reinhard Mucha. *Flak*. 1981. Felt, glass, and wood. Hamburger Kunsthalle, Hamburg, Germany.

D

Edgar Degas. *Dancer looking at the sole of her right foot*. 1919–21. Bronze.

and in its articulation of formal relationships, it continues one of sculpture's grand traditions: the exploration of gravity and balance **(D)**.

Asymmetrical Balance

While balance often implies **symmetry**, *Cascading Spines* **(B)** is clearly not symmetrical. With its visually heavy disks on one side and thin rods hanging down on the other, it is asymmetrical. It is nonetheless visually balanced—the many small elements equal the few large elements. This kind of balance is called **asymmetrical balance**.

Balance—Implied

The sculpture in **E**, from David Smith's Cubi series, does not achieve equilibrium in any classic sense; it is intended to be more dynamic than that. It doesn't need to be perfectly balanced like a Calder mobile, because it is welded together. It can initiate a conversation about gravity and balance but never has to become embroiled in gravity's relentless demands. The David Smith piece deals with the visual issues of implied balance (in 2D design this is referred to as pictorial balance).

 E

David Smith. *Cubi XVIII*. 1964. Stainless steel. Art Resource, New York © Estate of David Smith/Licensed by VAGA, New York.

CORRESPONDENCE ACROSS A DIVIDE

Symmetry occurs when there is formal correspondence on opposite sides of an object's central dividing line—in simpler terms, when left and right sides are mirror images. This definition refers specifically to **bilateral symmetry,** but it will serve as a workable starting point. Symmetry is a widely used organizing tool closely tied to issues of balance; sometime these terms are used interchangeably. There are many distinct kinds of symmetry. We will examine some of the most common forms.

Bilateral Symmetry

Bilateral symmetry is undoubtedly the most important and ubiquitous form of symmetry. Faces, bodies, mammals, insects, and many other living things, as well as numerous built forms are all structured bilaterally. This is the symmetry of classical architecture; it is stable and familiar. Bilateral symmetry cuts one way. For example, a horse is symmetrical when looked at straight on. Imagine a plane that divides the horse from his ears down to the space between his two front hooves and projects through him to his rear. That is the dividing plane that virtually splits our horse into two symmetrical halves, but look at the horse from the side and there is no symmetry at all.

The rear view of the Silver Arrow automobile **(A)** is perfectly symmetrical, bilaterally, just like a face, which it clearly resembles. Like the horse, cars express no symmetry when viewed from the side. Seen frontally, bilateral symmetry commands our attention. It is also balanced, and most often, static (as opposed to dynamic).

A

Pierce-Arrow. *Silver Arrow.* 1933. Design concept Philip Wright, body engineer James Hughes. Pierce-Arrow Motor Car Company.

B

Matthew Ames, designer. Spring 2010. New York Fashion Week.

C

Ettore Sottsass. Transparent, turquoise and yellow vase *Alioth.* 1983. For Memphis, executed by Compagnia Vetraria Muranese.

The outfit worn by the model in **B** is a bit more complicated. The *form* of the jacket is symmetrical, like most jackets, but its *color* is delightfully and unexpectedly asymmetrical (devoid of symmetry). This serves to remind us that most objects are rich amalgams of more than one operating design principle—objects are bundles of forces.

Radial and Spherical Symmetry

Radial symmetry is based on symmetry around a central axis. Trees, flowers, many circular patterns, and most cylindrical configurations, such as the glass vase in **C**, are radially symmetrical.

Spherical symmetry is the condition of having similar form arranged regularly around a single point. The greatly enlarged image of a grain of pollen **(D)** is an example of spherical symmetry. Any cut that passes through the center point of the pollen grain will split it into two identical halves.

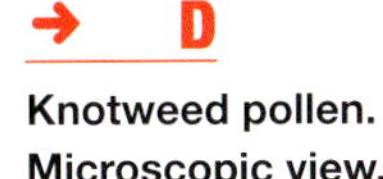

D

Knotweed pollen. Microscopic view.

DYNAMIC FORM

Every configuration that isn't symmetrical is asymmetrical. **Asymmetry** is symmetry's evil twin—it is off center, out of whack, and confrontational. Asymmetry prefers the dynamism and danger of the diagonal, to the stability of the vertical and the horizontal. If symmetry is associated with all things good, like balance and harmony, does that make asymmetry something to avoid? Absolutely not! Asymmetry is a powerful design principle, and it is in synch with contemporary ideas.

The Extension to the Denver Art Museum **(A)** is a dynamic wedge that appears as if it fell from the sky and embedded itself in the ground. This building is a high-energy cluster of abstract forms that derives power from an asymmetrical, diagonal configuration. The extreme, cantilevered triangle that hovers precariously overhead provides the spectacle that modern engineering makes possible.

Daniel Libeskind. Extension to the Denver Art Museum, Frederic C. Hamilton Building.

Alexander Calder's *Flamingo* **(B)** is an arching, stable sculpture that touches the ground in five places. It is nonetheless asymmetrical with most of its weight planted firmly on one side. *Flamingo* has an off-center grace that energizes a form that would otherwise be a staid, tripod-like structure. As discussed in the section on *Symmetry*, most animals have bilateral symmetry (including flamingos), but such symmetry is only apparent when viewed head-on, eye to eye. Living, moving animals assume many positions that hardly ever approach perfect symmetry—life is dynamic, rarely static.

The asymmetrical suspension bridge in **C** reminds us of the convention that all bridges and many other designed objects be symmetrical. When convention becomes rule, it is time to reconsider, as did Santiago Calatrava in designing the Campo Volantin footbridge, an inclining parabolic arch that achieves a new kind of resolution—asymmetrical equilibrium.

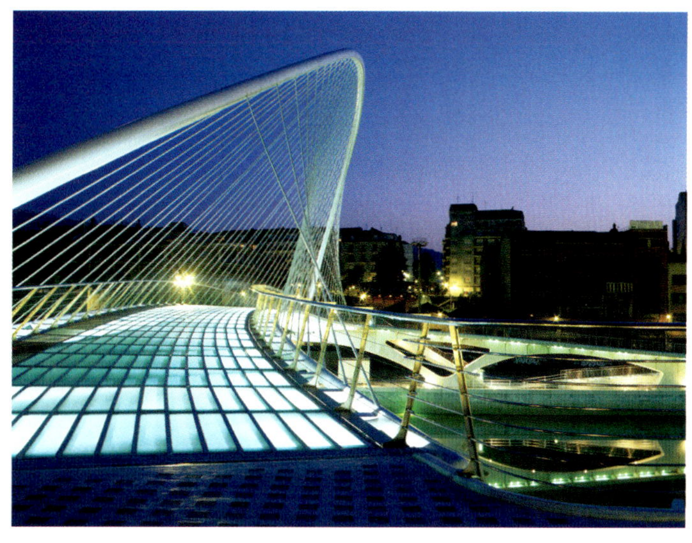

Santiago Calatrava. Campo Volantin Footbridge. 1997. Bilbao, Spain.

Alexander Calder. ***Flamingo.*** **1974. Chicago. © 2011 Calder Foundation, New York/Artists Rights Society (ARS), New York.**

UNITY, BALANCE, ORDER

The following are some traditional definitions of harmony:

- Harmony is unity; its elements form an integrated whole.
- Harmony is balanced proportion.
- Harmony is a pleasing or orderly arrangement of parts.

Informed by aesthetics as remote as those of the ancient Greeks, ideas of harmony are still useful and continue to attract adherents. Nevertheless, harmony, as a principle of organization, has a diminished role in contemporary art and design, partly due to the vagueness of its defining principles, and, to a greater extent, because of the numerous competing ideas and principles in modern and contemporary design culture that are increasingly useful and compelling.

In any case, artists and designers interested in harmony have produced some remarkable objects. The silver decanter in **A** is a perfectly resolved object. The negative shape situated between the handle and the body of the vessel is equal in expressive form to that of the mass of the vessel itself, and it is seamlessly integrated. The decanter is holistic and biomorphic—it appears to be the result of a natural process of growth, rather than something fabricated. Its width-to-height proportion is 3:5, a proportion seen as harmonious since ancient Greece.

→ A

Kay Fisker. Decanter. 1926. Silver. Also octagonal tobacco jar. Manufactured by Anton Michelsen.

Idealism

Plato believed that objects in the world were flawed reflections of forms that were true and ideal, and these perfect forms could exist only in the mental realm of ideas. These thoughts influenced Greek artists and architects who strove for a perfection beyond mere imitation, a perfection that sought deep, essential form. This approach to form, called **idealism**, is apparent in many temples, artifacts and sculpture **(B)** of Greek antiquity.

The silver decanter **(A)** and the humble record player **(C)** both embody qualities of idealism: essential form (stripped of any unnecessary elements) and sublime proportions that would please the gods on Mount Olympus.

See also *Sources: Geometry and Mathematics*, page 54.

→ **B**

Greek, bronze statuette of a horse. Late Hellenistic, late 2nd–1st century BC. Bronze, 1' $3\frac{13}{16}$" high. The Metropolitan Museum of Art, New York.

← **C**

Wilhelm Wagenfeld, Dieter Rams and Gerd Alfred Muller, designers. Braun record player. 1957.

AN ORGANIZATIONAL TOOL

Looking up at the night sky we see stars. Some groups appear formless; some appear as specific configurations; some seem to connect, appearing to form lines or triangles; and some constitute the well-known constellations. Two related phenomena contribute to these perceptions. One is the powerful pattern-forming aptitude of the human mind. The other is the principle of proximity, which visually unites things that are near one another and excludes those more distant. Venus and Jupiter in the center of the night sky in **A** are firmly locked together, perceptually, due to proximity (other configurations present themselves as terrestrial bodies and Earthly lights form distinct patterns).

Use proximity to do the important work of linking elements, forming groups and sub-groups, and creating hierarchies.

→ **A**

Night sky showing Venus and Jupiter in conjunction.

Tension

Proximity contributes to the creation and nature of visual tension. Standing too close or too far from someone you are having a conversation with significantly influences the nature of the interaction. The proximity of the two figures in **B**, a king and a falcon/god, creates an electrically charged space, like the gap between the electrodes of a spark plug. Placing the king, who is making an offering, and the falcon farther apart would completely alter our perception of this relationship.

Proximity and Function

The principle of proximity is especially important in such fields as architecture, product design, city planning, and landscape architecture. It is in these disciplines that the visual, perceptual aspects of proximity are joined by the functional. If you design a hospital or an anesthesiologist's control unit, it *must* have various rooms and equipment or instruments in close proximity.

Walking through Central Park in New York City **(C)** appears to be a walk through a bucolic, natural landscape, but this is far from the truth. Central park is a completely designed, artificial wilderness. "During the initial 20 years of construction, 10 million cartloads of dirt were shifted, 4–5 million trees of 632 species . . . were planted, and half a million cubic yards of topsoil were spread over the existing poor soil (some of it recovered from the organic refuse of the garbage dump)."*

Proximity in the park is not something you can see at a glance, but it is a carefully planned arrangement of sites that can be understood only by strolling its winding paths repeatedly over time, from the rambles to the lake (formerly a swamp), to the sheep meadow, and so on. This 843-acre park, designed by Frederick Law Olmsted, places various natural environments—woodlands, meadows, and scenic views—into a series of interconnected experiences.

B

King Taharga Offering a Libation. **Egypt.**

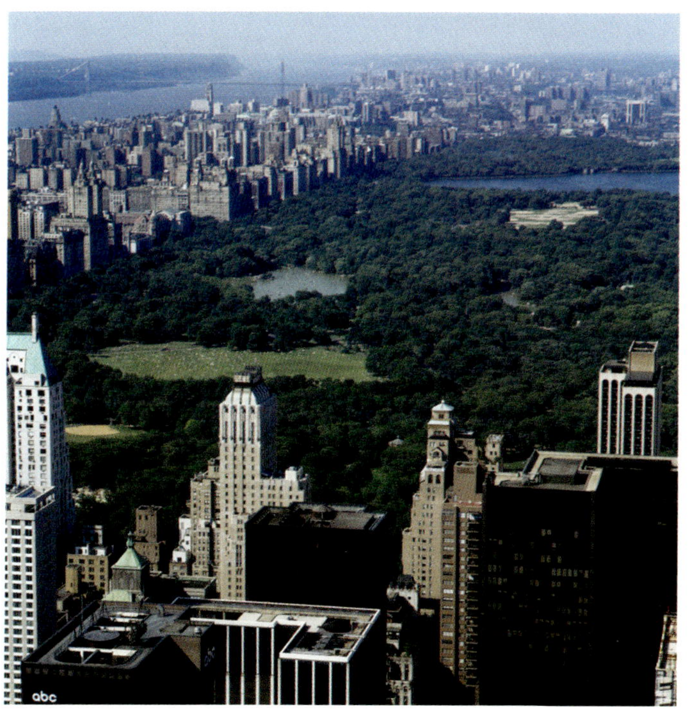

C

Central Park. New York.

*Carol von Pressentin Wright, *Blue Guide New York*. 1991, 2nd Ed.

CONTRAST

Emphasis is essential in design and art, as it is in life. Try telling a story with a completely even tone of voice, and you will be reminded of the significant role emphasis plays in all forms of expression and communication. Emphasis is similar to the pictorial idea of focal point. There are numerous strategies for achieving emphasis—differences of color, texture, shape, and size, as well as isolation and placement, are commonly employed.

To differentiate one aspect of form from another by the use of contrasting elements is to emphasize both. Contrast is the underlying force behind the design principle emphasis. In Le Corbusier's celebrated chapel **(A)**, the dark cast-concrete roof appears heavier, more imposing and dramatic when juxtaposed with the whitewashed, ethereal walls that support it.

Emphasis by Color

The chest of drawers in **B** uses paint and color to emphasize unexpected parts. While primarily playful, one can imagine that the highlighted drawers might be used for special items, serving as an eccentric filing system of sorts.

 **A**

Le Corbusier. Notre Dame du Haut. 1955. Ronchamp, France.

B

Roy McMakin. Dresser.

Emphasis by Size and Placement

The Palette of King Narmer **(C)**, an Egyptian relief sculpture, emphasizes the image of King Narmer by size and placement. The King is placed in the important central position, and he is larger than all the other figures depicted. In ancient Egyptian art, figures were not larger because they were closer to the viewer, as is common in perspective; size was based on status—kings, pharaohs, and other dignitaries were always the largest figures; peasants and enemies the smallest. The **ideoplastic** system of representation employed in Egyptian art is not unlike the front page of your daily newspaper, in which the largest photographs represent the most important news events.

Compound Emphasis

Ken Price creates emphasis in a number of ways in his ceramic vessel **(D)**. The penetrating hole is made prominent by surrounding it with a smooth flat shape that contrasts sharply with the bulbous forms of the vessel. In addition to texture contrast, the emphasized shape is a different color. It is also a geometric shape, a triangle, surrounded by distinctly organic form.

Narmer Palette. 1st dynasty, 3100–2890 BC. 2' 1" high. Egypt.

Ken Price. ***Sweet Paste.*** **1994. Fired and painted clay, 1' 6" h.**

RATIO

Proportion refers to the comparative relationship of size. It can be observed by comparing one form to another, or one part to the whole, and can be expressed as a numerical ratio—for example, the ratio of a yardstick compared to a twelve-inch ruler is 3:1.

Villa Savoye **(A)** displays carefully considered variations in proportion. The height of the house to its width, the long, thin rectangle of windows in relationship to the façade, and the lightness and height of the supporting columns all contribute to a reductive sensibility made profound by the fine tuning of proportional relationships.

The Hong Kong cityscape in **B** presents itself as a kind of three-dimensional pie chart. Like most big cities, Hong Kong is an arrangement of buildings of various sizes (heights and widths), masses, and shapes; it gets almost all its visual power from its display of proportional relationships. Like many works of art and design, Hong Kong's range of proportional variation creates an invigorating visual music.

B

Hong Kong cityscape.

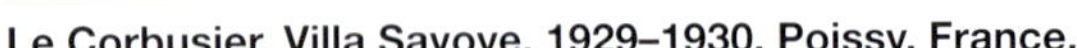

A

Le Corbusier. Villa Savoye. 1929–1930. Poissy, France.

Ideal Proportion and Convention

The ancient Greeks believed that certain proportions of the human body were ideal. We still have many beliefs and preconceptions concerning the contested realm of ideal physical beauty, and many of these beliefs are based on proportional standards.

We have expectations concerning the way things should look. The notion of "correct" proportion is often based on familiarity, norms, and convention. Many beliefs are well-founded; some turn out to be biases. Artists and designers take pride in their willingness to examine and challenge their preconceptions, and many use skepticism as a design strategy. The high-fashion design of the extremely oversized lace ruff collar **(C)** is not a radical work of art; it is more whimsical than that, but it does play on and subvert our expectations of what a collar should be, and it has a lot of fun with proportion along the way.

↑ **C**

Junya Nutanake. Lace ruff collar. Comme des Garçons.

COMPARATIVE SIZE

The word ***scale*** as used by artists, designers, and architects refers to the relative size of an object or a volume of space in relationship to the viewer, in relationship to other objects in the vicinity, or to the object's environment in general. Scale is a design principle that wields a great deal of power.

The photograph of the Kensu Valley **(A)** makes clear the contextual nature of scale. The Celestial Mountains dwarf a hunting cabin, and the mountains are understood to be immense only because we can compare them to the cabin. Scale is all about context—perceiving size depends on comparison.

From atoms with diameters of 0.1 to 0.5 nanometers, to a galaxy that is six million light-years wide, the full range of scale in the universe is exhilarating and perhaps beyond real comprehension. Human beings utilize an infinitesimal segment of the universal scale continuum.

The film *Powers of Ten* is an excellent guide to the relative nature of cosmic scale. As seen in the selection of stills from the film **(B)**, *Powers of Ten* takes the viewer on a journey from the proton of an atom in a sleeping man's hand to the outer reaches of the universe.

Human Scale

Monumental and miniature objects represent the extremes of scale in daily life. Most objects and spaces occupy a place in between these extremes. This more domestic realm is often referred to as human scale, and it is here that slight discrepancies in size or expected size can profoundly impact viewers. The human body remains the default benchmark when perceiving scale.

If you have ever sat at a table that is too high, you have experienced the disconcerting feeling that you are smaller than you actually are. The scale of the table has virtually altered your size—scale is a potent design tool. Scale's ability to make a viewer feel and appear larger or smaller brings to mind each individual's own human development—entering the world as infants and growing to adulthood, we have all experienced a wide range of scale relationships with the world. The oversize table not only alters your perception of your own body size, but it can make you feel childlike.

↑ **A**

Kensu Valley. Staton R. Winter, photographer. Kyrgyzstan.

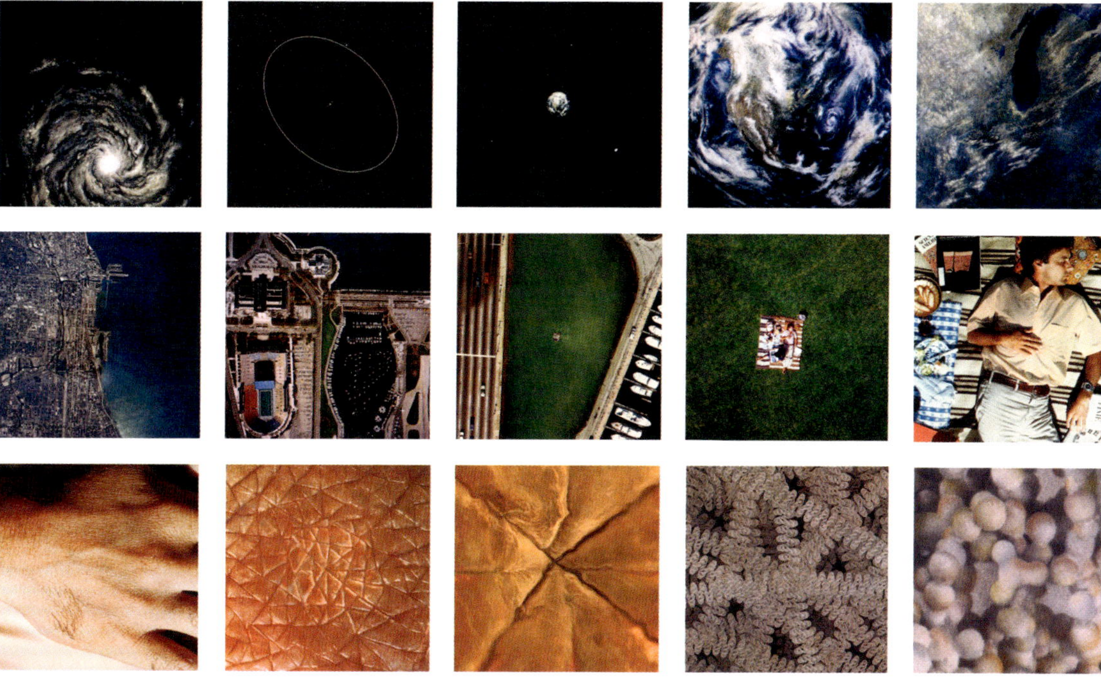

Charles and Ray Eames. Images from the film *Powers of Ten.* 1977.

Space

Architects are especially involved with scale. The void or volume of space contained within architectural structures influences perception. The experience of being in a room with very low ceilings can be oppressive and claustrophobic. Entering a gothic cathedral **(C)** can fill one with a sense of wonderment. The scale of the soaring space, in relationship to the viewer's body, was designed to inspire awe.

Scale Drawings

The word *scale* is also used to explain the difference in size between an object or environment and its representation. This is a vital aspect of maps, models, and diagrams. If a designer draws a chair three inches tall and determines that the scale is *one inch equals one foot*, using the drawing as a guide, the chair that is constructed from it will be three feet tall. Measuring the scale drawing will provide all of the information required to construct the chair at the intended size.

> *. . . In that Empire, the Art of Cartography attained such Perfection that the map of a single Province occupied the entirety of a City, and the map of the Empire, the entirety of a Province. In time, those Unconscionable Maps no longer satisfied, and the Cartographers Guilds struck a Map of the Empire whose size was that of the Empire, and which coincided point for point with it.*

—From On Exactitude in Science, *by Jorge Luis Borges, 1960*

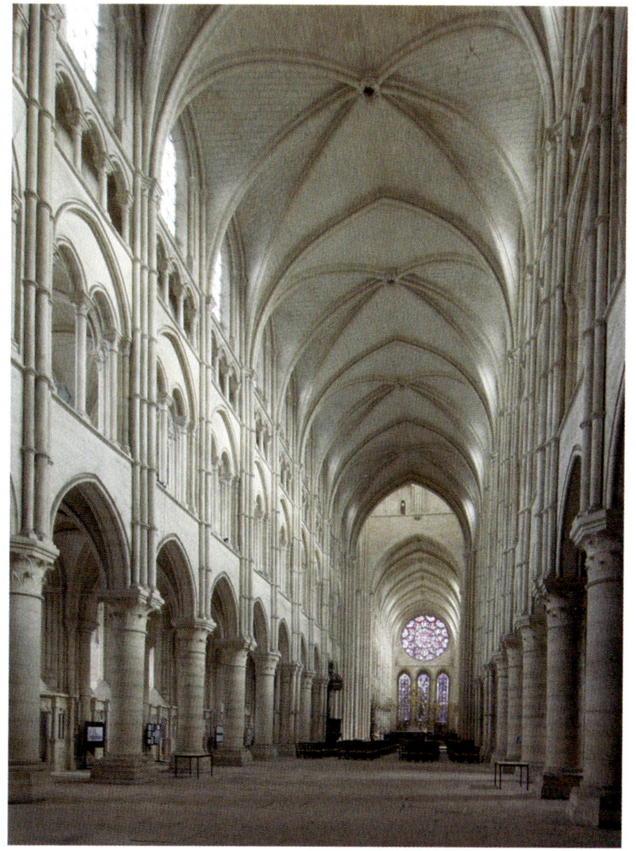

Interior of Laon Cathedral (looking northeast). Begun c. 1190. Laon, France.

THE MINIATURE

Miniatures are frequently encountered in daily life—children's figurines, toys, educational models, tabletop figurative sculpture, and souvenirs are just some of the objects often produced in a scale that is smaller than life-size.

A model train set is an interesting example of an installation that can be quite large, and also understood to be scaled down many times over. Miniature scale doesn't just mean small, but small relative to a point of reference. The miniature can generate a counter perception—the operator of the train set becomes a giant with total control.

Viewing *Two Women* **(A)**, we struggle to resolve a perceptual conundrum. Have these figures been somehow shrunken and preserved by alchemy or incantation? Are they simply life-sized representations of tiny women? These figures are highly detailed representations and we can get up close and examine every wrinkle, but their diminutive size (approximately one-half life-size) leads us to feel as if we are not close, but viewing them from a distance. When scale is carefully employed, complex plays of perceptual ambiguity can be achieved. Why is **B** included? To illustrate the scale of *Two Women*, of course.

The Effects of Scale

Scale alters one's relationship to the world. The water strider **(C)** can walk on water. The same insect scaled up to a larger size would fall through the surface of the water. The relationship between the surface tension and the surface-to-weight ratio of the insect (scale!) determines successful water walking.

Extremes

How small can you go? From the minuscule to the infinitesimal, some craftspeople are pushing the envelope. Willard Wigan carves diminutive sculptures that fit in the eye of a needle **(D)**. According to his website, "Willard enters a meditative state in which his heartbeat is slowed, allowing him to reduce hand tremors and sculpt between pulse beats. Even the reverberation caused by traffic outside can affect Willard's work."

A

Ron Mueck. ***Two Women.*** **2005. Mixed media, 2' 9½" high.**

B

Ron Mueck's ***Two Women*** **with viewers at the Royal Scottish Academy. Edinburgh, Scotland.**

C

Water strider.

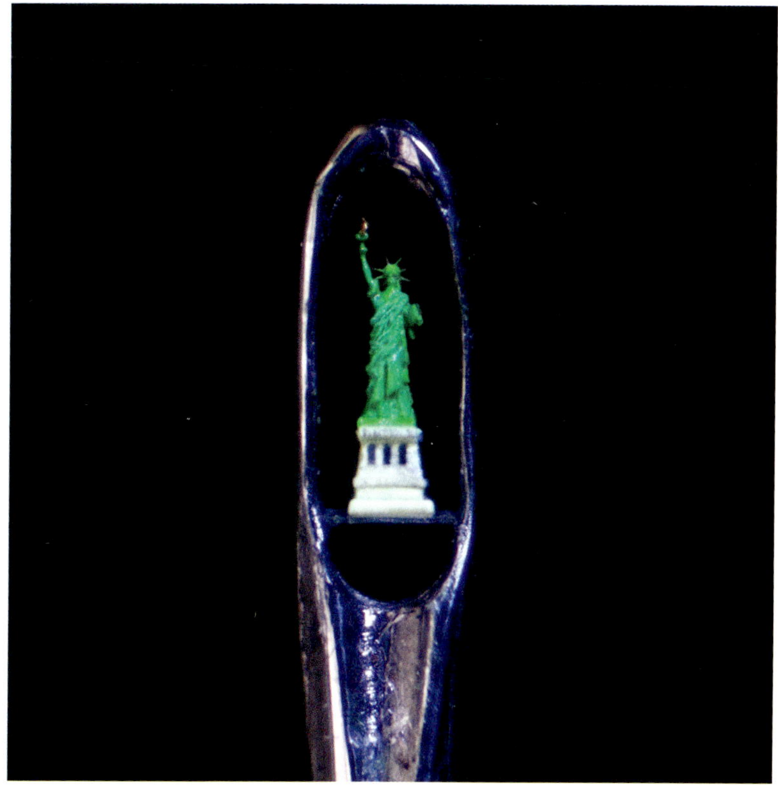

D

Willard Wigan. *Statue of Liberty* in the eye of a needle.

MONUMENTAL

The power of scale can be well observed in monumental things. The image of the worshiper at the foot of the 70-foot-tall statue of Gomateshwara in India **(A)** clearly indicates, even in a photograph, how forcefully scale can impact observers and how that can be experienced in extremely visceral ways. The statue is at least eleven times larger than life. Scale-increases of this magnitude are humbling and exhilarating. It is for such reasons that monumental scale is often used for political and propaganda purposes. The statue of Kim Il Sung **(B)**, former prime minister of North Korea, looms over a saluting soldier, not only expressing grandeur and power but dwarfing and diminishing all viewers—we feel like mere specks in its presence.

Making the Familiar Strange

Monumental scale isn't always about power; it is often playful, as in the Claes Oldenburg/Coosje Van Bruggen binocular entrance **(C)** incorporated into the facade of a building in Venice, California. The artists utilized the classic Pop Art strategy of appropriating and super-sizing a **quotidian** object. By their choice of subject matter, they not only mock the idea of the classical facade with columns, but they use scale to breathe life into the esteemed art world **tenet**, "make the familiar strange."

Sculptor Urs Fischer also makes the familiar strange by scaling up the miniature **(D)**. After squeezing a small piece of clay in his hand, he used a 3D computer scanner to record these casual lumps, increase scale, and produce molds. The final aluminum sculpture is over thirteen feet tall. This work evokes numerous references, from cocoons and rock formations to body parts and abstract sculpture, but these readings are disrupted, ominously or hilariously—massive fingerprints are clearly visible on the surface.

↑ **A**

Statue of Gomateshwara with worshipper. Shravanbelagola, Karnataka, India.

  **C**

Claes Oldenburg and Coosje Van Bruggen. Binocular entrance to Chiat/Day Building designed by Frank O. Gehry. 1991. Steel frame. Exterior: concrete and cement plaster painted with elastomeric paint, 45' × 44' × 18'. Venice, California.

↑ **B**

Kim Il Sung monument. North Korea.

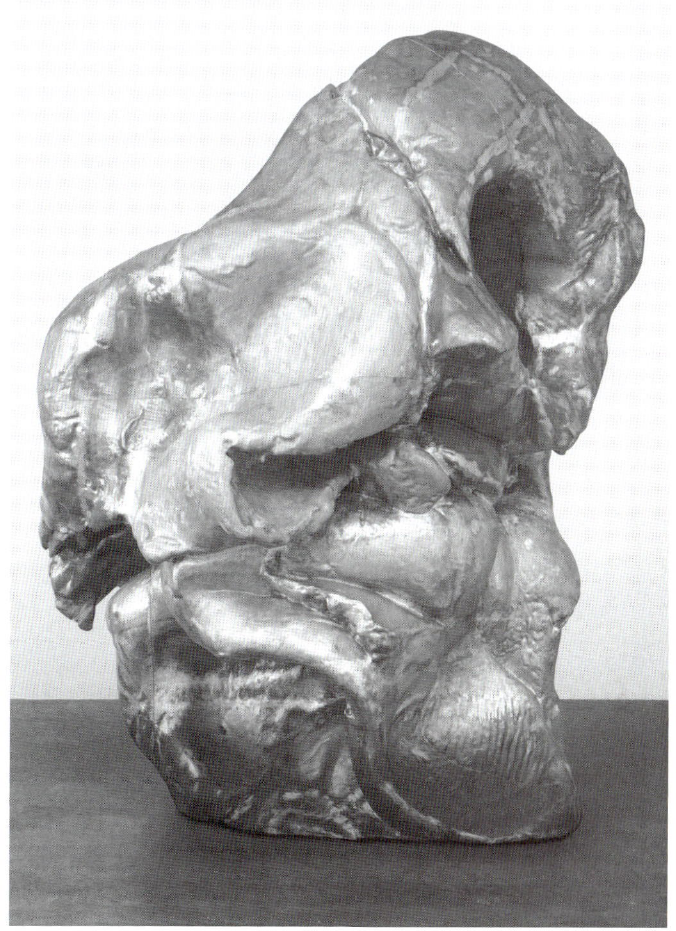

 **D**

Urs Fischer. *Marguerite de Ponty.* 2006–2008. Cast aluminum, 13' 1½".

Camille Seaman. Photograph from *The Last Iceberg*. 2006.

CHAPTER

5 MATERIAL

MATERIAL CARRIES MEANING

Selecting the right materials, the appropriate materials for your purpose, is critical—it is, in itself, an art. Selecting the right stone will allow easy shaping with your chisel, the wrong wood will warp, the appropriate plastic will bend as you require, and perhaps only one metal will oxidize to become the color you require. Selecting material demands that you accumulate knowledge through research, experiment, and experience. Good ideas can be brought down by the wrong materials.

Material is not only a substance to build with; material carries meaning, contains **content**. Think how different the painting/sculpture *Corvette of My Heart* **(A)** would be if it were made of carved wood, then painted red, or if it consisted of stacked red cloth instead of its actual material, paint—layers and layers of thick, red paint. Knowing and sensing that *Corvette* is solid paint impacts our experience of it. We can see that it was made with viscous paint, applied over time, until it became a colossal, tongue-like wedge on an industrial cart. Paint contains the weight of history, and this paint is literally and virtually heavy, dark, and loaded.

Puppy **(B)**, a public sculpture that has been installed in a number of locations since it was first created in 1992, depicts a West Highland terrier. It is constructed from approximately 70,000 living plants arranged on a stainless steel armature. Flowering plants, the basic building material, are light, colorful, and aromatic—they flutter gently in the wind. No other material would generate the same associations—formal gardens, topiary, and spring—and no other material would evoke such smiles of pure delight.

↑ **A**

Scott Richter. *Corvette of My Heart.* **2000. 3' 6" × 5' × 2' 3".**

Similarly, the sculpture *Self* in **C** derives its meaning more from its unusual material than from its form. It is made with ten pints of the artist's blood and must be kept frozen perpetually to maintain its shape. *Self* in another material is simply not an option. As Marshall McLuhan said, in a different but related context, "The medium is the message."

Truth to Materials

Truth to materials is a modernist tenet suggesting that materials should be used in ways that take advantage of their intrinsic properties. Modernist architects demanded that concrete be unpainted and unadorned, and that the process of its fabrication remain exposed on its surface. Truth to materials stands against making plastic, for example, look like wood or another material. If plastic is used, it should explore and celebrate its unique properties, its "plasticness." Today, truth to materials remains a valuable notion but it is no longer utilized systematically. The postmodernism wind has blown in more open, permissive, and playful attitudes.

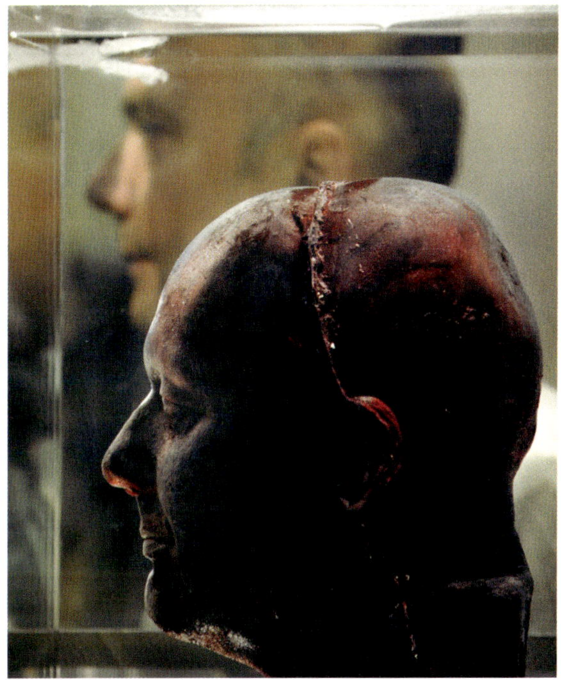

 **C**

Marc Quinn. *Self.* 1966. Self-portrait. Frozen blood, vitrine, and refrigeration unit. The artist poses in background.

 **B**

Jeff Koons. *Puppy.* 1992. Stainless steel, soil, and flowering plants, 40' $8\frac{3}{16}$" × 27' $2\frac{3}{4}$" × 29' $10\frac{1}{4}$".

EASE OF USE

Most materials fall into one of these groups: wood, fiber, and paper-based products; metals; earth-based materials such as clay, stone, concrete, plaster, and glass; plastics, foams; dyes and pigments. As makers, we are fortunate to have an extensive range of widely available materials to select from.

For those who craft objects, especially beginners, one of the first requirements for selecting materials is workability. Material that is easy to form, permitting alteration of your developing ideas, allows work to proceed most effectively. Cost and availability might also be factors. It is no accident that plaster, Styrofoam, clay, wood, cardboard, and wire **(A)** are widely used in foundation programs. They are workable.

In **B**, sculptor Henry Moore is seen working on a massive polystyrene version of *Large Spindle Piece*. A small, preliminary plaster maquette served as a model for the large foam piece. Both plaster and foam are supremely adjustable and easy to form. The foam can be shaped with handsaws and rasps, allowing for quick progress on any scale. When this foam sculpture was fully resolved, molds were made and the piece was cast in bronze.

Health Hazards in Design and the Arts

It is a serious mistake to think that art and design materials, unlike industrial, workplace substances, are free of toxins or

A

Alexander Calder bending wire to create a self-portrait in his studio in Sache, France. 1968.

health hazards. Just about anything sprayed or sanded requires a respirator. For many processes, proper ventilation is necessary. Most activities, especially in the woodshop, require safety glasses. If you eat or smoke with various materials on your hands, such as lead or cadmium pigments, you will endanger your health. If not handled properly, art materials are dangerous—there is a lot to learn. Purchasing a good book on health hazards in the arts is a smart investment, one that will be useful as long as you continue to make things.

See also *Introduction: Making*, page 170.

Henry Moore working on polystyrene version of *Large Spindle Piece.* 1968–1969. © 2011 The Henry Moore Foundation. All Rights Reserved/ARS, New York/DACS, London.

BAMBOO

You might think bamboo is an archaic building material, or that it is used only in developing nations, but due to its renewability, versatility, and global presence many believe it is the material of the future. Bamboo has been clocked growing up to two feet in a 24-hour period and can attain a height of eighty feet. Not actually a tree (it's in the grass family), it proliferates by spreading rhizomes and grows in abundance in warm climates all over the world.

The meeting house **(A)** illustrates the structural possibilities of large-scale bamboo construction. Here bamboo is used as a rigid support as well as a gracefully flexing network. This image shows the meeting house during its construction in New Guinea. The bamboo poles have yet to be covered with thatch. Indigenous fabrication methods developed over long periods, utilizing local materials, produce extremely sophisticated structures. Bamboo is still used in large-scale projects; it is a perfect scaffolding material and is used for this purpose worldwide. In **B** bamboo scaffolding is employed on a massive bridge construction project in China.

↑ **B**

Bamboo scaffolding for bridge construction. China.

↑ **A**

Men's clubhouse. Bamboo structure. New Guinea.

↑ **C**

Woven bamboo fish trap anchored by a rock. Alor, Indonesia.

D

Bamboo tea whisk. Japan.

The range of bamboo products is astounding. The Indonesian fish trap in **C** has been used for generations. Fish swim in, but can't escape the funnel within. Here the trap is shown underwater, anchored by a rock. The ingenious tea whisk **(D)** is used in the Japanese tea ceremony and conforms to the reductive esthetic required by that Zen ritual. It is made from a single segment of bamboo, the whisk end formed by slicing the bamboo into wafer-thin tines.

The contemporary bicycle in **E** is made from bamboo that has been smoked and heat-treated; it is not just a novelty product—it's a high-performance bike for daily use as well as racing. It is strong and light, and its production process claims an extremely small **carbon footprint**. The company that produces this bicycle is now helping entrepreneurs in Ghana build their own bikes from locally sourced bamboo.

↑ E

Calfee Design. Bamboo bicycle.

TECHNOLOGICAL DEVELOPMENT

The evolution of material for sculpture, products, and structures has a long and interesting history. Reinforced concrete (concrete with embedded steel rods or wire) was a new and exciting material in the late 1800s, and it contributed to the development of modernist architecture, allowing ever larger, lighter, and more daring structures to be built. Today, technology has accelerated the development of new materials. An interesting company, Material ConneXion, is responding to the deluge of new materials entering the field. It houses a fast-growing library of materials that designers can actually see and touch.

Aerogel

A .07-ounce piece of aerogel supports a five-and-one-half-pound brick in **A**. A human body, if composed of aerogel, would weigh approximately one pound. Aerogel, the lightest known solid, nicknamed solid blue smoke, is a new material with many special properties. Aerogel was used on the *Stardust* spacecraft to capture particles from Comet Wild 2. Aside from the esoteric task of trapping comet particles, it is being used as a thermal insulator; other uses continue to be discovered.

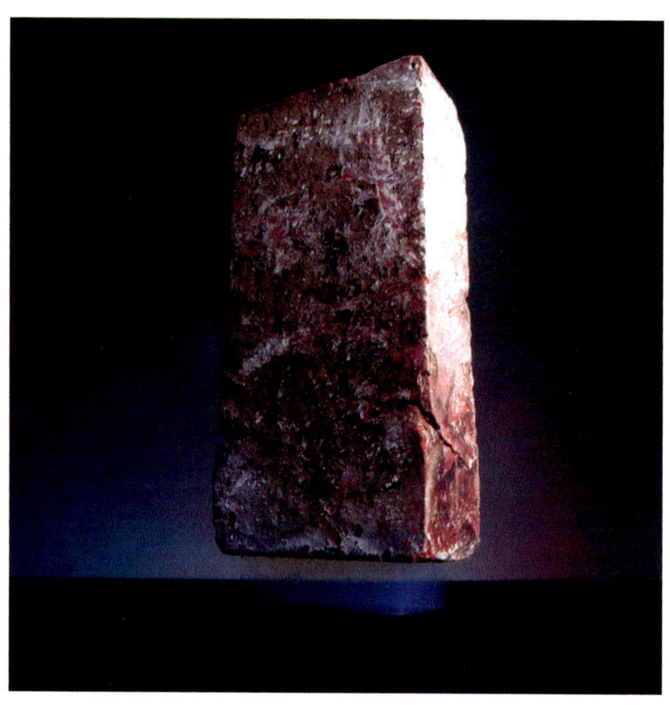

↑ A

Aerogel supporting a brick. A 2.5-kg brick is supported on top of a piece of aerogel weighing only 2 grams.

↑ B

***Alinghi 5* and *USA 17* (on left) during the 33rd America's Cup.**

Carbon Fiber

Carbon fiber and epoxy resin have been revolutionizing the fields of boatbuilding, aeronautical engineering, and sports and racing equipment for many years. Carbon fiber is a threadlike material with a very high strength-to-weight ratio. It can be woven, wound, or used as a composite (in combination with other materials). Carbon fiber is replacing fiberglass, which is heavy and bulky in comparison, in many high-performance products and vehicles. The thirty-third America's Cup was won by *USA 17* **(B)**, a ninety-foot trimaran sailboat that utilized cutting-edge design and carbon fiber construction.

Synthetic Skin

Many laboratories are working to perfect living, synthetic skin, and a number of skin substitutes are already available. They are effective in healing burn victims, for example. The artificial skin in **C** is INTEGRA® Dermal Regeneration Template. It provides a scaffold for skin growth. Skin replacement technology is concurrent with exciting developments in tissue engineering, the cultivation of replacement body parts from living human cells.

Designing Material

Composite materials, laminates, new polymers, nanotechnology, biotechnology, fiber optics, new textiles, porous ceramics, super-hard materials, and specialized adhesives are just some of the exciting developments in material science. Materials are no longer simply raw stuff awaiting the designer's hand. Today, materials themselves are being designed, the result—smart materials.

 **C**

Synthetic skin. Integra® Dermal Regeneration Template. Integra LifeSciences Corporation.

REUSE AND GREEN DESIGN

Sustainability is an important idea with worldwide significance. Sustainable or green materials refer to products such as sorghum plywood made from reclaimed agricultural fiber, or bamboo (discussed in a previous section), which grows rapidly and can be renewed or regrown as fast as it is consumed. A green material may also be one that has a local source, or has been made from recycled material, or is itself recyclable. The concept of designing the sustainable aspects of the complete life span of a building or a product is referred to as **cradle to cradle** design. Reductive design, the old idea of doing more with less, takes on new life in this context.

It is good that plastic bottles and aluminum cans have been getting thinner and thinner—many have had so much material eliminated, it seems more appropriate to call them bags. Some designers are seeking solutions to global problems in the social and behavioral realm—if we simply didn't buy bottled water, those bottles, no matter how thin, would neither have to be manufactured, nor, as often is the case, shipped across the Atlantic.

Sustainability is a critical issue in the field of design, where mass production magnifies even small incidents of wastefulness, and in architecture, where the scale of projects can involve mass quantities of building materials. Artists, as makers of unique objects, have tended to view these issues less urgently. Today, however, they are becoming more engaged.

Reuse

El Anatsui, a Ghanaian artist, uses aluminum screw-tops from discarded liquor bottles and copper wire to create enormous sculptures **(A** and **B)** that resemble metallic textiles. These abstract configurations are loaded with meaning, from the traditions of kente cloth to the history of liquor and slavery in Africa. Artists have long realized the value of found and discarded objects, but today the added idea of reuse is an important sustainability issue.

The WOBO or world bottle **(C)** was an attempt in the 1960s by the Heineken Brewing Company to make bottles that would have a second life, in this case as bricks! It was an idea that was ahead of its time; no beer was ever sold in the world bottle.

Green Design

Cook+Fox Architects, advocates of **green design**, created an energy-efficient, environmentally sustainable house **(D)**. Inspired by natural systems, the architects employed a reactive skin (an outer screen designed to interact with changes in daylight), as well as pivoting interior screens, moveable partitions to collect and block light, and skylight tubes.

A

El Anatsui. *Dusasa I.* **2007. Aluminum liquor bottle caps and copper wire, 20' × 30'. Venice Biennale.**

B

El Anatsui. *Dusasa I.* **Detail. 2007. Aluminum liquor bottle caps and copper wire, 20' × 30'. Venice Biennale.**

C

John Habraken, designer. Heineken WOBO (world bottle).

Environmental Guardianship

Some cultures deserve an A+ in environmental guardianship. Here, Vietnamese fishermen transport their bamboo fish traps on bicycles **(E)**.

Ideas of sustainability, sustainable materials, and conservation are issues that are changing the face of design, art, and architecture. Even if there were no global warming and resources were endless, we would still have to dispose of massive amounts of waste every day, and we would have to worry about its impact on the environment. So . . . the things your grandmother taught you remain valuable in life and design—don't be wasteful!

See also *Simplicity: Reductive Sensibility*, page 42.

D

Cook + Fox Architects. *LiveWorkHome* house. Eco-friendly house.

E

Fishermen carry several bamboo fish traps on their bicycles on a road in Hai Hung province, Northern Vietnam.

Crab Nebula. Photograph from NASA Hubble Space Telescope.

CHAPTER

6 STRUCTURE

STRUCTURAL PRINCIPLES

If you create sculpture, build a table, or design a house, your first obligation is, inevitably, structural. The ever-present force of gravity must be dealt with in order to achieve structural integrity. No matter how wonderful your table design may be, if it wobbles, sags, or leans over like a parallelogram when you place a load on it, it will fail to be a viable structure.

The Inherent Strength of Forms

Some forms are inherently weak, such as squares, rectangles, and rectangular solids; others, like triangles, pyramids, arches, cylinders, domes, and spheres, achieve stability quite naturally. One of the earliest types of construction is **post and lintel**; it is a building system in which a lintel (horizontal beam) is supported by two posts (columns). Stonehenge and Greek Temples are constructed in this manner, and since right angles have inherent structural deficiencies, the columns must be substantial. When post and lintel construction (also referred to as post and beam) is utilized in contemporary, wood frame houses, corners are always reinforced by bracing that forms triangles. The old, leaning barn in **A** has taken on the familiar shape of the stressed, unstable rectangle—a parallelogram.

The Arch

If the lintel, resting on its supporting columns, is too long, it will bend or break. The length of a lintel is limited. If you want to create a span with an exceptionally long lintel, such as a bridge, for example, you must resort to another structural type—the arch. An arched bridge can span approximately four times the distance and support more weight than a flat beam bridge, and a suspension bridge is far more efficient than an arch.

↑ **A**

Leaning barn.

B

Shigeru Ban. Paper Bridge. Remoulin, France. 2007.

The Arch and the Truss

The architect Shigeru Ban and his students built a bridge of paper and cardboard that could hold up to twenty people **(B)**. For this amazing feat, they utilized the power of the arch. To make this bridge even stronger, another stable form was also employed—triangular structure. When triangles are repeated to form an extended configuration, an extremely sturdy structure, the **truss**, is formed; and in this case the truss is curved. In the background of **B** there is a Roman aqueduct that, though an ancient masonry structure, utilizes the same efficient arch.

The Truss

The longest continuous truss bridge in North America **(C)** harnesses the strength of the triangle—try to count the number of diagonal braces and triangles in this structure. The truss is a widely used structural configuration that adds rigidity to beams and prevents such unwelcome deformation as the parallelograming of the old barn.

C

Astoria-Megler Bridge, detail. Connects Astoria, Oregon, and Megler, Washington.

EFFICIENT FORM

The line of beauty is the result of perfect economy. The cell of the bee is built at that angle which gives the most strength with the least wax. The bone or the quill of the bird gives the most alar (wing) strength with the least weight. . . . There is not a particle to spare in natural structures.

—*Ralph Waldo Emerson*

From the galaxy to a crystal of salt, the exuberance of nature takes billions of forms, but study discloses that stupefying variety has been achieved with stringent economy of means. All things both great and small evolve in a few simple patterns—among them spirals, meanders, branchings, angles of 120 degrees. Why the preference for elegant simplicity? In three-dimensional space, only a few basic shapes will combine to build stable structures or do useful work. These patterns prevail because they make the most efficient use of energy. They are purposeful.

—*Horace Freeland Judson*

Towers

The radio transmission tower in **A**, the tallest structure in Louisiana, at close to 2,000 feet, is an example of extreme structural economy. It is an efficient vertical truss (under **compression**) that must be kept perfectly upright to remain stable. Most towers, like the Eiffel Tower in Paris, remain perpendicular to the surface of the earth by virtue of being considerably wider at the bottom, thus creating the necessary stability. Exceptionally tall towers, like the one in **A**, are often a consistent width from the top to the bottom. Guy wires are the key to keeping these improbably thin towers straight up. Observe the numerous cables (under **tension**) connecting the tower to the ground.

Domes

From igloos to cathedrals, the dome is a stable structure widely used in architecture, design, and the arts. The **geodesic dome (B)** designed by Buckminster Fuller, takes advantage of the inherent strength of both the dome and the triangle. Fuller strove to use the smallest quantity of material to span the greatest area. The weight of the dome is distributed by its web of triangles, spreading the load evenly and efficiently throughout the entire structure. Efficient and cost-effective, geodesic domes have been constructed worldwide for purposes ranging from world's fairs to emergency shelter.

Extreme Economy

Flying for about nine days, the *Voyager* **(C)** was the first aircraft to circumnavigate the world nonstop without refueling. To do this it had to have low drag, be light in weight, and carry an enormous amount of fuel. Formed by a composite material consisting of graphite, Kevlar, and fiberglass, the *Voyager* weighed approximately 2,250 pounds, incredibly light considering its wingspan of 110 feet. When it took off, fully fueled, it weighed 9,700 pounds! To obtain maximum lift, the *Voyager* utilized a double-wing design, not unlike the designs of the Wright brothers. Aeronautical design has always required stringent attention to structural economy; it is an area of design in which there is no place for the superfluous.

← **A**

Radio transmission tower near Houma, Louisiana.

Buckminster Fuller. Biosphere of Environment Canada. 1967. Montreal, Quebec, Canada.

↑ C

Burt Rutan, designer. *Voyager* aircraft. Built by Rutan Aircraft Factory, Inc., 1984.

PHYSICAL FORCES

The increased understanding of the applied physical forces of tension and compression resulted in important advances in structural engineering and design. Tension is the force that stretches. Pulling each end of a rubber band places it under tension—tension acts to expand. Compression is the application of pressure. If you stand on a stack of books, squeezing it downward, it is being compressed.

The sculpture in **A** was designed by the engineer/architect Santiago Calatrava who is renowned for elevating engineering to a high art. It is no surprise, therefore, that this sculpture happens to be an extremely clear demonstration of the principles of tension and compression. The two tall cones at the base are under compression; the weight of the entire sculpture rests upon them.

What kind of force is acting on the supporting cables? They are not being compressed, they are being pulled from one end to the other; they are under tension, like our example of the rubber band. Cut these cables, and the sculpture will come crashing down.

↑ **A**

Santiago Calatrava. ***Bou.*** **2007. Palma, Spain.**

The Suspension Bridge

This structural system that keeps the Calatrava sculpture upright is closely related to the design principles of suspension bridges. The Brooklyn Bridge **(B)**, one of the earliest suspension bridges, is an interesting case. It was built with twin masonry towers. Today, steel is commonly used for suspension bridge towers. If you compare the Brooklyn Bridge towers to the more modern suspension bridges you have seen, you can't help noticing how squat and bulky the Brooklyn Bridge towers seem. Stone is simply not as efficient as steel as a supporting, compressive material, so more stone was required. The steel cables are under tension, and the stone towers are under compression. In this way, all suspension bridges find their **equilibrium**. Many believe that the modern suspension bridge is among the most beautiful objects in the built world.

Tensile Strength and Load Bearing

Spider webs **(C)** are structures under tension and tension alone. These engineering marvels are incredibly strong and super lightweight. Webs must support their own weight as well as that of anything in it (engineers call this a dead load). In addition, webs, as traps for insects, need to withstand the sudden, moving forces of their prey. Any such load that involves moving forces (wiggling insects in a web or cars driving over a bridge) is called a live load. All structures need to deal with dead and live loads. The spider's silk has a very high **tensile strength**, as does steel. In fact, pound for pound, spider silk is stronger than steel. Stone, concrete, and wood have low tensile strength. When designing and fabricating, one must be aware of material properties. On small-scale structures, casual testing is usually sufficient to get an understanding of material strength. Large projects require research and a more rigorous approach to material testing.

  B

Brooklyn Bridge. John A. Roebling, designing engineer. New York.

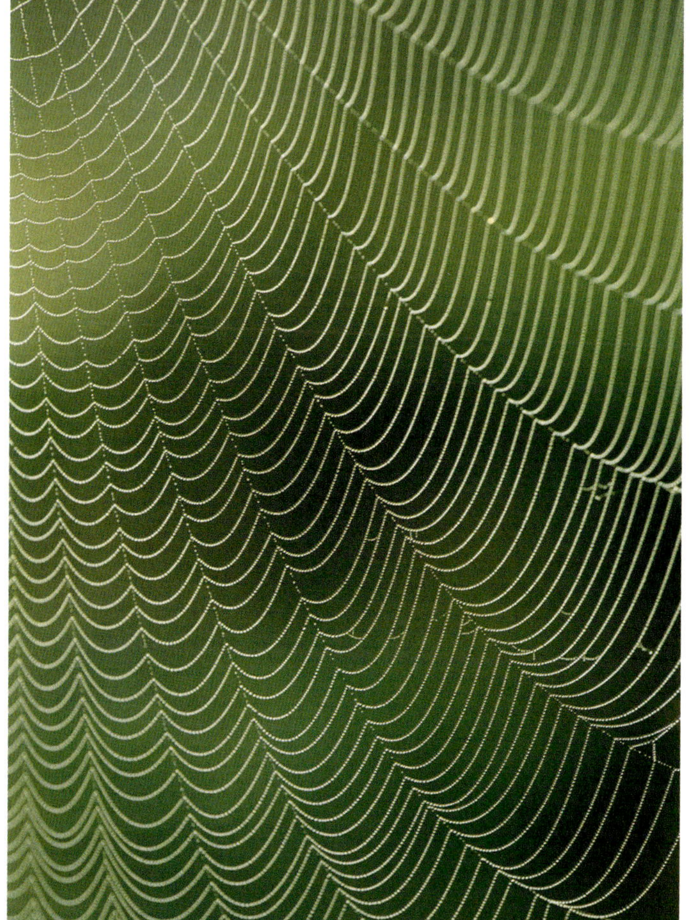

 C

Spider web.

STRUCTURAL CONNECTION

Joinery refers to how parts of a form are held together, how elements are attached. If you have ever built anything, you already know how challenging joinery can be. A common method in antiquity was simply tying things together with rope or cord. Even more basic is the use of gravity. Many ancient structures, such as masonry walls and monumental forms, were made with carefully cut stone—no mortar; just weight and a close fit held everything together. Both methods are still in use today.

Nails, screws, staples, bolts, rivets, clamps, binding, tape, adhesives, welding, soldering, brazing, heat-sealing, and mechanical splicing are just some of the many joinery methods now available. One of the challenges of the designer or artist is to find the appropriate method for the task at hand.

Joinery was considered so important at the Bauhaus that it was the subject of numerous projects. In **A**, Josef Albers had his students build structures with extremely unusual (and dangerous) materials, double-edge razor blades and wood dowels only. The students were forced to be inventive. The tension of the flexed razor blade and its two holes were harnessed to become efficient connectors.

Rivets, however basic, are still used in steel construction **(B)**. They are perhaps your fundamental fastener. Each end of a small steel rod is pounded flat, serving to clamp two pieces of steel together. Rivets have been wtidely replaced by welding, a process in which two pieces of metal are melted together, usually by a bead of applied molten metal. Welding has revolutionized steel construction, allowing for fabrication of almost any configuration.

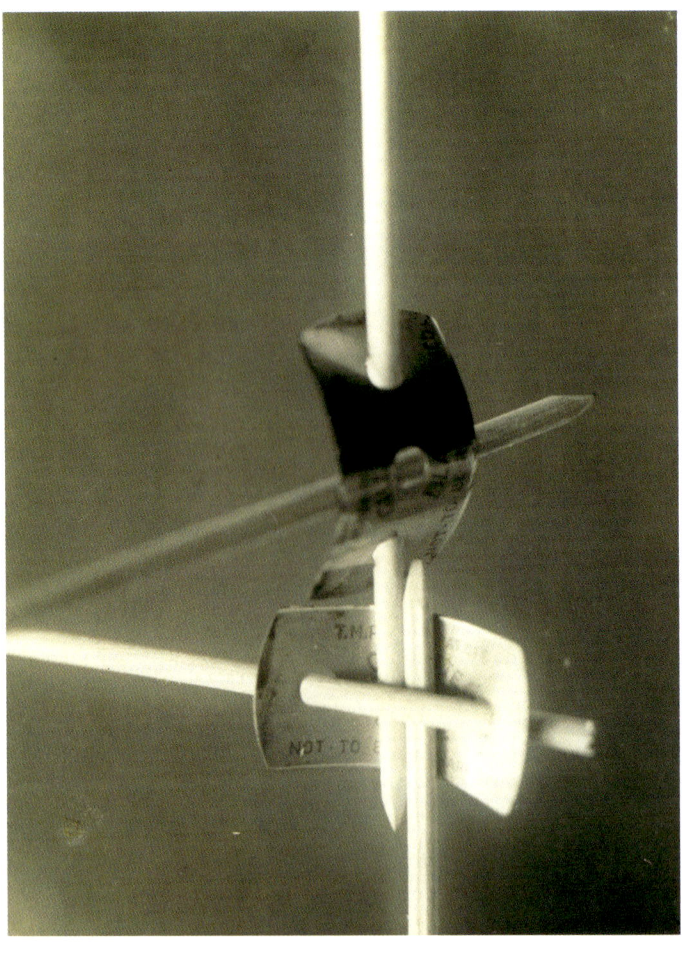

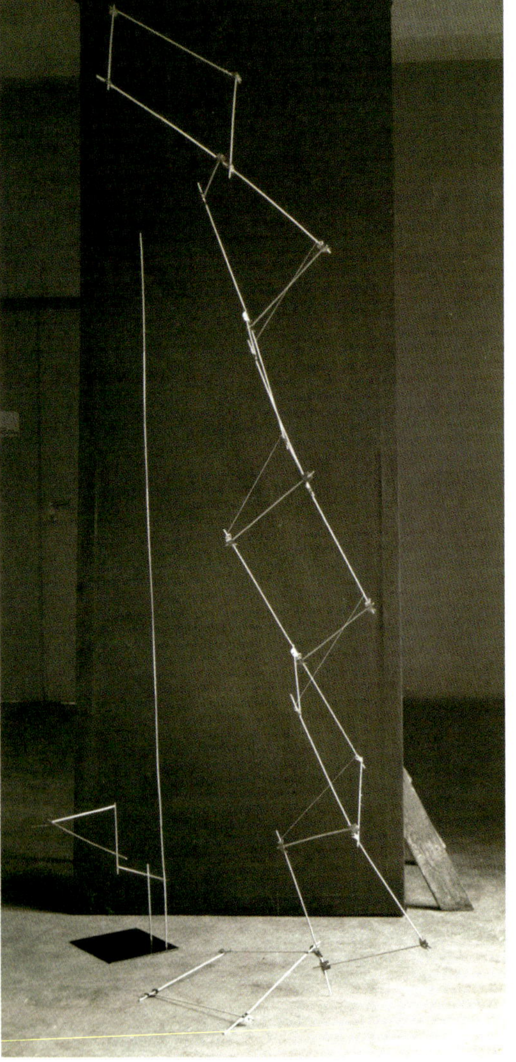

 **A**

Construction from Josef Alber's preliminary course at the Bauhaus. Detail on left; 9' high construction on right. 1938. © 2011 The Josef and Anni Albers Foundation/Artists Rights Society (ARS), New York.

Woodworkers utilize many kinds of joints: miter, spline, dovetail, tongue and groove, and dado are just a small selection. Some joints require glue, and some can do without. The dovetail joint in **C** that is being fitted in place will be held together by the logic of its design (which is purely mechanical) and the precision of its artisanry (along with a little glue).

Richard Deacon, a master fabricator, used epoxy to join slabs of wood in his sculpture *Kiss and Tell* **(D)**. Epoxy adhesives are increasingly valuable in art and design. Different kinds of stone are being epoxied together to form new, layered materials; and epoxied composite materials are routine in airplane and boat construction.

← **B**

Ben Franklin Bridge. Philadelphia, PA.

↑ **C**

Woodworker fitting dovetail joint.

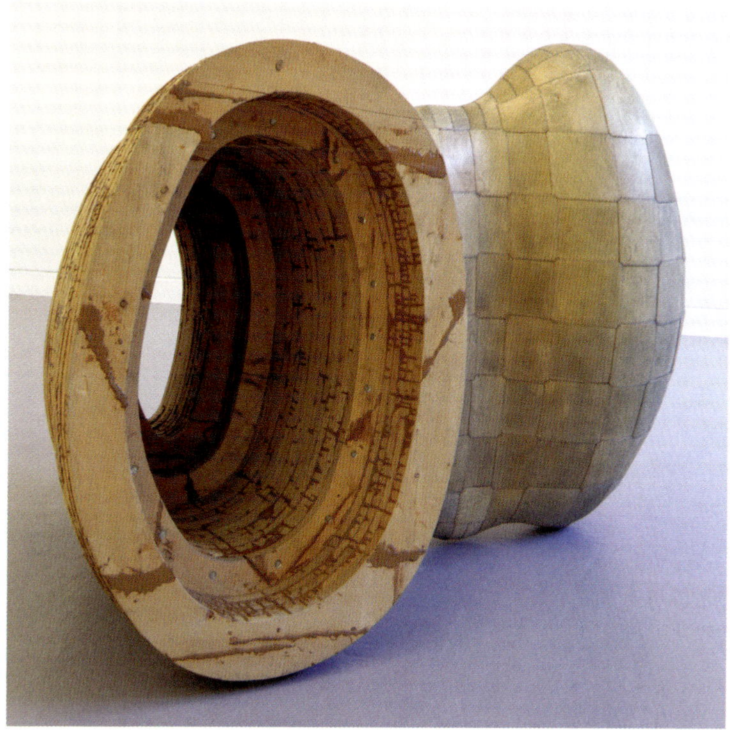

↑ **D**

Richard Deacon. *Kiss and Tell.* **1989. Epoxy, plywood, steel, timber, 5' $9\frac{11}{32}$" × 7' 5" × 8' $10\frac{11}{32}$". Collection, Arts Council of Great Britain, London.**

COLLAPSIBLE AND EXPANDABLE STRUCTURE

From simple folding chairs to high-tech tents, objects that transform are increasingly important. Form is not simply a static mass; it can be collapsible, expandable, inflatable, and foldable. Objects that collapse for economical shipping or for carrying in your car or in your backpack are extremely useful. Ikea, the giant Swedish furniture manufacturer, loves flat-pack shipping, and has claimed that this allows them to reduce costs by not shipping air.

The *Blue Heron* decoy **(A)** that we've seen before in its assembled form is shown again here, but this time paired with an image of it in its disassembled state. Hunters could easily carry this decoy disassembled into remote areas where its component parts, three sticks, an oval form, and a ball, could be assembled to create a full-size heron.

Martha Graham, the legendary dancer choreographer, created new forms of movement that often involved an inventive use of costumes. In the performance depicted in **B**, the dancer wears a stretchable tube that becomes the vehicle for the formation of transforming sequences of extraordinary form.

A

***Blue Heron* decoy. Assembled, left. A rendering of the decoy unassembled, right.**

B

Herta Moselsio, photographer. *Lamentation*. Choreographer, Martha Graham. c. 1937. Silver gelatin print.

Expandable Structures

The Hoberman Sphere is a toy that expands from nine to thirty inches in diameter **(C)**. Not simply an amusement, the sphere employs ingenious folding mechanisms that have led the designer to major projects involving rapidly deployable tents and adaptive buildings with roofs that open and close and facades that retract.

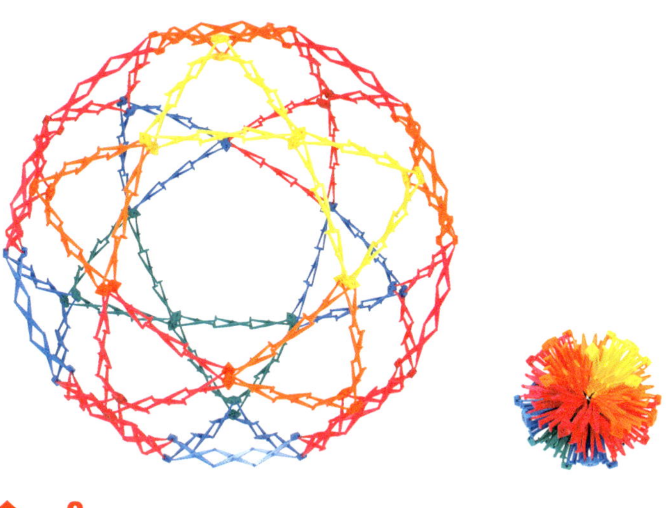

C

Hoberman Sphere. Toy. Expanded and contracted views. Chuck Hoberman, designer. Plastic, 9"–30".

Raumlaborberlin, Art and architecture collective. ***Portavilion 2010: Rosy (the ballerina)*****. London, U.K.**

Nomadic Structures

Portable dwellings such as Bedouin tents, or those built for temporary use, like igloos and huts, are a necessity for **nomadic** people. In today's world of widespread international travel, we are all becoming nomads. Suitcases with wheels, collapsible camping cups and bowls, tents, domes, inflatable structures, mobile homes, and the lunar lander are all contemporary manifestations of nomadic culture.

Consisting of an air-supported membrane and a sustaining trailer, the nomadic pavilion in **D** toured London parks, serving as a temporary, pneumatic event space. With this pavilion, the designers continued to explore what they refer to as "bubbletecture." For sheer ingeniousness, however, it would be difficult to surpass the makers of the "raft" in **E**, who brought their harvest of coconuts to a mill, downstream, using their cargo as its own transporting vessel!

Raft of coconuts. The Philippines.

Rollercoaster.

CHAPTER 7

FUNCTION

UTILITY

Beauty rests on utility.

All beauty that has not a foundation in use, soon grows distasteful, and needs continual replacement with something new.

—*Shaker Maxims*

Shaker Design

It would be impossible to discuss utility without acknowledging the Shakers' contribution to contemporary art and design. The **Shakers** created an alternative religious community that flourished in the nineteenth century. They produced tools, furniture, and architecture that embodied their devout religious beliefs. Shaker design is revered for its reductive form, exquisite craft, and its plain and humble focus on use. Shaker furniture has been referred to as "religion in wood."

↑ A

Double Trustee's Desk. Shaker. Mount Lebanon, New York. c. 1840.

"That which has in itself the highest use, possesses the greatest beauty." This Shaker maxim makes objects such as the double desk **(A)**, combining a cabinet and side-by-side fold-down work surfaces, inevitable. If you believe **utility** simulates the order of heaven, as did the Shakers, then what could be better than an object that is multifunctional?

Utilitarianism

Shaker design ideas (and utility in general) relate in interesting ways to the philosophy of utilitarianism, which posits that one should act so as to provide the greatest happiness (and least pain) for the greatest number of people.

The Greatest Good for the Greatest Number of People

There are many designers, architects, and artists dealing with utility. And if you care about utility, why design a new silver-plated wine cork extractor, however functional, when there are more pressing problems facing humanity? Donald G. McNeil Jr. reported in an article in the *New York Times*, "Design That Solves the Problems for the World's Poor":

The world's cleverest designers, said Dr. Polak, a former psychiatrist who now runs an organization helping poor farmers become entrepreneurs, "cater to the globe's richest 10 percent, creating items like wine labels, couture and Maseratis. "We need a revolution to reverse that silly ratio," he said.

"A billion customers in the world," Dr. Paul Polak told a crowd of inventors recently, "are waiting for a $2 pair of eyeglasses, a $10 solar lantern and a $100 house."

One of the products in the Cooper-Hewitt National Design Museum exhibition that McNeil discusses is a simple and elegant design solution, the *Q Drum* **(B)**. It is a 20-gallon water can that is easily towed by an individual, potentially saving millions of people worldwide, mostly women and children, the arduous and dangerous task of carrying heavy vessels.

In **C**, Dean Kamen, inventor of the Segway, operates an iBOT, the motorized wheelchair he designed. The iBOT allows the user to participate in conversations at eye-level, and due to its innovative gyroscopic, self-balancing technology, it can even navigate stairs. All this is extremely valuable, but the design of the iBOT attempts to accomplish more than that, it seeks to provide dignity to the disabled users' experience.

Design as Social Action

Good contemporary, utilitarian design need not involve a product. Socially concerned citizens and designers are finding innovative, alternative methods for creating solutions to pressing problems, as did the group of law students that purchased industrial pollution rights at auction and let them expire unused (preventing the emission of many tons of sulfur dioxide).

B

P. J. and J. P. S. Hendrikse, designers. *Q Drum.* 1993.

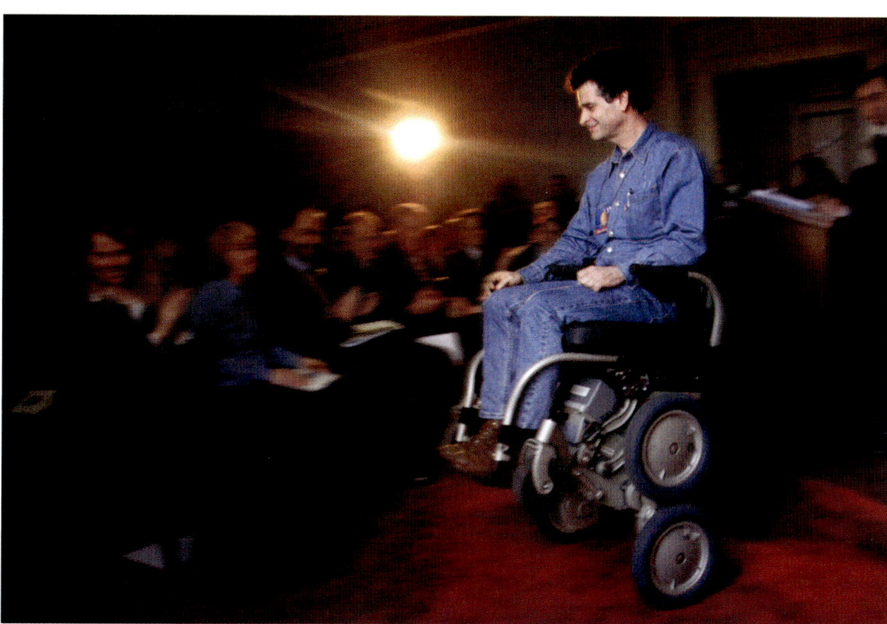

C

Dean Kamen riding the *iBOT* motorized wheelchair he invented.

DESIGN AND ART COMPARED

It is commonly believed that the difference between art and design is utility—design has a function and art does not . . . but that is a simplification. While, yes, a great deal of design is clearly about function first and foremost, the difference between art and design can be ambiguous. Let's look at clothing as an example. The production of clothing is a design discipline, and clothing has a clear utilitarian purpose. It conceals and protects our bodies, and keeps us warm in the winter. If this were the entire truth about clothing's purpose, factories would need only produce a few shirt styles for different activities, and we would all be wearing something like white Ts or blue denim work shirts every day. The fact is, there are thousands and thousands of shirt designs produced annually, in every conceivable shape and pattern, and different versions in countries the world over. What is going on here? Whatever it is, it is certainly not all about utility. Clothing design is about so much more than function, and it does not stand alone among the design disciplines.

↑ A

Philip Treacy. Hat. Fall/Winter 2001/2002.

We all know that fashion design has a high end, experimental, haute couture faction, but what do you think Philip Treacy is up to with his outrageous, delightful hat in **A**? The cell phone coffin in **B** is from Ghana, where some have opted for burial in playful, custom coffins—beer bottle coffins, lizard coffins, running shoes, pineapples, and automobiles.

The Philip Treacy hat and the coffin illustrate the blurred boundaries of art and design. The hat, like any intelligent, formal sculpture, inventively explores form and structure; and the coffin confronts death with celebratory, pop humor, while both also serve utilitarian objectives, however diminished they may be. To understand the full complexity of the utilitarian–nonutilitarian interface, remember that most things, such as shirts, for example, are also signs, identifying your personal style, social class, subcultural affiliations, and so on.

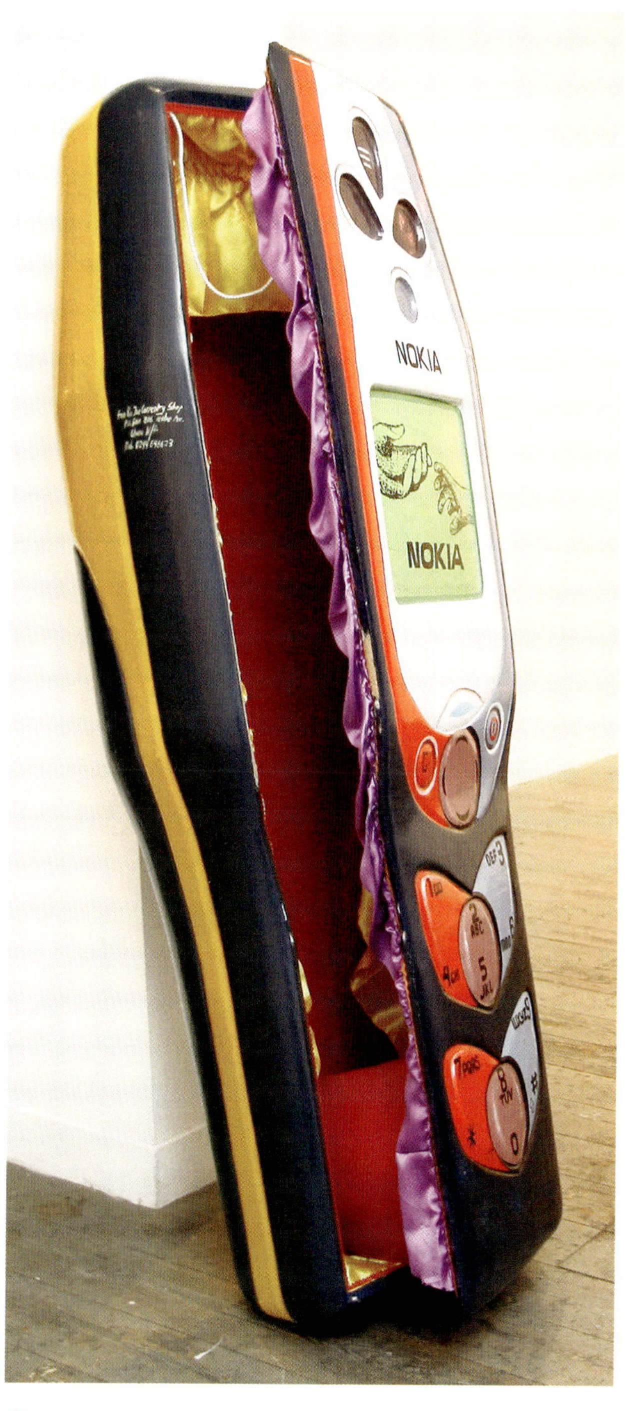

↑ **B**

Contemporary cell phone coffin. Ghana.

ART

Let's consider the notion that art has no utility. Yes, bronze sculpture is really not very good for driving to work in or for opening cans, but if you examine the proposition more carefully, you might agree that art is full to the brim with utility. For its audience, art provides delight, intellectual stimulation, and information; it challenges preconceptions and provokes passionate emotion and even political action. For artists there is a different range of functionality at work. The artist may celebrate or investigate various aspects of phenomena, form and perception, and psychological and social structure, as well as her or his own deepest nature. Art practice remains a quite useful method for self-development. It is a path to self-awareness, often reminiscent of Zen in its approach.

Mark Tansey. *The Innocent Eye Test.* 1981.

Isomorphism

Humanist psychologist Abraham Maslow describes his idea of **isomorphism** (similarity of structure or form) in this way: you can only know that which you are "up to" (or what you are). We see the sum of our experiences in the world around us and understand and identify with those things that reflect our outlook. Mark Tansey shrewdly comments on such matters in **A**, *The Innocent Eye Test*. To know more, to see farther, requires that we attend to the task of becoming more informed and receptive beings. The practice of art naturally facilitates this process of self-development.

Memes

Richard Dawkins explains that **memes** are similar to genes, and they replicate by being spread from mind to mind. Memes can be ideas, styles, art works, tunes, or theories. Good memes survive for long periods of time because they continue to be spread, and as Dawkins says, they "parasitize" your mind.

The work of Marcel Duchamp and Dadaism turned the art world on its head. After one hundred years, Duchamp remains important because artists continue to explore, spread, and reinterpret his ideas. Duchamp's ready-mades, such as *Fountain* in **B**, are a highly successful meme. His ideas, like certain Web images, have gone viral in art history. Let's get to the studio and make some good memes.

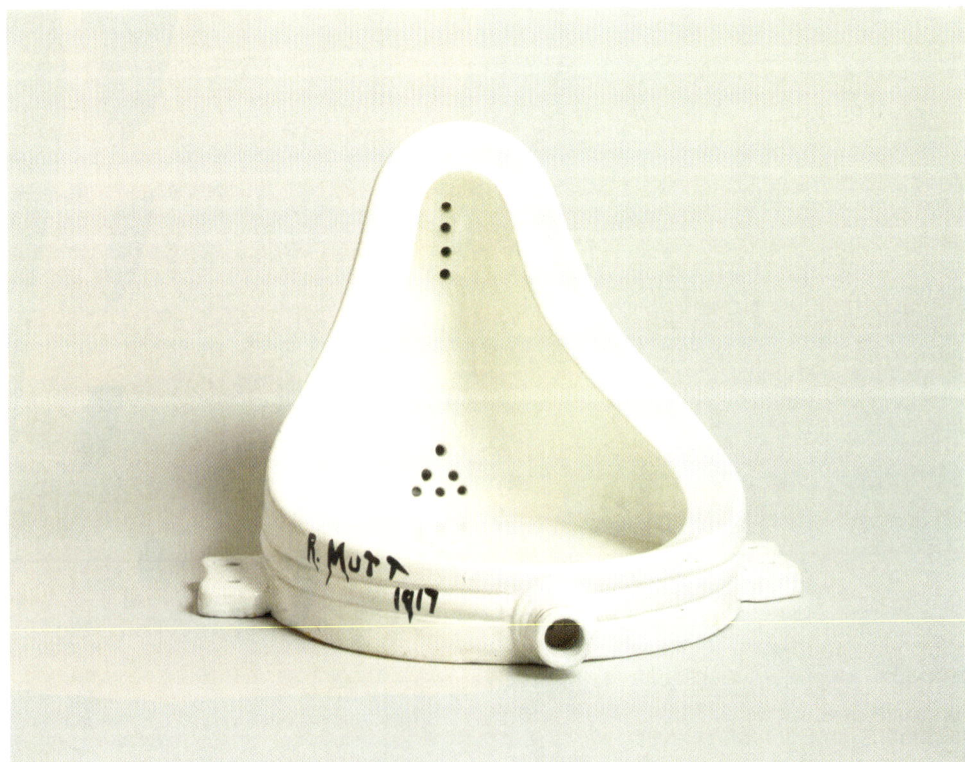

Marcel Duchamp. *Fountain.* 1917. © 2011 Artists Rights Society (ARS), New York/ADAGP, Paris/ Succession Marcel Duchamp.

The Gap between Art and Design

The things that exist in the gap between art and design are informative. They make us aware of the richness of human production and the shortcomings of categorization. The finger **prosthesis** in **C** is a utilitarian device—it conceals missing fingers. This prosthesis is successful by virtue of its degree of **verisimilitude**. The maker had to have more than skill; he or she had to carefully observe the form, proportions, color, and texture of the model, as would any good figurative artist.

The trout fishing fly **(D)** speaks eloquently in the languages of both art and design. It has a clear purpose, to assist in the successful capture of a wily trout. The fly must be tied, as the prosthesis was made, by carefully observing actual insects that the trout are feeding on. The more accurate the representation, the better the fly. But in this case things are a bit more complicated—the fly doesn't have to look lifelike to us; it has to look lifelike to trout! Furthermore, it must be realistic when wet, and it must move through the water like the real insect it mimics (it is a behavioral mimic as well as a visual one). The lesson of the prosthesis and the fishing fly is intended to encourage us to remain open to the complexities inherent in the relationship of art, design, and utility.

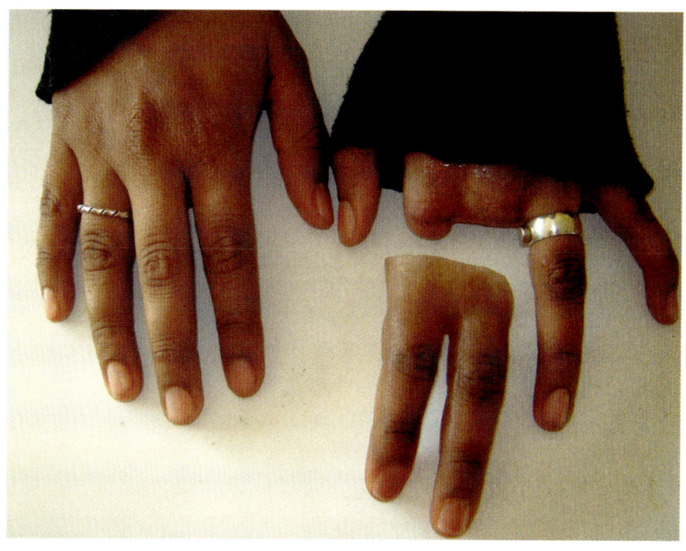

↑ C

Prosthetic fingers. Dianceht Company. Guadalajara, Jalisco, Mexico.

↑ D

A trout fishing wet fly known as an Invicta secured in a fly-tying vice.

FORM AND FUNCTION

Form and function is a term used to express the relationship between the form of an object and its use.

Form Follows Function

A closely related notion is **form follows function**—a **dictum** of Modernist architects who, turning their backs on the styles of the past, sought new principles to shape their architecture. It is, however, an idea that has been used throughout history, especially in the creation of tools and structures.

Ergonomic Design

Form derived from function is most evident in objects created for disciplines requiring highly specific uses—air and space travel, medical equipment, transportation, and sports equipment. The handle of the ski pole **(A)** has not been designed to look cool; it has been designed only to function, to fit the hand of the skier and allow him or her to wield the poles effectively and comfortably in all required positions. **Ergonomic** design engages the idea that designed objects must interact compatibly with the user's body.

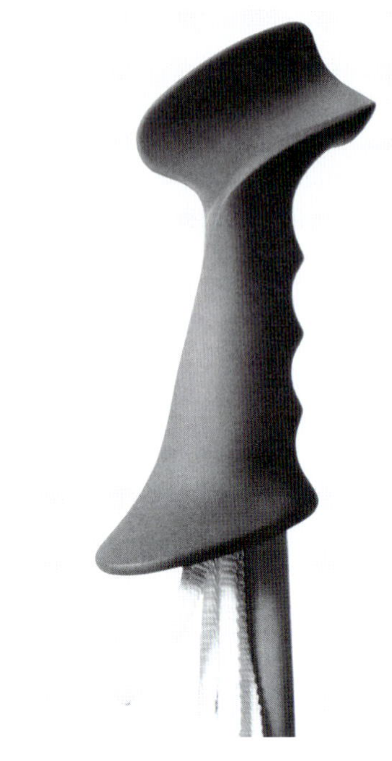

↑ A

Peter Stathis, designer. ***"Thumb Sparing" Ski-Pole Grip.*** **1991. The Museum of Modern Art, New York.**

↑ B

Paul MacCready, designer. ***Gossamer Penguin*** **in flight. 1979.**

Functionality Determines Form

In 1980 Paul MacCready's experimental solar-powered airplane, the *Gossamer Penguin* **(B)**, flew a few miles over a dry lake bed. It had a seventy-one-foot wingspan and weighed a mere sixty-eight pounds—it weighed less than its pilot! Every inch of its stripped-down form was determined by its functional requirements. It is interesting to note that the *Penguin's* subsequent iteration, the *Solar Challenger*, integrated the solar panels into the wings, improving its aerodynamics, enabling it to fly across the English Channel.

From the complexities of solar-powered flight to the simplicity of domestic products, functionality determines form. The humble paper clip **(C)** performs its simple task with elegant efficiency. It is even a design icon—an 1899 GEM paperclip has been included in the Museum of Modern Art design collection.

Form and Function in Nature

Evidence of the close relationship of form to function is seen everywhere in nature. Uniquely specialized insects and animals evolve in order to take advantage of specific opportunities in the ecosystem.

 **C**

Paper clip.

While feeding on the nectar of orchids, moths simultaneously pollinate those orchids. Pollen sticks to the bodies of the moths, and when they proceed to other orchids, they unwittingly disseminate pollen. Some orchids have developed longer nectar spurs to guarantee pollination through body contact. The moths in turn must develop longer tongues to reach the nectar. This is an example of the biological concept of **coevolution**, and it illustrates the interaction between function and the development of form in nature.

The Madagascar Star Orchid **(D)** evolved a slim, exceptionally long eleven-inch throat with nectar at the bottom. When Charles Darwin first saw it, he predicted that there must be a pollinating moth that evolved an equally long tongue, though no such moth was known at that time—fellow scientists were extremely skeptical. In 1903, forty years after Darwin's prediction, a hawk moth with a ten-inch tongue was discovered in Madagascar!

 **D**

Madagascar Star Orchid (also known as Comet Orchid). Photo by Pete Oxford.

SIGNATURE AND TYPOLOGY

Style is a simple way of saying complicated things.

—Jean Cocteau

Style, neurologically, is the deepest part of one's being.

—Dr. Oliver Sacks

God is really only another artist. He invented the giraffe, the elephant and the cat. He has no real style, he just goes on trying other things.

—Pablo Picasso

Style as Signature

In art and design, style is usually considered to be a particular manner or technique evident in the work. If you are looking at a work for the first time and its creator is not identified, you will know who made the work if you are aware of the style of the artist or designer. Style can be that unique, like a fingerprint. If you have seen a few Giacometti sculpture's, such as *Man Walking* **(A)**, based on your observation of the artist's signature elongation of the figure and forms built by hesitant accumulation, you will always be able to spot a Giacometti.

Style as Typology

Style is also a type of artwork, object, or architecture with distinguishing characteristics that may be associated with a general concept or historical period. Such classifications are known as **typologies**. The styles of gothic and modernist architecture, for example, are easy to discern. The **streamline style** of the 1930s was based on useful aerodynamic ideas, but eventually this style became a visual *look*, separated from its initial function. Streamlined airplanes and trains make sense, but when toasters are streamlined, you know things have taken a strange turn. The 1935 concept motorcycle in **B** is clearly an example of streamlining. It is, however, a more decorative example of this style, not unlike the toaster; this tendency is often referred to disparagingly as **stylized**. Sacrificing functional design elements (the BMW R7 in **B** is excessively heavy and has purely decorative accessories), the designers of the R7 created a vehicle with high-spirited style, but only the *illusion* of speed.

The young woman in **C** might be included in a typology of style—contemporary Japanese youth street fashion. But she also reminds us of the other uses of the word style—a manner of conducting oneself; popular artifacts *of the moment* (things that are in style); or fashionable elegance. These notions tend to be fleeting, like fads. Does that make them less important?

Dick Hebdige, in a fascinating little book, *Subculture: The Meaning of Style*, explains how style is more than frivolity—subcultures recontextualize commodities "subverting their conventional uses and inventing new ones." The style of the young woman in **C** (like all styles, whether preppy or hip-hop) declares her allegiance to a certain group and her separation from others, at the same time celebrating exuberant color and presenting a dizzying array of pop culture **signs**.

Style usually comes to the emerging artist or designer naturally, as a by-product of a sensibility; simply mimicking a style is not a replacement for genuine discovery. General wisdom suggests: style is not something to be forced.

A

Alberto Giacometti. ***Man Walking (Version I).*** **1960. Bronze, overall (with base), 5' 11¾" × 10½" × 3' 2". © 2011 Succession Giacometti/Artists Rights Society (ARS), New York/ADAGP, Paris.**

B

BMW R7 Motorcycle. 1935.

→ C

Young woman. Tokyo, Japan

Plastic snowman on suburban lawn.

CHAPTER 8

FIGURATION

REPRESENTATION

Representation and Abstraction

To shape material into a form resembling a preexisting thing (object or figure) is to represent it—to make a representation (**representational** art is also commonly referred to as **realism** or figuration). Representational sculpture dates back to prehistory and is one of the principal modes of three-dimensional expression. **Abstraction** (nonrepresentational art) is another major approach to 3D expression. Perhaps all art can be divided into these two fundamental categories: the representational and the abstract.

Abstraction

The abstract realm exists in tandem with the representational, and of course there are countless overlaps, hybrids, and interactions. Like representation, abstraction is a vast category with a wide range of expressions, from preexisting forms that have been altered, simplified, or exaggerated by their creators (an apple presented as a red sphere, or more profoundly Brancusi's *Bird in Space*—see page 8) to the manipulation of pure form for its own sake, also referred to as **nonobjective** or **concrete** art (Anthony Caro sculpture is an example; see page 176). In many ways this book is about abstraction, abstraction as the language of form, and abstraction as the structural basis for representational art as well.

↑ A

Gianlorenzo Bernini. *David.* 1623. Marble, approx. 5' 7" high. Galleria Borghese, Rome, Italy.

Verisimilitude

The representational artist attempts to reproduce or express, feature by feature, the essential aspects of the form of the observed subject—often attempting not only to represent the subject in general but to capture its unique and specific features. The more sensitive and skillful the observer, the more convincing the representation.

There are many kinds and degrees of realism. Bernini's *David* **(A)**, for example, represents a high point of verisimilitude. Not only is this sculpture extremely accurate in its depiction of the figure, but the position of the body and the gesture perfectly express that poised moment between winding up and throwing. The facial expression accurately portrays that of a man concentrating intensely.

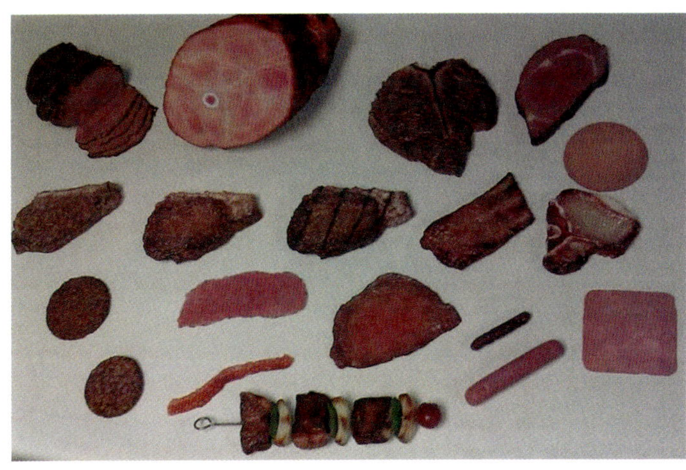

Faux food. Iwasaki Images of America.

Ubiquitous Realism

Realism, of course, exists across the cultural spectrum, from the classical artworks of antiquity to present-day **kitsch** artifacts. The plastic **faux** food items in **B** have a high degree of verisimilitude in spite of their simple task of displaying food available in restaurants and stores. These faux meats occupy a very specific niche in the realism universe—they are all life-size, full-color, three-dimensional replicas. It is quite uplifting to see such a high degree of care expressed in the fabrication of such lowly items as individual slices of ham or bologna, for example.

Experiential Realism

A child in central Africa created the wire car in **C**. Not only is it an excellent linear representation of a car (a kind of drawing in space) but it is a representation that *functions* as a car. It is a good example of the category of objects that attempts to represent objects experientially as well as visually. This homemade toy was driven around the streets of Malawi by its maker—its full-size, operational steering wheel allowing the user to push the little car and steer it nimbly. The wire car also reminds us of the expansive range of realistic objects, from high verisimilitude, to those that are abstractions of reality. This car is both a representation and an abstraction.

Wire car. Created by a child in Malawi. Copper wire, bamboo, tin can lids. c. 1967. Photograph: Travis Fullerton, 2010.

CAMOUFLAGE

Illusion may be less prevalent in the three-dimensional realm than on the two-dimensional plane, where it is a seminal issue, but there are, surprisingly, many manifestations of illusion involving 3D form and space.

Camouflage in Nature

Nature is the ultimate master of illusion. Many creatures must hide their form, their dimensionality, in order to be rendered invisible to predators. There are countless examples of camouflage in nature, in which insects and animals assume the color and patterns of their surroundings in order to disappear into the specific environment they inhabit. We are most familiar with this form of camouflage, but there are other kinds such as countershading. Deer, for example, have white bellies and dark backs. This serves to counteract and neutralize the inevitable shadow underneath. Shadows reveal form—obliterate shadow and so will form be obliterated.

Similarly, birds and fish tend to have lighter undersides and darker tops in order to be less visible from below (looking up at them against the light) as well as from above (viewed against the darker ground). In **A**, Atlantic spotted dolphins blend in against the lighted ocean surface. The military often adopts this kind of coloration for airplanes for the same reason nature does—protective coloration offers survival advantages.

Camouflage in the Built World

Camouflage is also used in the built world. Hunters and soldiers do exactly what nature does in order to visually blend into an environment. In some communities, electrical utility boxes are considered unsightly. Well, why not camouflage them? Using digital prints of the surrounding site and adhesive vinyl, this is exactly what an artist did to many utility boxes in California **(B)**.

Yet another category of camouflage, and one also first used by nature, is a kind of hiding in plain sight. The butterfly that mimics a dead leaf remains visible on the plant where it rests, but simply looks like something other than a meal for a bird, and thus it is protected. Similarly, the cell phone towers in **C** and **D** are completely visible, but they no longer look like cell phone towers; they look like pine and palm trees, however out of scale they may be. Still there, still huge objects, but now they are objects that don't offend. Camouflaging utility boxes and cell towers may be a surreal, cosmetic solution to the unwanted elements in our environment; nevertheless, it employs basic forms of illusion.

 **A**

Atlantic spotted dolphins.

B

Joshua Callaghan. Camouflaged utility box.

C

Artificial pine tree concealing cellular telephone tower.

D

Cell phone tower disguised as palm tree.

ART AND ARCHITECTURE

Impossible Objects

Robert Lazzarini's *Payphone* **(A)** is a compound distortion of an ordinary, life-size pay phone. After the original object was digitally scanned and electronically distorted, 3D models were generated, and the final piece was fabricated with the very same materials used in the original pay phone. The resulting illusion is similar to **anamorphic** projection in which an image is coherent only when viewed from a single, fixed point; from other viewpoints it appears strangely stretched or radically distorted. The end result of Lazzarini's sleight of hand is a paradoxical object that situates the viewer in an impossible place. There is no vantage point from which the viewer of *Payphone* can account for the visual information received; the result: an image that hovers disconcertingly. Like all illusions, *Payphone* is as much about human perception as it is about the image observed.

Reflected Distortion

Looking at *Cloud Gate* **(B)** for a second time in this book—this time a view from below, looking up at its underbelly—we are lost in a maze of reflected distortions, and these distortions are in motion, coinciding with the movement of people below. This disorienting apparition stands in stark contrast to the distant view of *Cloud Gate*: a minimal form with reflected blue sky and clouds.

Defying Gravity

One element in the spectacular and theatrical fountain **(C)** by Isamu Noguchi appears to be a cube propelled skyward by its trail of water, miraculously levitating above the surface of the pool. In reality, pipes support the cube and supply the water cascading downward, hiding the trick. The other cube disperses water from above, becoming as ethereal as a floating chunk of fog.

Representing the Unrepresentable

The Klein bottle is not really a bottle; it is a mathematical concept that cannot exist in real 3D space. As a one-sided construct requiring a fourth dimension, it can only exist theoretically. Nonetheless, mathematicians have created fascinating representations to approximate this theoretical object **(D)**.

↑ **A**

Robert Lazzarini. *Payphone* and two viewers. **2002. 9' × 7' × 4' 8".**

B

Anish Kapoor. *Cloud Gate,* detail. 2004. 33' × 42' × 66'. Millennium Park, Chicago.

C

Isamu Noguchi. *Nine Floating Fountains,* detail. World Expo 70. Osaka, Japan. © 2011 The Isamu Noguchi Foundation and Garden Museum, New York/Artists Rights Society (ARS), New York.

D

Klein bottles made by Alan Bennett. 1995.

Construction worker releasing concrete from a hopper.

CHAPTER **9**

FORMING AND FABRICATION

MAKING

The hand is the window on to the mind.

—Immanuel Kant

From the Stone Age to the present day, the history of objects and structures coincides with the history of making. Today there are numerous fabrication methodologies available, and new processes are continually being invented and utilized. The forming process is important for many reasons. Two especially significant aspects of making involve (1) process (the process of making determines form) and (2) thinking (the making process is a form of thought).

Process Determines Form

The objects you might make while manipulating clay with your hands will always be different than those made by manipulating sheets of steel and welding them together. The making process you use will determine, a priori, a great deal about the resulting object.

Making Is Thinking

One of the most important aspects of making is the fact that it promotes thought; in fact, many today believe that making *is* a kind of thought. The process of manipulating material generates ideas and presents new visual and tactile information for the maker to react to. In addition, the particular process used determines the nature of the ideas generated. To develop ideas, don't just think—do! Start drawing, glue two pieces of wood together, or boot up your computer!

This chapter will examine the principal types of making—additive, subtractive, constructive, **bricolage**, hybrid approaches, industrial methods, computer aided design, replication technologies, and new approaches to replication. Keep in mind, however, that these ways of making seldom stand alone; they are mostly used in combination. Additive clay sculpture (adding clay to clay to make a form) is also used together with subtraction. You add a piece of clay and then you pull or carve off a chunk, and then perhaps you add again. Additionally, you can simply squeeze the humble lump of clay into a desired shape—clay is plastic and malleable.

One contemporary sculptor who raises making and handcraft to a place of extreme thoughtfulness and sensitivity is Martin Puryear. His work **(A)** utilizes a variety of hand fabrication processes. In the sculpture visible on the far right in **A** he employs the very basic materials of tar on wire mesh to create a simple form that is rich with associations from both nature and traditional utilitarian craft. This sculpture uses a process of piecing wire mesh on a wood form—it is made as honestly and directly as a well-built cabin or a birch bark canoe. Puryear has said, "At a certain point, I just put the building and the art impulse together. I decided that building was a legitimate way to make sculpture."

Martin Puryear. Installation view of exhibition, "Martin Puryear" 2007. The Museum of Modern Art, New York.

ADDITIVE

Perhaps the most fundamental fabrication process is additive, and clay the oldest and most basic material used to make objects additively. Take a lump of clay and add other small pieces of clay to it, bit by bit, until it takes the desired form—a face, a sphere, or an invented form, for example. You can do the same with wax and plaster of paris.

Welding also suggests the additive. One piece of steel gets added to another and is welded in place, then another, and so on. The process ends when the sculpture—or bridge perhaps—is complete. Brazing, soldering, riveting, and gluing also involve additive processes.

In a film on Henry Moore, the distinguished British sculptor himself, amazingly, gives a very basic but informative demonstration on working with plaster of paris. He is clearly very excited about the versatility of plaster as a medium. He demonstrates how to mix plaster and how to build a form by adding wet plaster to an existing dry plaster, preliminary form, and he continues to trowel on plaster to develop his maquette. Moore then shows how to remove material by rasping and sanding, then adds more plaster, then rasps—continually adding and subtracting until the piece arrives at a satisfactory conclusion.

Alberto Giacometti similarly used the additive process to make *Dog* **(A)**. The sculptor attached small bits of clay to a wire armature to form a representation of the body of a dog. This simple process of **accretion** successfully expresses a very particular dog, following a scent with an ungainly lope, the clay a perfect vehicle for representing the droopy posture. The final work is a bronze cast of the clay original.

In architecture and engineering, the additive process is fundamental. Imagine the construction of a brick building—thousands and thousands of small additions, like the cumulative strokes of an impressionist painting, build the structure. The bridge under construction in **B** was built symmetrically from opposite sides of a river. Concrete was poured into forms that were extended incrementally until the two concrete arches met high over the Colorado River. As the concrete dried and cured, the forms were removed, and ultimately suspension cables and the stable structure of the arch stood to support the weight of the bridge and its traffic.

 **A**

Alberto Giacometti. *Dog.* c. 1951. Bronze (cast 1957). © 2011 Succession Giacometti/Artists Rights Society (ARS), New York/ADAGP, Paris.

Colorado River Bridge under construction (Hoover Dam in background).
2009. Design: HDR Engineering, T.Y. Lin International, Jacobs Engineering.

SUBTRACTIVE

The subtractive process allows us to make things not by adding or attaching, but, counterintuitively, by removing material! A dug-out canoe is made by the simple act of hollowing a log. Carving is the most common subtractive fabrication process, but it is not the only one.

To create a figure in stone, stone carvers chip from the block all the stone that is not the figure, leaving behind only the material that resembles the figure they wish to make. Michelangelo imagined the figure within the block and believed his task was simply to release it. Michelangelo's *Unfinished Captive* **(A)** from his series of unfinished slaves is a good example of making by subtraction because he left remnants of the marble block intact, clearly illustrating the relationship of the stone block and the carving process to the "imprisoned" figure.

Similarly Giuseppe Penone carves **(B)** to expose the core of the younger tree contained in the heart of the wood **(C)**. He has said, "My artwork shows, with the language of sculpture, the essence of matter and tries to reveal with the work, the hidden life within."

The installation/**intervention** *Conical Intersect* **(D)**, in which artist Gordon Matta-Clark cut a series of circles out of the shell of an abandoned Paris house, is a subtractive process that doesn't involve traditional carving. Matta-Clark made *Conical Intersect* with industrial saws, creating a kind of poetic, partial demolition that produced startling vistas by literally punching holes in the domestic domain.

In **E** Tom Friedman attacked an ordinary school chair with an electric drill, subtracting so much material that the chair can barely stand. It has been dematerialized to the brink of collapse. Subtraction here equates with loss—this is a chair becoming a poignant memory.

Michelangelo. *Unfinished Captive.* **1527–1528. Marble, 8' 7½" h. Accademia, Florence, Italy.**

Giuseppe Penone at work on an Atlas cedar weighing 5 tons.

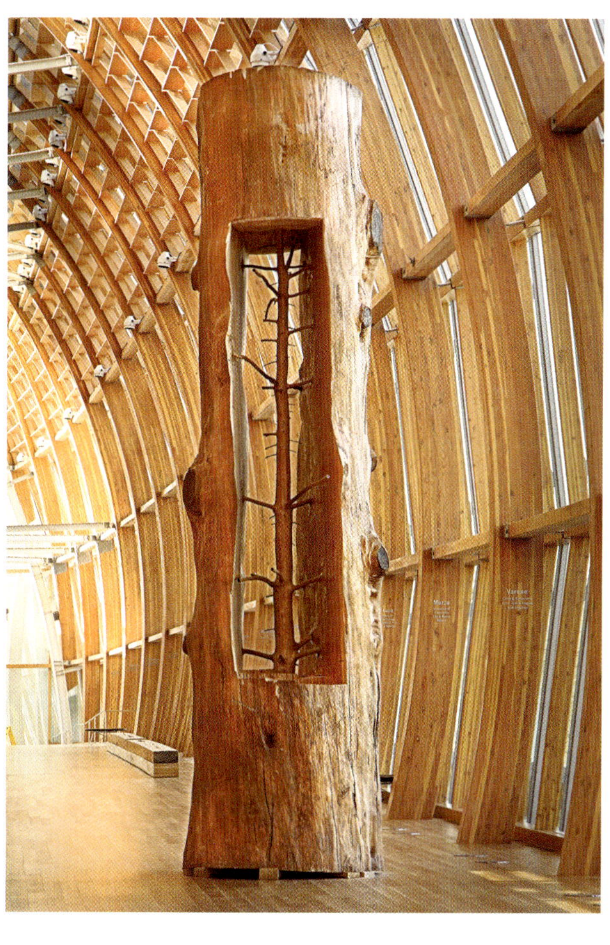

Giuseppe Penone. *Cedro di Versailles* (Versailles Cedar). 2000–2003. 20' 8" × 5' 3". Art Gallery of Ontario. Toronto, Ontario, Canada.

Tom Friedman. *Untitled.* 1999/2002. Wooden school chair, 2' 11" × 1' 4½" × 2' ½". Courtesy Mary Boone Gallery.

↑ D

Gordon Matta-Clark. Documentation of *Conical Intersect* in Paris, four detail views. 1975. Paris courtesy of David Zwirner, New York, and the Estate of Gordon Matta-Clark/© 2011 Estate of Gordon Matta-Clark/Artists Rights Society (ARS), New York.

CONSTRUCTIVE

Other then shaping malleable materials, making can generally be explained by the two fabrication processes discussed in the preceding sections—additive and subtractive. The **constructive** process involves addition and subtraction, but it does not involve the traditional methods of modeling and carving. Constructive making involves joinery—it is a process of adding and adjusting elements that are ultimately fixed in place to form a structure. These elements are usually welded, fastened mechanically, or glued together to form a sculpture, product, or building.

The constructive method might best be understood in relationship to its two-dimensional counterpart—collage. The constructive approach was revitalized by modernism, the availability of prefabricated materials, and new methods for joining materials. Constructive method is a combinative idea.

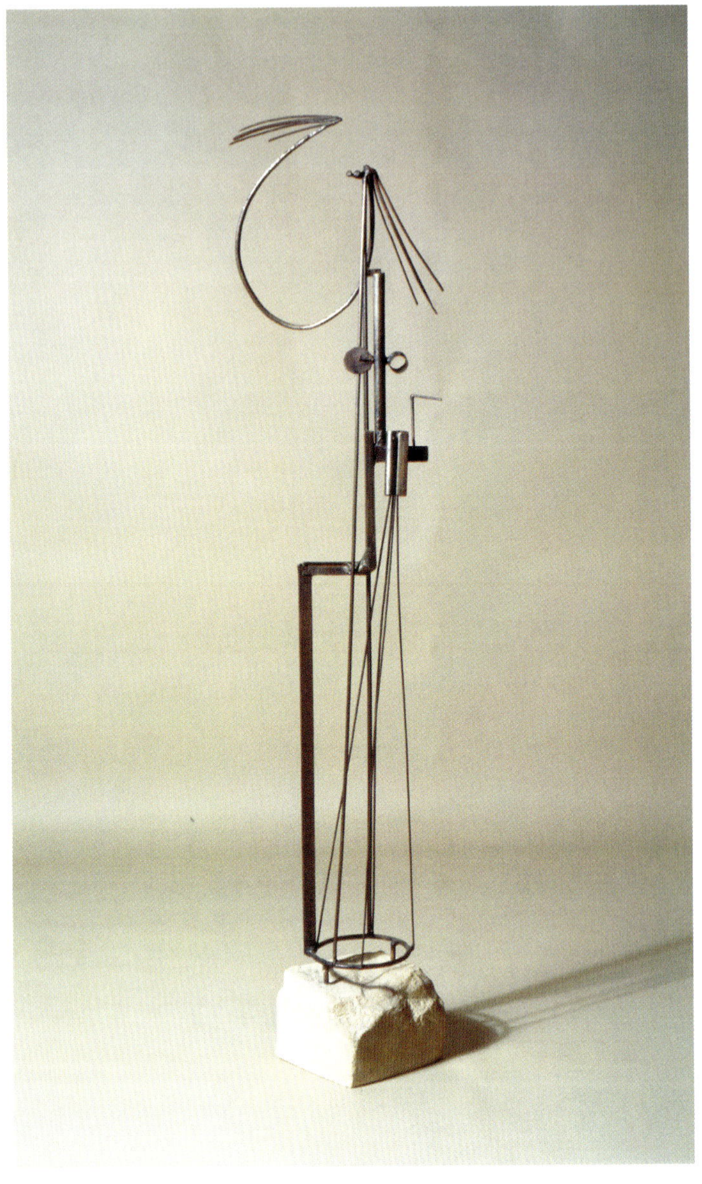

Julio Gonzalez. *Maternity.* 1934. Steel. 4' 3⅓" × 1' 4" × 9¼". © 2011 Artists Rights Society (ARS), New York/ADAGP, Paris.

Anthony Caro. *Early One Morning.* 1962. Painted steel and aluminum, 9' 6" × 20' 4" × 11'.

The industrial process of welding was quickly adopted by artists. Welding radically altered ideas of what a sculpture can be. Julio Gonzalez **(A)** and Anthony Caro **(B)** used welding to create sculpture that took full advantage of the basic materials of metal rods, beams, and planes, and the newfound freedom of welded joinery. Welding and oxy-fuel metal cutting were perfectly suited to the constructive process and contributed to the growing excitement about abstraction.

Chairs may be carved from wood, heavily upholstered, or cast in plastic. The classic modernist chair in **C**, however, is the product of a constructive approach—wood planes and linear elements mechanically joined.

Most buildings and products are made constructively—consider the suburban house with its wood frame, aluminum siding, sheetrock, and plumbing. The Eiffel Tower is a good example of early constructive fabrication—its iron lattice is held together by approximately 2.5 million rivets. **D** shows the tower under construction.

C

Gerrit Rietveld. ***Armchair Red and Blue.*** **1918. Wood, paint.**

D

Drawing by unknown artist. Eiffel Tower during construction. Designed by Gustave Eiffel. 1889. Paris, France.

THE READYMADE

Dada and Duchamp

In the early 1900s Marcel Duchamp claimed various objects to be works of art. This simple act has dramatically impacted the art world for a century. The Duchamp work in **A** involves the appropriation of an ordinary coat rack. While no physical alterations have been made, a significant change was made to its context. It was removed from its natural place on the wall and placed in a gallery (a site that is accompanied by very specific, viewer expectations) and presented on the floor, robbed of its utility and introduced as a sculptural object. Duchamp and the found objects he referred to as Readymades created fascinating philosophical conundrums; they are puzzles that challenge viewers instead of reinforcing preconceptions. Surrealist painter Rene Magritte would describe this experience as a "crisis of the object." Magritte said an artist could transform the common object and evoke this experience through "isolation, modification, hybridization, scale change, accidental encounters, double image puns, paradox, double viewpoints in one."

Context and the Found Object

One of the most recent and audacious manifestations of the found object is Damien Hirst's thirteen-foot tiger shark in a tank containing 4,360 gallons of formaldehyde, here installed at the Metropolitan Museum of Art **(B)**. Concerning context and the found object, Roberta Smith wrote in the *New York Times*, "On its own the shark looks a bit tamer than usual, though at the Met, of course, it still shocks. If you passed it at the American Museum of Natural History across Central Park, you might not look twice."

 **A**

Marcel Duchamp. ***Trap.*** **1917/1964. © 2011 Artists Rights Society (ARS), New York/ADAGP, Paris/Succession Marcel Duchamp.**

Precursors

Duchamp and other **Dadaists,** however, did not invent the found object; they just made it central to their art practice. In some sense, most artists have always had an interest in the found object—subject matter and source material, such as objects for still life, are essential to the art-making process. Consider Vincent Van Gogh's view on this subject in a letter to a friend:

> *This morning I visited the place where the street cleaners dump the rubbish. My God, it was beautiful! Tomorrow they are bringing a couple of interesting pieces from the garbage pile, including some broken street lamps, for me to admire or, if you wish, to use as models. . . . It would make a fine subject for a fairy tale by Andersen, that mass of garbage cans, baskets, pots, serving bowls, metal pitchers, wires, lanterns, pipes and flues that people have thrown away. I really believe I shall dream about it tonight, and in winter I shall have much to do with it in my work. . . . it would be a real pleasure to take you there, and to a few other places that are a real paradise for the artist, however unsightly they may be.*

In his book *The Unknown Craftsman: A Japanese Insight into Beauty*, Sōetsu Yanagi discusses the the Kizaemon Ido tea-bowl, a bowl made in Korea in the sixteenth century and selected by Japanese tea masters in the early seventeenth century to be used as an artifact in the tea ceremony. In Japan today the Kizaemon bowl (a found object) is a national treasure.

> *This single Tea-bowl is considered to be the finest in the world. . . . to contain the essence of Tea. . . .*
>
> *In 1931 I was shown this bowl in company with my friend, the potter Kanjirō Kawai. For a long time I had wished to see this Kizaemon bowl. I had expected to see that "essence of Tea," the seeing eye of Tea masters, and to test my own perception; for it is the embodiment in miniature of beauty, of the love of beauty, of the philosophy of beauty, and of the relationship of beauty and life. It was within box after box, five deep, buried in wool and wrapped in purple silk.*
>
> *When I saw it, my heart fell. A good Tea-bowl, yes, but how ordinary! So simple, no more ordinary thing could be imagined. There is not a trace of ornament, not a trace of calculation. It is just a Korean food bowl . . . that a poor man would use everyday. . .*

A typical thing for his use; costing next to nothing . . . an article without the flavor of personality; used carelessly by its owner; bought without pride; something anyone could have bought anywhere and everywhere. . . . The kiln was a wretched affair; the firing careless. Sand had stuck to the pot, but nobody minded; no one invested the thing with any dreams. It is enough to make one give up working as a potter. . . .

But that was as it should be. The plain and unagitated, the uncalculated, the harmless, the straightforward, the natural, the innocent, the humble, the modest: where does beauty lie if not in these qualities? The meek, the austere, the unornate—they are the natural characteristics that gain man's affection and respect.

More than anything else, this pot is healthy. Made for a purpose, made to do work. Sold to be used in everyday life. . . . Only a commonplace practicality can guarantee health in something made. . . .

Emerging from a squalid kitchen, the Ido bowl took its seat on the highest throne of beauty. The Koreans laughed. That was to be expected, but both laughter and praise are right, for had they not laughed they would not have been the people who could have made such bowls . . . The Koreans made rice bowls; the Japanese masters made them into Tea-bowls. . . .

—*Excerpts from* The Unknown Craftsman *by Sōetsu Yanagi*

Damien Hirst. ***The Physical Impossibility of Death in the Mind of Someone Living.*** **Installed at the Metropolitan Museum of Art, New York. 1991.**

THE ALTERED READYMADE AND BRICOLAGE

The Altered Readymade

The combination of two or more found objects is often referred to as an altered or assisted Readymade (a term coined by Marcel Duchamp). Earlier in this book we looked at Picasso's *Bull's Head* **(A)**, an assemblage constructed of a bicycle seat and handlebars, in the context of play; here we reconsider it as an example of an altered Readymade (though it preceded such work by Duchamp). In **A** two found, functional components of a bicycle were brought together to form a completely realistic figurative sculpture, a bull's head. What is responsible for a work such as this? It is neither skill nor hard work. It is an intellect that makes creative connections, discovering new meaning in that which has been discarded and overlooked. A later version of *Bull's Head* was cast in bronze from the original objects, complicating its status as found object and connecting it to the tradition of figurative sculpture that is cast from life.

Bricolage

A bricoleur is someone who tinkers or putters about. Bricolage is generally used to describe a constructed object that is made with only materials at hand, regardless of their origin or purpose. The bricoleur is clever, proficient at combining preexisting things in new ways. Makers of Readymades and assisted Readymades are bricoleurs, as are many contemporary artists and designers today (bricolage suits the postmodern temperament).

Collecting

Artists who exhibit collections and who practice art as if they were curators are also bricoleurs. To make art from available material suggests that artist-bricoleurs must harvest material to fuel their combinatorial inventions. Joseph Cornell, famous for glass-fronted boxes containing arrangements of ephemera from art history and popular culture **(B)**, maintained extensive collections of found objects in his Utopia Parkway apartment **(C)**.

 A

Pablo Picasso. *Bull's Head.* Assemblage, bicycle seat and handlebars. 1' 1½" × 1' × 7½". © 2011 Estate of Pablo Picasso/Artists Rights Society (ARS), New York.

 B

Joseph Cornell. *Medici Slot Machine.* 1942. Mixed media construction, 1' 3½" × 1' × 4⅜". Edward Owen/Art Resource, NY © The Joseph and Robert Cornell Memorial Foundation/Licensed by VAGA, New York, NY.

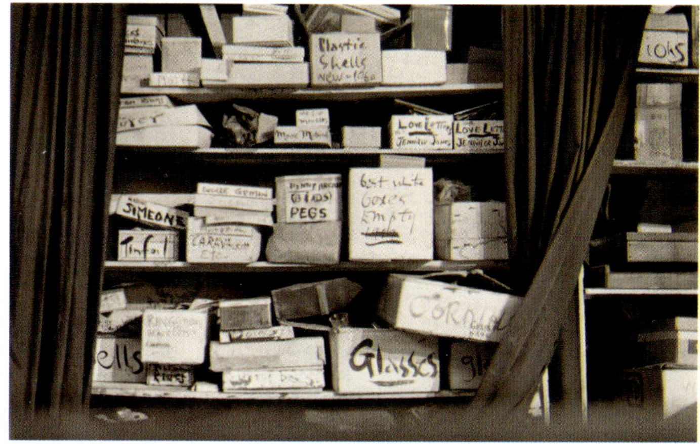

Joseph Cornell's studio. Utopia Parkway, Queens, New York.

The sculptor Sarah Sze, a classic bricoleur, creates sprawling installations of found objects **(D)** utilizing material from a vast array of sources. Tree limbs, cardboard gift boxes, electric lamps, water bottles, plastic tubs, and fire extinguishers are just a few of the items used to build her structures, precariously held together with not much more than hardware store clamps. At first glance, the piece in **D** appears to consist of constellations of color/form that utilize the principle of unity and variety as they activate space; upon closer inspection we are delighted to see the quite ordinary materials that have been summoned to perform these formal acrobatics.

Sarah Sze. *Tilting Planet,* detail. 2008. Mixed media. Dimensions variable.

Found Objects and Reuse

Contemporary designers are also interested in found objects. The base of the lamp in **E** consists of skewered figurines and ornamental boxes, a vacuum cleaner part, and a faux pear. While found objects in design today are often used humorously, the interest in ordinary and discarded objects is growing, primarily because of the idea of reuse, an aspect of green design. Many designers and D.I.Y. practitioners are repurposing existing objects and utilizing found and discarded materials instead of using new resources.

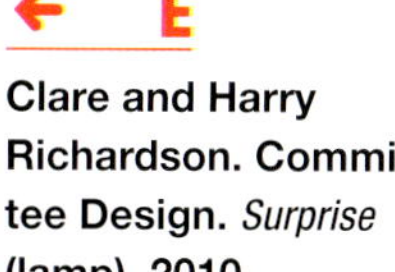

Clare and Harry Richardson. Committee Design. *Surprise* (lamp). 2010.

ART AND EVERYDAY EXPERIENCE

> *I am for an art that is political-erotical-mystical, that does something other than sit on its ass in a museum. . . .*
>
> *I am for an art that embroils itself with the everyday crap & still comes out on top. . . .*
>
> *I am for an art that takes its form from the lines of life itself, that twists and extends and accumulates and spits and drips, and is heavy and coarse and blunt and sweet and stupid as life itself. . . .*
>
> —*Claes Oldenburg*

Design and architecture are inherently more actively involved with everyday life than art. We drive cars, live in houses and apartments, and use countless products and appliances daily (and often quite intimately). Art nonetheless has its own passionate and complex relationship with life.

Life as Model

Artists have long desired to create lifelike experience to rival nature. The painter Albert Pinkham Ryder expressed his frustration with painting:

> *When I grew weary with the futile struggle to imitate the canvases of the past, I went out into the fields, determined to serve nature as faithfully as I had served art. In my desire to be accurate I became lost in a maze of detail. Try as I would, my colors were not those of nature. My leaves were infinitely below the standard of a leaf, my finest strokes were coarse and crude.*

Edgar Degas challenged the conventions of traditional figure sculpture by dressing his bronze figure **(A)** in an actual cloth bodice, tutu, and satin hair ribbon. Reality meets the virtual, provoking a complex dialogue. Boundary-blurring is part of the fun of those hybrid works that aim to bridge art and life; it increases the demands on viewers who must decide how to approach a work intellectually.

Happenings and Social Events

Allan Kaprow created **Happenings** in the 1970s, performance-like activities in which the artist gave his full attention to ordinary, ephemeral life experiences, attempting to raise them to a plateau of intensified awareness. According to Kaprow, "nonart is more art than Art art." With a similar mind-set, Tom Marioni created a work titled *The Act of Drinking Beer with Friends is the Highest Form of Art*, and that is exactly what this work consisted of—a social gathering involving the artist, friends, and beer.

A

Edgar Degas. *The Little Fourteen Year Old Dancer.* **Bronze (cast 1932), cloth dress and ribbon. Representing Marie van Goethem. 3' ½" × 1' 2" × 9½".**

 **B**

Michael Mercil. *The Virtual Pasture.* 2008–2011. The Wexner Center for the Arts, The Ohio State University, Columbus, Ohio. Photograph by Rachel Heberling.

Art in the Flow of Life

The Virtual Pasture **(B)** was an artwork installed at the Wexner Center for the Arts on the campus of The Ohio State University. It involved a flock of sheep that visited the campus intermittently as well as virtually, through a live video feed. Less than a hundred years ago cows, sheep, and horses were part of daily life; today they are invisible. The introduction of sheep to a university campus is more than surreal juxtaposition; it is a proposal for a balanced life. Additionally, *The Virtual Pasture* enabled its creator, Michael Mercil, to integrate his life, his job (university professor), and his art.

Artist David Hammons offered snowballs for sale in Cooper Square, New York City **(C)**. To viewers he was just another street vendor; he was not in a gallery that would declare "this is an artwork." This real-life performance was both confrontational and extremely poetic. Titled *Bliz-aard Ball Sale*, Hammons's anti-commodity commodities were presented to everyday New Yorkers . . . in winter. Devoid of institutional structure, labels, and protocol, the artist thrust himself into the unpredictable flow of daily life, challenging his viewers to accept the responsibility for determining meaning. They had no choice but to engage with the work as active participants in its very realization. Today, work like *Bliz-aard Ball Sale* is increasingly being labeled *relational*. In **relational aesthetics** the artist is viewed as a catalyst of social experiences.

 **C**

David Hammons (left) performing *Bliz-aard Ball Sale.* 1983. Cooper Square, New York. Photograph by Dawoud Bey.

BLURRING BOUNDARIES

Many contemporary artists, designers, and architects utilize hybrid form. They feel free to use various styles and media within a single work, and they don't worry if the work is called sculpture, painting, or design—in fact, they often combine or hybridize disciplines. It's not that working within disciplinary boundaries is no longer useful; it's just that it is no longer obligatory.

Ann Hamilton's *mattering* **(A)** might be seen as installation, sculpture, or performance—it uses aspects of all these disciplines—or perhaps it is simply a new form, an enveloping environment that is sprawling and complex. A massive sheet of red-orange silk undulates like ocean waves, peacocks strut freely about, and a solo performer sits atop a pole winding typewriter ribbon around his hand, periodically letting the knot of ribbon drop to the floor. This piece exists in time, appropriates living animals, utilizes a performer, includes recorded sound, and has a powerful formal and chromatic presence—all driven by an otherworldly, dreamlike structure.

The work in **B** is a kind of mammoth musical organ constructed of plastic tubes and huge bladders attached to horns, each playing a different octave. Long scrolls of dots and dashes are interpreted by the organ/artwork to play non-repeating variations of old tunes. It is at once a sculpture, musical instrument, installation, and sound experience.

A very different kind of hybrid object exists in the realm of contemporary electronic products—it involves combining functions that previously existed as separate products. This hybrid

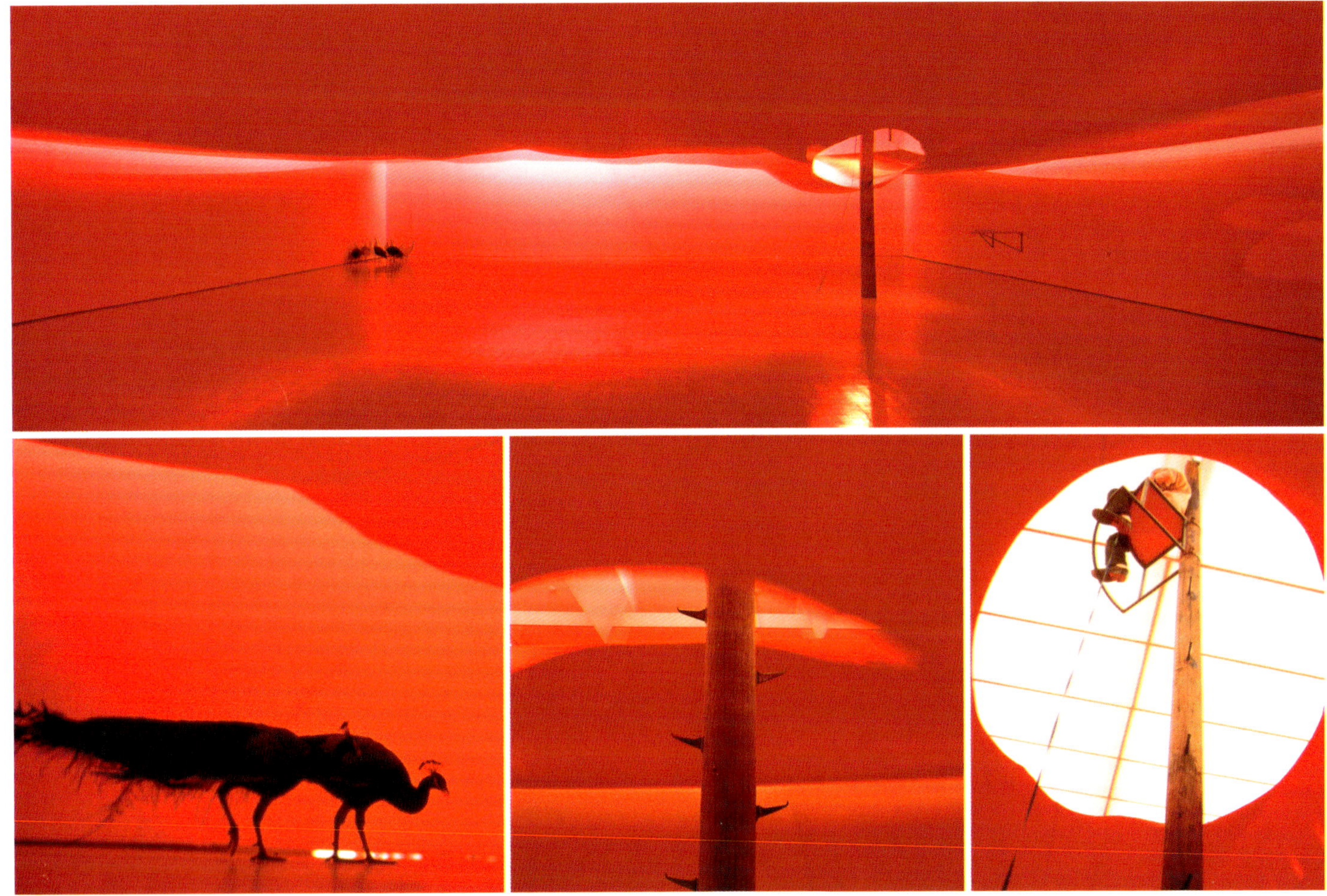

A

Ann Hamilton. *mattering* (four views). Multimedia installation, 16' × 105' × 58'. 1997. Musee d'Art Contemporain de Lyon, France.

tendency in electronic product design is referred to as convergence. Consider the Apple iPhone **(C)**. It is first of all a mobile telephone but also a computer with e-mail and World Wide Web access. It tacks on numerous additional functions such as GPS, calendar, and calculator; and with its menu of apps it can even serve as a carpenter's level. Many have used its lighted face as an emergency flashlight. Smart phones are the Swiss army knives of the electronic product marketplace.

There are a great many hybrid forms in popular culture as well. Perhaps one of the more interesting and powerful hybrids is Disney World, an amusement park that might easily be considered a work of art, a theatrical production, or in any case, a grand spectacle. Disney World combines installation, live performance, film, sound, animatronic figures, artifacts, and architecture tied together by popular thematic fantasies and completed by interacting viewers.

Hybrid form may become the new norm; in any case, **hybridity** opens doors for artists and designers and expands imaginative possibilities.

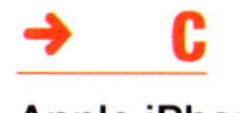
C

Apple iPhone.

B

Tim Hawkinson. *Überorgan*. 2000. Woven polyethylene, nylon net, cardboard tubing, and various mechanical components, size variable. Installation in the entrance of the Getty Center. 2007. Los Angeles, California.

THE MACHINE AESTHETIC

In 1908 the French writer Octave Mirbeau wrote of his admiration for machines:

> *Machines appear to me, more than books, statues, paintings, to be works of the imagination. When I look at, when I hear the life of the admirable organism that is the motor of my automobile, with its steel lungs and heart, its rubber and copper vascular system, its electrical nervous system, don't I have a more moving idea of the imaginative and creative human genius than when I consider the banal, infinitely useless books of M. Paul Bourget, the statues, if one can call them that, of M. Denys Puech, the paintings—a euphemism—of M. Detaille?*

↑ A

Moving assembly line (top) and assembly line outdoor body drop (bottom) at Ford Highland Park plant, Michigan. c. 1914.

Octave Mirbeau's impassioned statement provides a glimpse of the widespread public enthusiasm for the machines and new inventions of the early 1900s. The automobile, the airplane, radio, the electric light bulb, the skyscraper, and motion pictures were all either invented or came into wider use at approximately this time. The architect Corbusier said, "A house is a machine for living," and product design as we know it today developed then and was widely known as industrial design.

Artists too caught the excitement—the machine metaphor was everywhere. Artists and photographers lovingly depicted the new industrial subject matter of factories, skyscrapers, bridges, locomotives, automobiles, and airplanes, and they began to utilize the materials and fabrication processes of industry.

The industrial assembly line **(A)** replaced the individual craftsperson, a maker of unique products. The assembly line utilized machine-made parts assembled by many workers, each playing a small role in the greater process. Efficiency and mass production replaced handcraft and the pride of the individual maker. But machine-made things have their own kind of beauty, and it is a new beauty for our time—the machine aesthetic has many devotees.

The chair in **B** is a clear example of the influence of industrial fabrication and the assembly line process. Like the Model T Ford, this chair consists of discrete parts that have been joined together to form a whole, and each part utilizes the material most suitable to its purpose and fabrication method; each part can be made more efficiently by a unique fabrication technology and by workers who are specialists in welding or wood-bending, for example.

Many artworks today would never have been conceived or made had there been no Industrial Revolution. Industrial mass-produced forms are the source of countless contemporary artworks. The monumental public sculpture *Sea Change* by Mark di Suvero **(C)** not only employs unadorned industrial H-beams and is installed with heavy-construction equipment, but it takes its very identity and its energy from industrial structures such as the San Francisco-Oakland Bay Bridge visible behind it in image **C**.

Jean Prouvé. ***Antony Chair.*** **1950. Enameled steel and molded beech plywood. The Museum of Modern Art, New York.**

Mark di Suvero. ***Sea Change.*** **1995. Steel, 70' h. San Francisco, California.**

THE FUTURE IS HERE

Today computers are handling an ever-increasing number of tasks in a growing number of disciplines. Art, design, and architecture are not exceptions to the trend toward computer dependency.

It is commonly understood that a great deal of architecture today could never have been made in any other time; that is, a time without computers. Frank Gehry's Guggenheim Museum in Bilbao **(A)** is so complex—consisting of numerous curving and interlocking forms—that its design required an expert group of programmers and an advanced computer-aided design system, CATIA (Computer Aided Three-dimensional Interactive Application), which combines CAD with manufacturing and engineering programs. Every curving beam and custom component had to be drawn in the CATIA program, which was required to keep track of every part and all adjacent parts as well as the whole, determine structural requirements, and monitor all components and their dimensions—a truly herculean task.

The computer rendering of *Embryologic House* **(B)** is an example of the forms achievable using CAD. Not only are complex biomorphic forms possible with CAD, but CAD can provide blueprints (fabrication drawings), structural analysis, and cost estimates.

The artist Karin Sander used a different kind of computer input to realize her one-tenth scale 3D representations of specific people **(C1, C2, C3)**. She used a laser scanner to provide relevant data and a rapid prototyper to transfer that data into actual 3D plastic figures. These portraits, made entirely by mechanical means, are like three-dimensional photographs, and like photographs, they provide us with likenesses that were previously obtainable only by means of an observer who engaged in the act of recreating observed form with skilled hands.

↑ **A**

Frank Gehry. Guggenheim Museum. Bilbao, Spain. 1997.

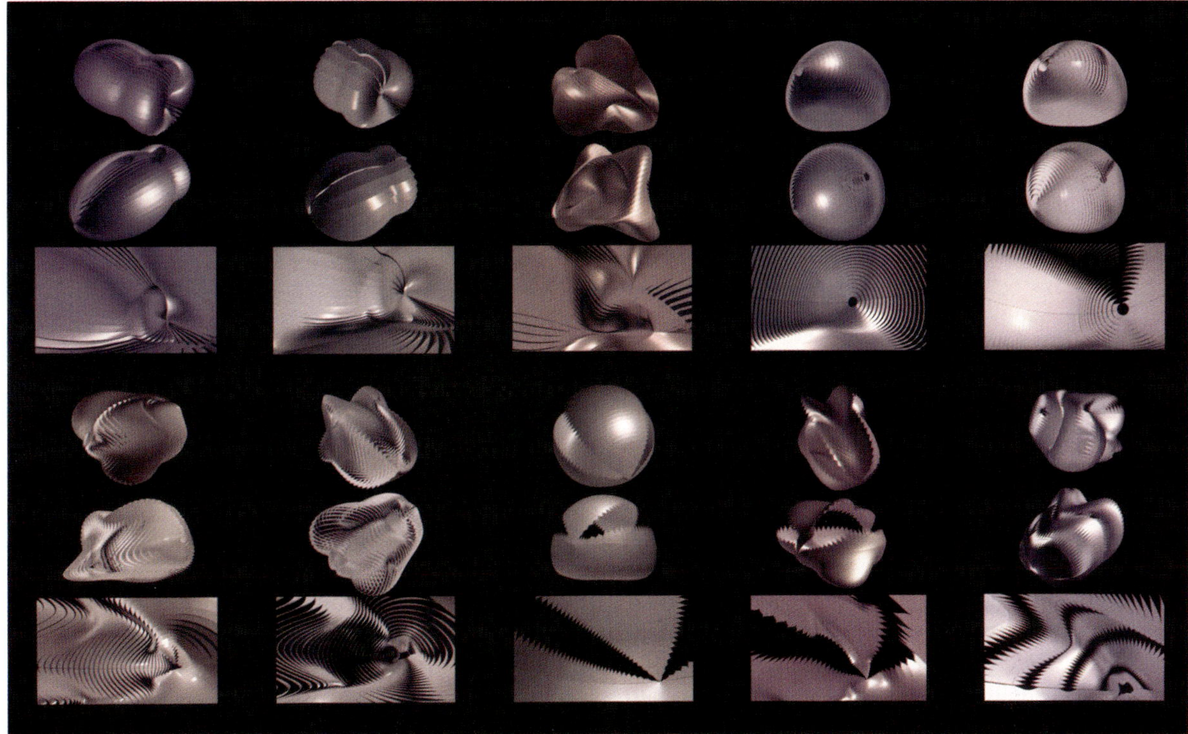

↑ B

Greg Lynn. *Embryologic House* [computer rendering]. 1998. Architectural Drawing, inkjet print.

↑ C1

Karin Sander. *Annemarie Becker* 1:10, 1999. 3D Bodyscan of the living person. FDM (Fused Deposition Modeling), Rapid Prototyping, ABS (Acryl-Butadien-Nityl-Styrol), Airbrush, Scale 1:10, Size ca. 17 cm.

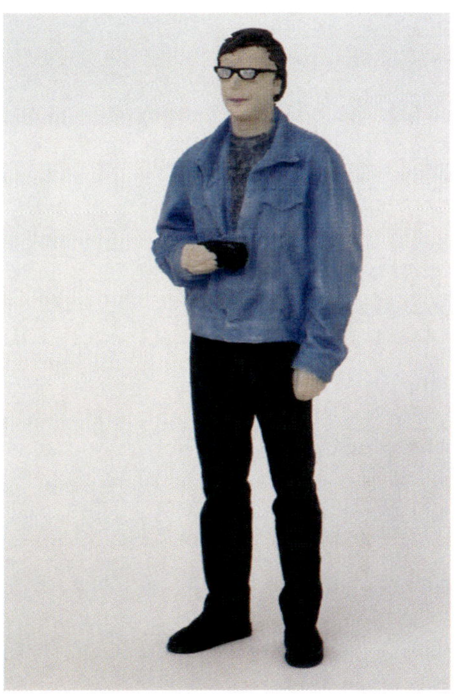

↑ C2

Karin Sander. *Georg Winter* 1:10, 1998. 3D Bodyscan of the living person. FDM (Fused Deposition Modeling), Rapid Prototyping, ABS (Acryl-Butadien-Nityl-Styrol), Airbrush, Scale 1:10, Size ca. 18 cm.

↑ C3

Karin Sander. *Dr. Ulla Klippel* 1:10, 1999. 3D Bodyscan of the living person. FDM (Fused Deposition Modeling), Rapid Prototyping, ABS (Acryl-Butadien-Nityl-Styrol), Airbrush, Scale 1:10, Size ca. 18 cm.

BASIC AND TRADITIONAL

2D Replication

If you wish to repeat an element or replicate an image in the realm of two dimensions, on the most basic level you might use a straightedge as a guide to make straight lines, a compass to create circles, or stencils to form letters. On a more advanced level, you can use one of the various printmaking techniques to replicate images, and today, of course, there are cameras and computers as well.

3D Replication

Similar processes exist in the three-dimensional realm. One fundamental tool that allows us to form identical units is the **jig**. Jigs are simple devices that serve as guides for cutting, drilling, and other forming methods. The device in **A** is a rudimentary jig—by virtue of a stop block (here illustrated in red), it allows the user to cut equal-length boards, endlessly, eliminating the need to measure every length of wood.

Casting and Molds in Sculpture and Product Design

The most common process for recreating three-dimensional form involves **casting** and mold making. We are all familiar with **molds**, from cake and Jell-O molds to sand castle molds **(B)**. Molds are useful in daily life. They are also extremely important in industry **(C)**.

Sculptors and product designers have long depended on the technology of casting and mold making to make more durable versions of vulnerable clay or wax originals, and to create duplicate versions of sculpture and products.

Molds are commonly made of plaster **(D)** from original works created in clay, but many other materials such as latex and silicone rubber are also used to make molds. To make a plaster mold, a box-like form is built around part of the original object, the pattern, and filled with plaster and left to harden. This is repeated until all parts of the original have a corresponding mold section. The hardened plaster mold sections are then coated with a release agent to prevent them from adhering to the casting material. The sections are strapped together and filled with plaster or other material that hardens, and finally the mold is removed to reveal the final cast object. The mold for the teapot in **D** had slip (liquid clay) repeatedly poured in and out until a layer of clay formed inside the mold, ensuring a thin-walled, hollow teapot; this mold is a two-part mold—note the negative and positive "buttons" used to align the two halves. Mold making can get very complex, with multiple parts that might be required to avoid undercuts (shapes that would resist removal from the mold). Fine mold making is an art and a science.

There are numerous mold types and variations. Traditional bronze sculpture is often created with a one-piece ceramic shell mold that contains the original wax pattern. After the wax is melted out in an oven, molten bronze is poured into the mold, hardening as it cools. This casting method is referred to as the lost wax process. The ceramic shell is then cracked off the encased bronze, revealing the sculpture. Newer industrial casting methods include plastic injection molding and spin casting.

When designing an object that you intend to replicate as a multiple, it would be wise to understand and carefully consider the casting/mold-making process to which your product or sculpture will ultimately be subjected.

↑ **A**

Sizing board jig.

↑ **B**

Sand castle made with wet sand using a red castle-shaped bucket.

C

Molten steel being poured into a mold.

D

Eva Zeisel. *Tomorrow's Classic.* Hall China teapot and mold. 1952.

NEW APPROACHES

The Rapid Prototype

Many new replication technologies are available to the contemporary artist and designer, and they all involve computer technology. Rapid prototyping (also referred to as 3D printing) is an additive process in which digital instructions control a computerized printing device that deposits a material (usually plastic), layer upon layer, until the full three-dimensional object is complete. The initial design input can be either digitally created with CAD software or by laser scanning an original object. The 3D printer illustrated in **A** houses a fabricated duplicate toy horse (green) created by extruding layers of plastic one-hundredth of an inch thick. The black, original horse was first scanned to obtain the information required. In addition to extruding modeling material, this 3D printer lays down a darker material that acts as a support for the object being formed; the supporting material is easily removed after printing.

Laser Cutting

Computerized laser cutters allow for CAD data to control cutting flat shapes in numerous materials. A steel table can be cut from sheet steel and later folded into its final form. The advantages of laser cutting are accuracy and the freedom to fabricate either one table or one hundred at a time, all from the original digital input. Computerized fabrication has contributed to the growth of on-demand manufacturing.

The CNC Router

A CNC (computer numerical control) router is a machine that removes materials such as plastic, foam, wood, and aluminum by virtue of a spinning router bit that moves on three or more axes. The CNC router in **B** is carving a figure in foam.

Two Extraordinary Objects

Two extraordinary objects that were created with new computer-aided replication technologies would not only be all but unbuildable with traditional replication technologies but would also be unthinkable. The *C2 Solid Chair* in **C** is fabricated by means of the stereolithography process, a type of 3D printing in which a computer-controlled laser heats and solidifies a photosensitive epoxy resin. The *Cinderella Table* in **D** was CAD designed, the result of virtually morphing two individual antique pieces of furniture, then fabricated by a CNC router. Fifty-seven individual sections were formed by the router, then pieced together to complete the table. Like the *C2 Solid Chair*, the *Cinderella Table* is endlessly reproducible after the initial data input. Both table and chair are fantasies inspired by technology.

New technologies lead to new thoughts, new forms, and new products.

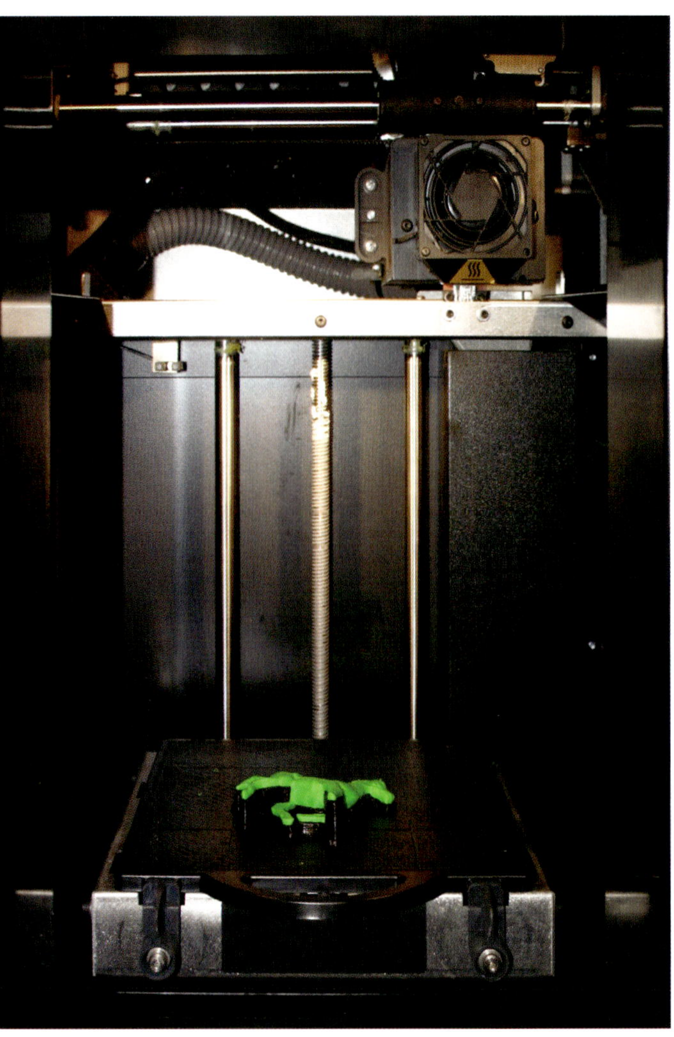

 **A**

Toy horse duplicate in a Dimension SST 3D printer at Virginia Commonwealth University, Sculpture Department (left). The SST printer uses a process called fused deposition modeling. Original black toy horse and green duplicate made by 3D printing (right). Photograph: R. Eric McMaster.

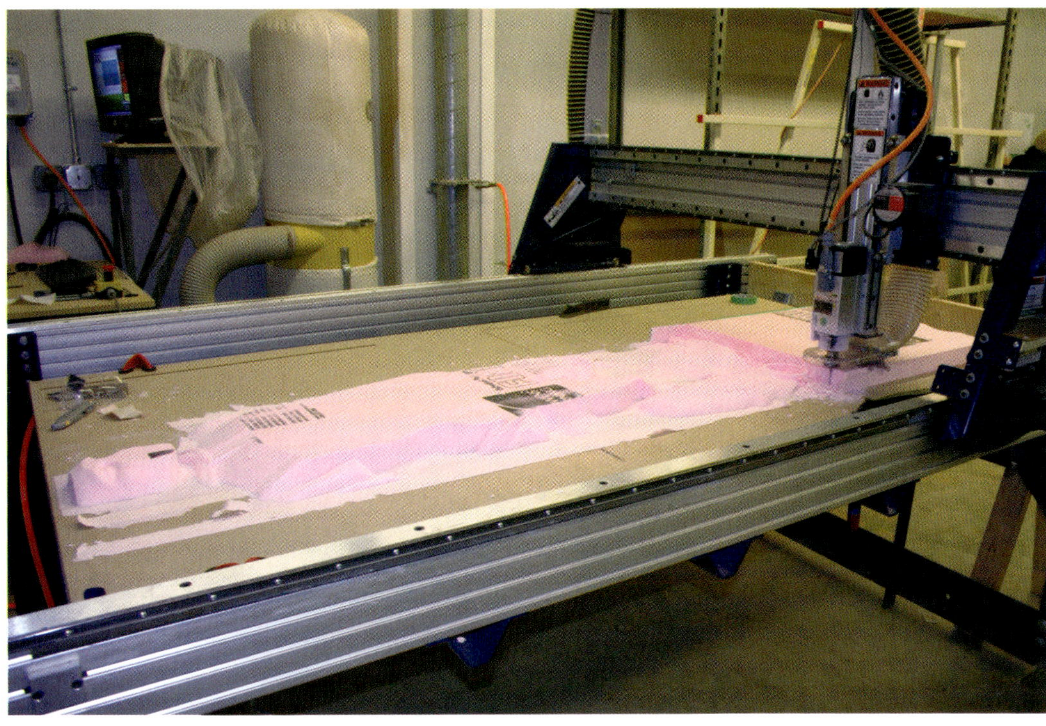

B

Shopbot PRS Standard CNC router with foam figure at Virginia Commonwealth University, Sculpture Department. Photograph: R. Eric McMaster.

C

Patrick Jouin. *C2 Solid Chair.* 2004. Epoxy resin, 2' 6⅞" × 1' 3⅞" × 1' 9¼". Manufactured by Materialise NV. The Museum of Modern Art, New York.

D

Jeroen Verhoeven. *Cinderella Table.* 2004. Birch, 2' 7½" × 4' 4" × 3' 4". Manufactured by Demakersvan. The Museum of Modern Art, New York.

GLOSSARY

Abstraction The presentation of form for its own sake, devoid of representation. Abstraction can occur through a process of simplification or distortion in an attempt to communicate an essential aspect of a form or concept.

Abstract Expressionism The abstract art movement of the mid-1900s characterized by energetic mark making motivated by the artist's subconscious impulses.

Accretion Building form by incremental additions.

Aerodynamic Objects designed to move through air or water with the least amount of drag (friction).

Aesthetics A branch of philosophy concerned with the beautiful in art and how the viewer experiences it.

Anamorphic Term used to describe an image that has been optically distorted.

Anthropomorphic Form that has human likeness or attributes.

Appropriate (e-´prō-prē-āt) The act of borrowing images, objects, or styles from pre-existing artworks or from culture in general for one's own creative use.

Archetype An ideal model.

Art Nouveau A late nineteenth-century style that emphasized organic shapes.

Ash-Can school American realist painters of the early 1900s who glorified daily life and ordinary people.

Asymmetrical balance Balance achieved with dissimilar objects that have equal visual weight or equal eye attraction.

Asymmetry Nonsymmetrical form.

Automatic writing The surrealist practice of writing or drawing without conscious control.

Balance The equilibrium of opposing or interacting forces in a pictorial composition.

Bauhaus Influential German school of architecture, design, and art.

Bilateral symmetry Balance with respect to a vertical axis.

Biomimcry Design that utilizes nature's methods to create new products.

Biomorphic Form derived from nature, often embodying organic growth.

Bricolage An assemblage of found materials and objects created by improvising with whatever material happens to be available.

CAD Computer Aided Design. Software programs that assist designers in the conception and execution of products and buildings.

Calligraphy Handwritten letterforms that are generally either geometric or cursive.

Cantilever A structural overhang that is counterbalanced at the opposite end.

Carbon footprint The amount of greenhouse gases produced by an activity or product, usually expressed in equivalent tons of carbon dioxide.

Casting The process of duplicating an original sculpture or object (the pattern) by means of a mold.

Ceramic An object of clay that has been fired at a high temperature, usually in a kiln.

CNC Computer Numerical Control. Machine tools that are operated by the programmed commands of a computer.

Coevolution The evolution of two or more species that adapt to changes in each other during an extended period of time.

Collage An artwork created by assembling and pasting a variety of materials onto a two-dimensional surface.

Compression The stresses associated with placing materials or structures under pressure.

Conceptual Artwork based on an idea. An art movement in which the idea is more important than the work's visual structure.

Concrete art Geometric abstraction.

Constructive A fabrication process that involves addition and subtraction (but not modeling or carving) by joining (usually welding, fastening mechanically, or gluing) to form a sculpture, product, or building.

Content An idea conveyed through the artwork that implies the subject matter, story, or information the artist communicates to the viewer.

Continuation A line or edge that continues, virtually, from one form to another, allowing the eye to move smoothly through a composition.

Cradle-to-Cradle design Design that considers sustainability, especially the entire life span of an object, from creation to disposal and ultimately to material recycling and reuse.

Crit An abbreviation of critique. A process of criticism for the purpose of evaluating and improving art and design.

Curvilinear Rounded and curving forms that tend to imply flowing shapes and compositions.

Dadaists International artists of the early 1900s that reflected the cynicism that followed WWI. They employed irrationality, humor, and irony.

Deformation The formal alteration of established forms or pre-existing elements.

Design A planned arrangement of visual elements to construct an organized visual pattern or structure.

Dictum A short pronouncement that expresses a general rule or principle.

Dynamic Energetic or forceful form, implying physical motion.

Equilibrium Visual balance between opposing compositional elements.

Ergonomic Design that considers the relationship of the body of the user to the product.

Faux Fake; an imitation.

Fetishism Extravagant devotion. The displacement of erotic interest to an object.

Figuration Realistic depiction in art.

Form and function The design elements that are often coupled because of their co-influence.

Form follows function Design in which the form of a product or building is dictated by its functional requirements.

Formal That which relates to visual form, such as the elements of shape, size, color, and composition.

Functional The usefulness or utility of an object.

Futurist Pertaining to the Italian art movement of the early 1900s that stressed speed, a machine aesthetic, dynamic form, and the rejection of the past.

Geodesic dome A dome constructed of a lattice of triangular elements that distributes stresses uniformly, creating a structure that is extremely efficient in its use of material.

Gestalt A unified configuration or pattern of visual elements whose properties cannot be derived from a simple summation of its parts.

Gesture A line that does not stay at the edges but moves freely within forms. These lines record movement of the eye as well as implying motion in the form.

Golden mean A mathematical ratio in which width is to length as length is to length plus width. This ratio has been employed in design since the time of the ancient Greeks. It can also be found in natural forms.

Green design Design that takes into consideration a product's energy consumption in its making, its use, and its disposal or re-use.

Grid A network of perpendicular intersecting lines that divides spaces and creates a framework of areas.

Happenings Informal and spontaneous art events, often involving ordinary daily activities.

Haptic Relating to the sense of touch.

Hybridity Relating to the phenomenon of composite identity, as when objects embody the characteristics of different genres or combine diverse functions.

Idealism An artistic theory in which the world is not reproduced as it is but as it should be. All flaws, accidents, and incongruities of the visual world are corrected.

Ideation The process that aids in the development of early-stage design ideas.

Ideoplastic Drawing what you know, not what you see. Also applies to figuration in general, when ideas eclipse perception.
Illusion A false perception. For example, perspective can create the illusion of deep space on a flat plane.
Interstitial The space between two things, usually a small gap.
Intervention In art, an intervention involves the act of altering an existing object, situation, or environment.
Irony The conflict between what seems to be communicated and what is really intended.
Isomorphism When objects share a formal resemblance, they are isomorphic.
Iteration The repetition of a process and the different stages that result.
Jig A device that regulates and maintains the relationship of a tool or machine to the work being formed.
Joinery The act of joining parts to form a single unit.
Juxtaposition When one image or shape is placed next to or in comparison to another image or shape.
Kinetic Structures that move or have moving parts.
Kitsch Low or common art forms that appeal to sentimentality.
Maquette A small-scale model that precedes the actual sculpture.
Memes Ideas that replicate by being spread from mind to mind. Memes can be ideas, styles, art works, tunes, or theories, for example.
Minimalism An artistic style that stresses purity of form above subject matter, emotion, or decoration.
Modernism The ideas, styles, and ideology of the modern epoch up to the 1960s. In art and design it is commonly associated with abstraction, the grid, and rationality.
Module A specific measured area or standard unit.
Mold An object made by enveloping an original object in a liquid such as plaster or resin that hardens. This hardened form, the mold, is then used to reproduce copies of the original.
Monolith A single, massive, and discrete form, such as an obelisk.
Negative space Unoccupied area or empty space surrounding objects or figures.
Nomadic A mobile or migratory life style.
Nonobjective A type of artwork with no reference to, or representation of, the natural world. The artwork is the reality.
Patina The color and surface changes resulting from the oxidation of metal, such as the green film that forms on copper. Also, any change in the surface of an object due to use or age.
Pattern The repetition of a visual element or module in a regular and anticipated sequence.
Polychrome Two or more colors occupying the surface of an object.
Post and lintel A building system in which a lintel (horizontal beam) is supported by two posts (columns).
Postmodernism The style and ideology of the current era, characterized by pluralism, appropriation, and irony. The idea of collage has come to be known as the signature structure of postmodern design.
Proportion Size measured against other elements or against a mental norm or standard.
Prosthesis A device to replace a missing or impaired part of the body.
Prototype A full-size working version of a product, created to test appearance and function through use, before general production.
Proximity The degree of closeness in the placement of elements.
Quotidian Everyday activity; ordinary objects.
Radial symmetry Symmetry of an object or organism around a central main axis. Such objects can be divided into identical halves by any vertical cut through its central axis.
Rapid prototyping Machine reproduction of objects by means of digital information and the layering of material. Also referred to as 3D printing.
Readymade An art object selected (appropriated) from the world of "ordinary" objects of daily use.
Realism An approach to artwork based on the faithful reproduction of surface appearances with a fidelity to visual perception.
Recontextualize Transforming the meaning of an object by transporting it from its natural environment to a new site.
Reductive An aesthetic of reduction that produces objects stripped of all but the necessary.
Relational aesthetics The artist is understood to be a catalyst of social experiences.
Representation The depiction of an object by approximating its characteristic physical attributes. Also, realism or figuration.
Rhythm An element of design based on the repetition of recurrent motifs.
Scale The relative size of an object or a volume of space in relationship to the viewer, to other objects in the vicinity, or to the object's environment in general.
Shakers An alternative Christian religious community that flourished in the 19th century; the Shakers produced tools, furniture, and architecture that embodied their devout religious beliefs.
Sign A fundamental visual or linguistic unit that designates an object or idea.
Site specific A work of art in which the content and aesthetic value is dependent on the artwork's location.
Source A place where creators seek information and inspiration. The source for many artists and designers is other art and design, but nature, geometry, and culture at large are also sources of special interest.
Spherical symmetry Symmetry around a central point. Any slice through the center of an object possessing spherical symmetry will produce identical halves, mirror images, such as when one bisects an orange.
Static Still, stable, or unchanging.
Streamline style The style associated with industrial design of the 1930s, inspired by the aerodynamic demands of the airplane and the automobile.
Stylized The application of stylistic elements to an object, usually associated with cosmetic as opposed to functional design considerations.
Surrealism An artistic style that stresses fantastic and subconscious approaches to art making and often results in images that cannot be rationally explained.
Sustainability Relating to the efficient use of resources, so as to sustain them, preventing depletion.
Symmetry A quality of a composition or form wherein a precise correspondence of elements exists on either side of a center axis or point.
Tenet A principle or belief held true by members of a group or discipline.
Tensile strength The ability of a material to withstand the pulling force of tension.
Tension Structurally, the stress resulting from stretching or pulling.
Texture The surface quality of objects that appeals to the tactile sense.
Truss A framework, typically consisting of triangulated struts, supporting a roof, bridge, or other structure.
Typology Classification by type or style.
Unity The degree of agreement existing among the elements in a design.
Utility The functionality or use-value of an object.
Verisimilitude Accuracy or faithfulness in depiction or representation.
Vernacular A prevailing or commonplace style in a specific geographical location, group of people, or time period.
Visceral Relating to deep inner feelings, as if experienced by the gut.
Zeitgeist The spirit of an era.
Zen A Japanese adaptation of Mahayana Buddhism that aims at enlightenment.

BIBLIOGRAPHY

General

Anderson, Walter Truett, ed. *The Truth About the Truth*. New York: G.P. Putnam's Sons, 1995.

Bachelard, Gaston. *The Poetics of Space*, trans. Maria Jolas. Boston: Beacon Press, 1994.

Battcock, Gregory. *Minimal Art: A Critical Anthology*. New York: E. P. Dutton & Co., Inc., 1968.

Barrett, Terry. *Criticizing Art: Understanding the Contemporary*, 3rd ed. New York: McGraw Hill, 2011.

Bayer, Herbert, Walter Gropius, and Ise Gropius, eds. *Bauhaus 1919–1928*. New York: The Museum of Modern Art, 1938.

Berger, John. *Ways of Seeing*. London: British Broadcast Corporation, 1987.

Chipp, Herschel B., ed. *Theories of Modern Art*. Los Angeles, CA: University of California Press, 1971.

Hall, Edward T. *The Hidden Dimension*. New York: Anchor Books, 1969.

Hebdige, Dick. *Subculture: The Meaning of Style*. London: Methuen & Co. Ltd, 1979.

Judson, Horace Freeland. *The Search for Solutions*. New York: Holt, Rinehart and Winston, 1980.

Koomler, Sharon Duane. *Shaker Style: Form, Function, and Furniture*. London: PRC Publishing Ltd., 2000.

Kostelanetz, Richard, ed. *Esthetics Contemporary*. Buffalo, NY: Prometheus Books, 1982.

Mau, Bruce, and the Institute without Boundaries. *Massive Change*. London: Phaidon Press Ltd., 2004.

McCann, Michael. *Health Hazards: Manual for Artists*, 6th ed. Guilford, CT: The Lyons Press, 2003.

Morrison, Philip and Phylis Morrison and The Office of Charles and Ray Eames. *Powers of Ten*. New York: Scientific American Books, 1982.

Nervi, Pier Luigi. *Aesthetics and Technology in Building*. Cambridge, MA: Harvard University Press, 1965.

Oka, Hideyuki. *How to Wrap Five Eggs*. Boston & London: Weatherhill, 2008.

Patin, Thomas, and Jennifer McLerran. *Artwords*. Westport, CT: Greenwood Press, 1997.

Rader, Melvin, ed. *A Modern Book of Esthetics.* New York: Holt, Rinehart and Winston, 1962.

Reps, Paul, ed. *Zen Flesh, Zen Bones*. Garden City, NY: Anchor Books, 1989.

Rossol, Monona. *The Artist's Complete Health and Safety Guide*, 3rd ed. New York: Allworth Press, 2001.

Roth, Richard, and Susan Roth, eds. *Beauty Is Nowhere: Ethical Issues in Art and Design*. Amsterdam: Gordon and Breach, 1998.

Rudofsky, Bernard. *Architecture without Architects*. Garden City, NY: The Museum of Modern Art, 1965.

Silk,Gerald. *The Automobile and Culture*. New York: Harry N. Abrams, 1984.

Thompson, D'Arcy Wentworth. *On Growth and Form: The Complete Revised Edition*. Mineola, NY: Dover Publications, 1992.

Drexler, Arthur. Introduction to *Twentieth Century Engineering*. New York: The Museum of Modern Art, 1964.

Yanagi, Sōetsu. *The Unknown Craftsman*. Tokyo: Kodansha International Ltd., 1972.

Art History

Arnason, H. H. *History of Modern Art*, 3rd rev. ed. New York: Harry N. Abrams, 1986.

Janson, H. W. *History of Art*, 4th rev. and enl. ed. New York: Harry N. Abrams, 1991.

Kleiner, Fred S. *Gardner's Art through the Ages*, 13th ed. Boston: Cengage Learning, 2009.

Nelson, Robert S., and Richard Shiff, eds. *Critical Terms for Art History*. Chicago: The University of Chicago Press, 1996.

Reimschneider, Burkhard, and Uta Grosenick, eds. *Art at the Turn of the Millennium*. Köln, Germany: Taschen GMBH, 1999.

General Design

Bevlin, Marjorie Elliot. *Design through Discovery*, 6th ed. Fort Worth, TX: Harcourt Brace College Publishers, 1994.

Itten, Johannes. *Design and Form: The Basic Course at the Bauhaus*, 2nd rev. ed. New York: Van Nostrand Reinhold, 1975.

Kepes, Gyorgy. *Language of Vision*. Chicago: Paul Theobald, 1969.

Lauer, David A., and Stephen Pentak. *Design Basics*. 8th ed. Boston: Wadsworth Cengage Learning, 2012.

Zelanski, Paul, and Mary Pat Fisher. *Shaping Space*. Belmont, CA: Thompson Wadsworth, 2007.

Visual Perception

Arnheim, Rudolf. *Art and Visual Perception: A Psychology of the Creative Eye, The New Version*, 2nd rev. and enl. ed. Berkeley: University of California Press, 1974.

Ehrenzweig, Anton. *The Hidden Order of Art: A Study in the Psychology of Artistic Imagination*. Berkeley: University of California Press, 1976.

Gombrich, E. H. *Art and Illusion: A Study in the Psychology of Pictorial Representation*. Princeton, NJ: Princeton University Press, 1961.

Köhler, Wolfgang. *Gestalt Psychology: An Introduction to New Concepts in Modern Psychology*. New York: Liveright Publishing Corporation, 1947.

Color

Albers, Josef. *Interaction of Color*, rev. ed. New Haven, CT: Yale University Press, 1975.

Porter, Tom, and Byron Mikellides. *Color for Architects*. New York: Van Nostrand Reinhold, 1976.

Pentak, Stephen, and Richard Roth. *Color Basics*. Belmont, CA: Wadsworth/Thomson, 2003.

Chapter 1: xii S. Department of Defense/Photo Researchers, Inc.; **2** Dimitri Vervitsiotis/Getty Images; **2** Just One Film/Getty Images; **2** Image Source/Getty Images; **3A** hammernet; **4A** Vanni/Art Resource, NY © 2011 Artists Rights Society (ARS), New York/VG Bild-Kunst, Bonn; **5B** © 2011 The Josef and Anni Albers Foundation, Artist's Rights Society (ARS), NY. Photo © Art Resource, NY; **6** William Wegman; **7A** Courtesy of Stephen Pentak; **7B** Courtesy of Stephen Pentak; **8A** Digital Image © 2009 Museum Associates/LACMA/Art Resource, NY © 2011 Artists Rights Society (ARS), New York/ADAGP, Paris; **9B** Historic New England; **10A** Tom McHugh/ Photo Researchers, Inc.; **10B** IndexStock/SuperStock; **11C** NASA, Hubble Heritage Team, (STScI/AURA), ESA, S. Beckwith (STScI). Additional Processing: Robert Gendler; **11D** Exactostock/SuperStock; **12A** Comstock Images/Jupiterimages/Getty Images; **13B** BMW PressClub; **14A** Haim Steinbach; **15B** Fred Wilson/The Pace Gallery; **16A** Art Resource, NY © 2011 Frank Lloyd Wright Foundation, Scottsdale, AZ/Artists Rights Society (ARS), NY; **17B** Wolfgang Volz © 1983 Christo; **17C** Wim Delvoye; **18A** Virginia Commonwealth University Art Foundation Program, photo: Matt King; **19B** Virginia Commonwealth University Art Foundation Program, photo: Matt King.

Chapter 2: 20 Jessica Hilltout; **22A** Russell Stewart; **22B** Courtesy of Cervèlo; **23C** Courtesy of Cervèlo; **23D** Natalie Jeremijenko/Massachusetts Museum of Contemporary Art; **24A** Digital Image Photo credit: The Museum of Modern Art/ Licensed by SCALA/Art Resource, NY; **24B** Digital Image © The Museum of Modern Art/Licensed by SCALA/Art Resource, NY; **25C** © Owen Franken/CORBIS; **25D** Joe McNally/Getty Images Entertainment/Getty Images; **26A** © Heritage Images/Corbis; **26B** Louie Psihoyos/Science Faction Jewels/Getty Images; **27C** Image copyright © The Metropolitan Museum of Art/Art Resource, NY; **27D** Photo: Marco Melander. Copyright Stefan Lindfors; **28A** Mike Quinn, National Park Service Photo; **29B** Bruce Barnbaum; **29C** Richard Barnes; **30A** Steve Gorton/ Dorling Kindersley/Getty Images; **31B** The Peck Tool Company; **31C** Yoshikazu Tsuno/AFP/Getty Images; **32A** Scala/Art Resource, NY; **33B** Photography courtesy The Pace Gallery © Tara Donovan, courtesy The Pace Gallery; **33C** Photography courtesy The Pace Gallery © Tara Donovan, courtesy The Pace Gallery; **33D** Allen Memorial Art Museum, Oberlin College, Ohio; Gift of Philip Droll, and the direction of Donald Droll, In Honor of Richard E. Spear, Director. © 2011 Estate of Scott Burton/Artists Rights Society (ARS), NY; **34A** Digital Image from The Museum of Modern Art/Licensed by SCALA/Art Resource, NY © 2011 Succession H. Matisse/ Artists Rights Society (ARS), New York; **34B** Digital Image from The Museum of Modern Art/Licensed by SCALA/Art Resource, NY © 2011 Succession H. Matisse/ Artists Rights Society (ARS), New York; **34C** Digital Image from The Museum of Modern Art/Licensed by SCALA/Art Resource, NY © 2011 Succession H. Matisse/ Artists Rights Society (ARS), New York; **34D** Digital Image from The Museum of Modern Art/Licensed by SCALA/Art Resource, NY © 2011 Succession H. Matisse/Artists Rights Society (ARS), New York; **35E** SITE | architecture, art & design; **35F** SITE: architecture, art & design; **35G** Collection of the Ohr-O'Keefe Museum of Art; **36A** © 2012 The LeWitt Estate/Artists Rights Society (ARS), New York; photo courtesy San Francisco Museum of Modern Art; **37B** Courtesy the artist and James Cohan Gallery, New York/Shanghai; **37C** Mike Kemp Images/ The Image Bank/Getty Images; **38A** © 2012 The LeWitt Estate/Artists Rights Society (ARS), New York; photo courtesy San Francisco Museum of Modern Art; **39B** Wim Delvoye; **40A** © Andrè Kertesz—RMN Photo: National Portrait Gallery, Smithsonian Institution/Art Resource, NY; **41B** Photo: R. Notkin; **41C** Rèunion des Musèes Nationaux/Art Resource, NY © 2011 Estate of Pablo Picasso/Artists Rights Society (ARS), New York; **42A** © Donald Judd Photography by Ellen Wilson, courtesy The Pace Gallery. © Judd Foundation. Licensed by VAGA, New York, NY; **43B** © Caste/SoFood/Corbis; **43C** Digital Image copyright The Museum of Modern Art/Licensed by SCALA/Art Resource, NY; **44A** © Photos 12/Alamy; **44B** © Estate of David Smith/Licensed by VAGA, New York, NY; **45C** © Estate of David Smith/Licensed by VAGA, New York, NY; **45D** Eva Zeisel Archive; **46B** Farrell Grehan/CORBIS; **47C** Courtesy of Intel®; **48A** Susan Spann/The New York Times; **49B** Jessica Hiltout; **50A** Digital Image © The Museum of Modern Art/Licensed by SCALA/Art Resource, NY © 2011 Artists Rights Society (ARS), New York/ADAGP, Paris/Succession Marcel Duchamp; **51B** The Art Archive/ Galerie Caron-Lestringant Louvre des Antiquaires/Gianni Dagli Ort © 2011 Artists Rights Society (ARS), New York/ADAGP, Paris; **51C** firstVIEW; **52A** Henry Moore Foundation © 2011 The Henry Moore Foundation. All Rights Reserved/ ARS, New York/DACS, London; **53B** Henry Moore Foundation © 2011 The Henry Moore Foundation. All Rights Reserved/ARS, New York/DACS, London; **53C** Andrea Jemolo/Scala/Art Resource, NY; **54B** Flirt/SuperStock; **55C** Cengage Learning; **55D** Exactostock/SuperStock; **55E** from "Illustration from On Growth and Form" by D'Arcy Wentworth Thompson, Courtesy of Dover Publications; **56A** The Museum of Modern Art/Licensed by SCALA/Art Resource, NY © 2011 The Andy Warhol Foundation for the Visual Arts, Inc./Artists Rights Society (ARS), New York; **57B** Photo Credit: William Watkins; **57C** Photo Credit: William Watkins; **58A** Digital Image © The Museum of Modern Art/Licensed by Scala/Art Resource, NY; **59B** Collection Walker Art Center, Minneapolis Gift of Kenneth E. Tyler © 2011 The Willem de Kooning Foundation/Artists Rights Society (ARS), New York; **60A** Tate, London/Art Resource, NY © Judd Foundation. Licensed by VAGA, New York, NY; **61B** © Eames Office, LLC (www.eamesoffice.com) Eames House: 1997, photographer, Eames Demetrios; **61C** Digital Image © The Museum of Modern Art/Licensed by SCALA/Art Resource, NY; **62A** Daniel Clowes/Fantagraphics Books Inc.; **63B** Harry Melchert/dpa/Corbis; **63C** Jenny Holzer/Art Resource, NY © 2011 Jenny Holzer, member Artists Rights Society (ARS), New York; **63D** Jason Miller Studio.

Chapter 3: 64 © Dan McCoy—Rainbow/Science Faction/Corbis; **66A** Photography by Richard Roth; **67B** Smithsonian American Art Museum, Washington, DC/Art Resource, NY; **67C** Kohler Wolfgang/Liveright Publishing Corporation; **67D** The Museum of Modern Art/Licensed by SCALA/Art Resource, NY © 2011 Richard Serra/Artists Rights Society (ARS), New York; **68A** © Ali Jarekji/Reuters/Corbis; **68B** Collection Walker Art Center, Minneapolis Gift of the T.B Walker Foundation, 1971 © Judd Foundation. Licensed by VAGA, New York, NY; **69C** © 1992 Janine Antoni. Courtesy of the artist and Luhring Augustine, NY; **69D** Koichi Kamoshida/Getty Images; **70A** Photograph by Richard Roth; **70B** Digital file from Getty Images. Maman, 2005 © Louise Bourgeois Trust/Licensed by VAGA, New York, NY; **70C** JPooreCollection/Cengage Learning; **71D** Nicolas Sapieha/Art Resource, NY © 2011 The Henry Moore Foundation. All Rights Reserved/ARS, New York/DACS, London; **71E** Courtesy of Rachel Whiteread and Luhring Augustine, New York. © 1994, Rachel Whiteread; **72A** © Charles Ray, Courtesy Matthew Marks Gallery, New York; **72B** The Museum of Modern Art/ Licensed by SCALA/Art Resource, NY © 2011 Calder Foundation, New York/ Artists Rights Society (ARS), New York; **72C** MARKA/Alamy; **73D** CNAC/MNAM/ Dist. Rèunion des Musèes Nationaux/Art Resource, NY; **73E** Chad Ehlers/Stone/ Getty Images; **74A** Digital Image © The Museum of Modern Art/Licensed by SCALA/Art Resource, NY; **75B** Xavier Florensa/age fotostock/Photolibrary; **75C** © Prisma/SuperStock; **76A** Robert J. Lang; **77B** Ufuk Keskin and Efecem Kutuk (efecemkutuk.com and ufukkeskin.com); **77C** Open Library; **77D** Google SketchUp; **78A** Diego Azubel/epa/Corbis; **78B** © Dennis Gilbert/VIEW/VIEW/Corbis; **79C** Richard Roth; **79D** © Clive Nichols/Corbis; **80A** Marie Mauzy/Art Resource, NY; **80B** © Clark Dunbar/Corbis; **81C** Fabrice Coffrini/AFP/Getty Images; **81D** Nicolas Sapieha/Art Resource, NY © 2011 Barragan Foundation, Switzerland/ Artists Rights Society (ARS), New York; **81E** Tapio Wirkkala/Venini spa Fondamenta Vetrai; **82A** © Terry Harris PCL/SuperStock; **82B** Albright-Knox Art Gallery/Art Resource, NY © 2011 Stephen Flavin/Artists Rights Society (ARS), New York; **83C** Courtesy of the artist; neugerriemschneider, Berlin; Tanya Bonakdar Gallery, New York; and Gallery Koyanagi, Tokyo © 2009 Olafur Eliasson; **83D** Elisabeth Pollaert Smith/Photographer's Choice/Getty Images; **84A** Digital Image © The Museum of Modern Art/Licensed by SCALA/Art Resource, NY; **84B** Harvard Art Museums/ Busch-Reisinger Museum, Gift of Sibyl Moholy-Nagy, BR56.5 Copyright: Photo: Junius Beebe © President and Fellows of Harvard College; **85C** Courtesy Tony Oursler and Metro Pictures; **85D** Getty Images; **85E** Chris Helgren/Reuters/Corbis.

Chapter 4: 86 Elliot Barnathan; **88A** Courtesy Modern Art Museum of Fort Worth; **88B** Portia Munson; **88C** Portia Munson; **89D** Portia Munson; **89E** Schroeder House, built in 1923-24 (photo), Rietveld, Gerrit (1888-1964)/Utrecht, Netherlands/The Bridgeman Art Library © 2011 Artists Rights Society (ARS),

New York; **90A** Courtesy of Tom Friedman, Luhring Augustine, New York and Stephen Friedman Gallery, London; **90B** Bettmann/CORBIS; **91C** © imagebroker/Alamy; **91D** Russell Mountford/Lonely Planet Images/Getty Images; **92A** Paul D. Slaughter/Photographer's Choice/Getty Images; **92B** Allan McCollum; **92C** Photo: Richard Roth; **93D** Musèe d'Orsay; **93E** Joel Shapiro; **94A** © Ian Griffiths/Robert Harding World Imagery/Corbis; **94B** Vanni/Art Resource, NY; **95C** Gregory Wrona PCL/SuperStock; **95D** © Gunter Marx Stock Photos; **95E** Tomoyuki Sugai/Getty Images; **96A** kokoroimages.com/Flickr/Getty Images; **96B** Bill O'Connell/Workbook Stock/Getty Images; **97C** A. Barrington Brown/Photo Researchers, Inc.; **97D** Safdie Architects photo by Timothy Hursley; **98A** Erwin Hauer; **98B** Courtesy of: Arte en la Charreria/Luis González Cárdenas; **99C** Mihrab [Isfahan, Iran] (39.20), Heilbrunn Timeline of Art History, The Metropolitan Museum of Art; **99D** Laura Wickenden/Dorling Kindersley/Getty Images; **99E** Ar.Shakti Nanda/Flickr/Getty Images; **100A** Copyright The Cleveland Museum of Art. Gift of the John Huntington Art and Polytechnic Trust 1928.856.a; **100B** Eva Hild © 2011 Artists Rights Society (ARS), New York/BUS, Stockholm; **101C** Erich Lessing/Art Resource, NY © 2011 Artists Rights Society (ARS), New York; **102A** Handout/Reuters/Corbis; **103B** Michael Lawrence/LonelyPlanet; **103C** © imac/Alamy; **103D** © Rubin Museum of Art/Art Resource, NY; **104A** Jean-Louis Blondeau/Polaris Images; **104D** Calder Foundation, New York/Art Resource, NY © 2011 Calder Foundation, New York/Artists Rights Society (ARS), New York; **105C** Flak, 1981 (felt, glass and wood) (see also 195073), Mucha, Reinhard (b.1950)/Hamburger Kunsthalle, Hamburg, Germany/The Bridgeman Art Library; **105D** Dancer looking at the sole of her right foot, 1919-21 (bronze), Degas, Edgar (1834-1917)/Art Gallery of New South Wales, Sydney, Australia /The Bridgeman Art Library; **105E** Art Resource, NY © Estate of David Smith/Licensed by VAGA, New York, NY; **106A** Design concept Philip Wright body engineer James Hughes. Pierce-Arrow Motor Car Company. Photograph by Stephen Pentak; **106B** © WWD/Condè Nast/Corbis; **107C** De Agostini/SuperStock; **107D** Science Faction/SuperStock; **108A** Studio Daniel Libeskind & © Bitter Bredt; **109B** DeA Picture Library/Art Resource, NY © 2011 Calder Foundation, New York/Artists Rights Society (ARS), New York; **109C** © Inigo Bujedo Aguirre/Arcaid/Corbis; **110A** © Condè Nast Archive/CORBIS; **111B** The Metropolitan Museum of Art/Art Resource, NY; **111C** SSPL/Getty Images; **112A** Ronald Zincone VWPics/SuperStock; **113B** Peter Willi/SuperStock; **113C** Ulf Sjostedt/Photographer's Choice RF/Getty Images; **114A** JPooreCollection; **114B** Courtesy of Roy McMakin; Matthew Marks Gallery; **115C** Werner Forman/Art Resource, NY; **115D** Courtesy L.A. Louver, Venice, CA; **116A** Jonathan Poore/Cengage Learning; **116B** Image Source /Getty Images; **117C** firstVIEW; **118A** Staton R. Winter/Redux Pictures; **119B** © Eames Office, LLC (www.eamesoffice.com); **119C** JPooreCollection; **120A** © Lebrecht Music and Arts Photo Library/Alamy; **120B** © Jeremy Sutton-Hibbert/Alamy; **121C** Charles Lewallen; **121D** Willard Wigan; **122A** Dinodia Picture Agency; **123B** REUTERS/Andrew Wong/CORBIS; **123C** Nik Wheeler/CORBIS; **123D** Gavin Brown's enterprise.

Chapter 5: 124 Camille Seaman; **126A** Scott Richter; **127B** Jeff Koons; **127C** AFP/Getty Images; **128A** Photo by Gjon Mili/Time Life Pictures/Getty Images; **129B** Henry Moore Foundation © 2011 The Henry Moore Foundation. All Rights Reserved/ARS, New York/DACS, London; **130A** Chicago Natural History Museum; **130B** John Lund/The Image Bank/Getty Images; **130C** Stuart Westmorland/Science Faction/Getty Images; **131D** Zen Shui/SuperStock; **131E** Paul Schraub; **132A** NASA/JPL; **132B** Guido Trombetta/Alinghi/NewSport/Corbis; **133C** Permission granted by Integra LifeSciences Corporation, Plainsboro, NJ; **134A** El Anatsui/NY Times; **134B** Photo by Richard Roth; **134C** John Habraken; **135D** © Cook+Fox Architects; **135E** Hoang Dinh Nam/AFP/Getty Images.

Chapter 6: 136 © Dennis Hallinan/Alamy; **138A** Comstock Images/Jupiterimages/Getty Images; **139B** Shigeru Ban Architects; **139C** Morey Milbradt/Brand X Pictures/Getty Images; **140A** © Chris Stelly/2006 225BatonRouge.com; **141B** Jean-Pierre Lescourret/Corbis; **141C** Apic/Hulton Archive/Getty Images; **142A** Josè Miguel Hernández; **143B** Nick Delaney/Axiom Photographic Agency/Getty Images; **143C** Felix Labhardt/Taxi/Getty Images; **144A** MoMA publication. © 1938. © 2011 The Josef and Anni Albers Foundation/Artists Rights Society (ARS), New York; **145B** Paul Marotta/Flickr/Getty Images; **145C** Jim Craigmyle/Corbis Edge/CORBIS; **145D** Richard Deacon; **146A** Historic New England; **146B** Herta Moselsio photographer. Lamentation. Choreographer Martha Graham. ca. summer 1937. Silver gelatin prints. Music Division Purchase, 2001 (233.2, 234.2). Library of Congress; **147C** Hoberman; **147D** Up Projects; **147E** Rob Oechsle Collection.

Chapter 7: 148 Lester Lefkowitz/Getty Images; **150A** Collection of Hancock Shaker Village, Pittsfield, Massachusetts/Photo by Michael Fredericks; **151B** Q Drum; **151C** Roll Call/Getty Images; **152A** © Orban Thierry/CORBIS SYGMA; **153B** AFP/Getty Images; **154A** © Mark Tansey. Courtesy Gagosian Gallery; **154B** Jerry L. Thompson/Art Resource, NY © 2011 Artists Rights Society (ARS), New York/ADAGP, Paris/Succession Marcel Duchamp; **155C** Copyright Dianceht, S.A. de C.V. www.manosydedos.com; **155D** John Warburton-Lee/JAI/Corbis; **156A** Peter Stathis Digital Image © The Museum of Modern Art/Licensed by SCALA/Art Resource, NY; **156B** NASA; **157C** Francesco Chinazzo /Shutterstock; **157D** Pete Oxford/Nature Picture Library; **158A** Albright-Knox Art Gallery/Art Resource, NY © 2011 Succession Giacometti/Artists Rights Society (ARS), New York/ADAGP, Paris; **159B** BMW Motorcycle Magazine; **159C** Ryan McVay/Stone/Getty Images.

Chapter 8: 160 Finn O'Hara/ Getty Images; **162A** Scala/Art Resource, NY; **163B** Iwasaki Images of America; **163C** Photographer: Travis Fullerton, 2010; **164A** Daniel Mcculloch/Digital Vision/Getty Images; **165B** Joshua Callaghan; **165C** Hans Georg Roth/Corbis; **165D** Nivek Neslo/Riser/Getty Images; **166A** Gustavo Caballero/Getty Images Entertainment/Getty Images; **167B** Photo: Richard Roth; **167C** The Noguchi Museum © 2011 The Isamu Noguchi Foundation and Garden Museum, New York/Artists Rights Society (ARS), New York; **167D** SSPL/Getty Images.

Chapter 9: 168 Lester Lefkowitz/ Getty Images; **171A** Digital Image © The Museum of Modern Art/Licensed by SCALA/Art Resource, NY; **172A** Scala/Art Resource, NY © 2011 Succession Giacometti/Artists Rights Society (ARS), New York/ADAGP, Paris; **173B** FHWA Central Federal Lands; **174A** Nimatallah/Art Resource, NY; **174B** Penone, Dèvoiler l'invisible; **175C** Giuseppe Penone/Art Gallery of Ontario; **175D** Paris courtesy of David Zwirner, NY, and the Estate of Gordon Matta-Clark; **175E** Image © the artist and courtesy of the artist and Stephen Friedman Gallery, London; **176A** Tate, London/Art Resource, NY © 2011 Artists Rights Society (ARS), New York/ADAGP, Paris; **176B** Barford Sculptures; **177C** Erich Lessing/Art Resource, NY © 2011 Artists Rights Society (ARS), New York; **177D** SuperStock/Getty Images; **178A** CNAC/MNAM/Dist. Rèunion des Musèes Nationaux/Art Resource, NY © 2011 Artists Rights Society (ARS), New York/ADAGP, Paris/Succession Marcel Duchamp; **179B** Rorbct Caplin for the *New York Times*; **180A** Rèunion des Musèes Nationaux/Art Resource, NY © 2011 Estate of Pablo Picasso/Artists Rights Society (ARS), New York; **180B** Edward Owen/Art Resource, NY © The Joseph and Robert Cornell Memorial Foundation/Licensed by VAGA, New York, NY; **181C** Harry Roseman; **181D** © Sarah Sze, Courtesy Tanya Bonakdar Gallery, New York; **181E** Gallop Workshop; **182A** Photo Credit: Rèunion des Musèes Nationaux/Art Resource, NY; **183B** Photo by Rachel Heberling. Reproduced with permission of Michael Mercil; **183C** Dawoud Bey; **184A** Ann Hamilton; **185B** © David Kennedy/Alamy; **185C** © David J. Green—technology/Alamy; **186A** Henry Ford Museum; **187B** The Museum of Modern Art/Licensed by SCALA/Art Resource, NY; **187C** © Ambient Images Inc./SuperStock; **188A** Allan Baxter/Photographer's Choice/Getty Images; **189B** SFMOMA; **189C** Image 1: courtesy: © Karin Sander, VG-Bildkunst, Bonn photography: © Studio Karin Sander. Image 2: courtesy: © Karin Sander, VG-Bildkunst, Bonn photography: © Studio Karin Sander collection: Sammlung LB-BW, Stuttgart, Germany. Image 3: courtesy: © Karin Sander, VG-Bildkunst, Bonn photography: © Studio Karin Sander collection: Private Collection, Aspen, USA; **190B** Steve Gorton and Gary Ombler/Dorling Kindersley/Getty Images; **191C** Stockbyte /Getty Images; **191D** The Schein-Joseph International Museum of Ceramic Art, photograph by Brian Oglesbee; **192A** Photos by R. Eric McMaster; **193B** R. Eric McMaster; **193C** Digital Image © The Museum of Modern Art/Licensed by SCALA/Art Resource, NY; **193D** Digital Image © The Museum of Modern Art/Licensed by SCALA/Art Resource, NY.